THE WITCH MUST DIE

THE WITCH MUST DIE

How Fairy Tales Shape Our Lives

SHELDON CASHDAN

BASIC
BOOKS

A Member of the Perseus Books Group

Basic Books

Copyright © 1999 by Sheldon Cashdan

Published by Basic Books,
A Member of the Perseus Books Group

The author acknowledges the following for permission to reprint excerpts and/or
illustrations from:

"The Little Girl and the Wolf" from FABLES IN OUR TIME, Copyright ©
1940 James Thurber. Copyright © renewed 1968 Helen Thurber and Rosemary A.
Thurber. Reprinted by arrangement with Rosemary A. Thurber and the Barbara
Hogenson Agency.

"Vasilisa the Beautiful" from RUSSIAN FAIRY TALES by Aleksander Afanas'ev,
translated by Norbert Guterman. Copyright © 1945 by Pantheon Books, Inc.
Reprint copyright © 1975 by Random House, Inc. Reprinted by permission of
Pantheon Books, a division of Random House, Inc.

"Little Snow White" and "The Juniper Tree" from THE COMPLETE
GRIMM'S FAIRY TALES by Margaret Hunt and James Stern (translators).
Copyright © 1944 by Pantheon Books, Inc. and renewed 1972 by Random House,
Inc. Reprinted by permission of Pantheon Books, a division of Random House, Inc.

C. Collodi, *Pinocchio: The Tale of a Puppet* (London: J. M. Dent, 1951) (originally
published in 1883).

Robert Coover's *Briar Rose* (New York: Grove/Atlantic, 1996).

Jeanne Desy, "The Princess Who Stood On Her Own Two Feet." Reprinted in
Stories for Free Children, edited by Betty Pogrebin (New York: McGraw-Hill, 1982).

FIRST EDITION

Designed by Jane Raese
Text set in 11/15 Janson

A CIP catalog record for this book is available from
the Library of Congress.
ISBN 0-465-09148-2

99 00 01 02 03 04 ❖/RRD 10 9 8 7 6 5 4 3 2 1

For Ariane,
who never tires of
The Frog Princess

OTHER WORKS BY SHELDON CASHDAN

Abnormal Psychology

Interactional Psychotherapy

Object Relations Therapy:
Using the Relationship

❖ CONTENTS ❖

❖ PREFACE ❖

$\mathcal{T}$hree is a special number in fairy tales. Snow White's stepmother, the queen, tempts Snow White with lethal gifts on three separate occasions. Cinderella, after repeatedly eluding the prince on her first two trips to the ball, loses her slipper on the third. And the miller's daughter promises Rumpelstiltskin her firstborn during the little man's third appearance. The number three is a staple of fairy tales: three visits, three trials, three promises.

I had three goals—three wishes, so to speak—when I set out to write *The Witch Must Die*. The first was to provide readers with a new way of understanding fairy tales. What do these age-old stories signify? What deeper meanings do they possess? Fairy tales are the first stories we hear, and though they are meant to enchant and entertain, they also offer us a means of addressing psychological conflicts. Using "the seven deadly sins of childhood" as a unifying theme, *The Witch Must Die* demonstrates how fairy tales help children deal with envy, greed, vanity, and other troublesome tendencies.

The second goal is to revisit the fairy tales of our youth in order to illuminate hidden meanings in the stories that were glossed over when we were young. Few children understand why Snow White lets the evil queen into the cottage three times in the face of the dwarfs' repeated warnings or why the princess in *The Frog Prince* refuses the frog's request to hop into bed. Is it merely that the frog is wet and clammy, or is there more to it than that? And it is not readily apparent that the reason the witch cuts off Rapunzel's tresses is to punish her for becoming pregnant, a condition that comes to light when the young girl's apron no longer fits about her waist. Adults have little trouble making these connections, but children do.

The third goal was to expose readers to lost fairy tales, stories that never found their way into children's storybooks. Because of their provocative, often sexual nature, stories like *The Juniper Tree* and *The Princess Who Couldn't Laugh* fell by the wayside and were lost to posterity. These powerful and poignant stories are nevertheless part of the rich heritage of fairy tales and storytelling. They also contain the seeds of the stories we know and cherish, including *Cinderella, Hansel and Gretel*, and *The Sleeping Beauty*.

When the three visits are completed, the three tasks successfully executed, and the three wishes fulfilled, a fairy tales ends with everyone—except perhaps the witch—living happily ever after. *The Witch Must Die* will also have a happy ending if the magic holds. And though it cannot be promised, some readers may even live happily ever after. There is no telling what makes wishes come true.

❧ ACKNOWLEDGMENTS ❧

$\mathcal{A}$ book is a fairy tale. It begins as a dream and ends up as a dream fulfilled. Like all fairy tales, *The Witch Must Die* has a cast of characters. The fairy godmothers are the women of the Linda Chester Literary Agency: Linda, Laurie Fox, and especially Joanna Pulcini. It was Joanna who saw the glint in my eye and realized it was a book. Not only was she a constant source of support and encouragement, she provided valuable input at various stages of the writing and helped sharpen many of my ideas. She is a wonderful person and an exceptional agent.

Jo Ann Miller, my editor at Basic Books, is the good witch in the story. Using her special brand of magic, she helped shape the final draft with her impressive knowledge of psychology and incisive wit. Her caring and expertise shine through on every page, and I feel fortunate to have had her at my side while I made my way through the woods. Just as Glinda saw Dorothy back to Kansas, Jo Ann saw the book home.

My wife, Eva, is the princess of the piece. She gave unstintingly of herself and never once complained. I don't know how many times she read and reread drafts of the manuscript or helped me hash out complex thoughts. Much of what is good in the book I owe to her. But I owe her much more. Years ago she transformed my life with a kiss. Were it not for her, I might still be sitting on a lily pad gazing at the moon.

Deeper meaning resides in the fairy tales
told to me in my childhood than in any
truth that is taught in life.

—*Friedrich Schiller*

I was Snow White, but then I drifted.

—*Mae West*

THE WITCH MUST DIE

1
Once Upon a Time

𝕴 came to fairy tales twice, first as a child and years later as an adult. Like mothers and fathers everywhere, my parents read *Hansel and Gretel*, *Jack and the Beanstalk*, and other popular tales to me. But my most vivid childhood memories of fairy tales came by way of Walt Disney. I remember sitting on the edge of my seat in a darkened movie theater watching *Snow White* and holding my breath as the gamekeeper prepared to cut out the heroine's heart. Like the children around me, I gasped with relief when he disobeyed the evil queen's edict and let Snow White escape. For weeks afterward, I chanted "Hi, ho, hi, ho, it's off to work we go." Today I may have trouble naming all the dwarfs, but the images of the evil queen, Snow White, and the seven dwarfs are forever emblazoned on my memory.

Many years passed before I came to fairy tales the second time. By then I was teaching at a university where I trained graduate students to do psychotherapy with children. As part of my duties I also taught undergraduate courses. One of my favorite courses, a seminar entitled "The Psychology of Fantasy and Folklore," grew out of my long-standing interest in the role that fantasy plays in children's lives. The purpose of the seminar was to explore the meaning of fairy tales and discover how they affect a child's psychological development. Sitting in a circle on Monday afternoons, the students and I discussed the classical tales of the Grimm brothers as well as that most famous twentieth-century fairy tale, *The Wizard of Oz*.

I was struck by how impassioned students would become when we talked about the stories. The atmosphere was different from that of other courses in which students merely sat back and took notes. Everyone had a favorite fairy tale from childhood that struck an emotional chord. One young woman recalled her mother reading *Cinderella* at bedtime and insisting that her mother repeat the sequence with the fairy godmother before turning off the lights. There was something about the silver and gold gown and the jewels that was irresistible.

Why do fairy tales trigger such strong reactions years after they are first encountered? Do they change us in some way, and if so, how? What is behind their enduring appeal? In trying to answer these questions, I discovered a number of myths that surround fairy tales, many of which my students and I held in common.

MYTH 1:
FAIRY TALES ARE CHILDREN'S STORIES

One thing I learned in studying fairy tales was that a substantial number never made their way into children's storybooks. On one level, this didn't come as a complete surprise. Some fairy-tale collections contain so many stories that they would become unwieldy if reproduced in their entirety. The Grimm brothers' *Kinder- und Hausmärchen* (Children's and Household Tales) contains well over two hundred fairy tales, of which only a dozen or so are ever included in children's books.

Yet the sheer volume of fairy tales is not the whole story. Charles Perrault's *Contes de ma Mère l'Oye* (Tales from Mother Goose) contains only twelve fairy tales, including *Cinderella*, *Little Red Riding Hood*, and *Sleeping Beauty*, yet some of the stories in his collection are mysteriously missing from modern storybooks. These omissions are especially perplexing since the stories left out are as captivating as the ones left in. One of the missing tales is *Donkeyskin*. It begins like this:

Once upon a time there lived a king who was so beloved by his subjects that he thought himself the happiest monarch in the world. He was rich beyond compare, and owned stables filled with the finest Arabian stallions. In one of the stables there lived a magic donkey. It was the king's most precious possession for it enjoyed a unique talent: it produced golden dung. When the king's servants arrived at the stable each morning, they found the animal's litter strewn with gold coins. Thus it was that the magic donkey provided the king with an endless source of riches.

After many years of prosperity, the king received the terrible news that his wife was dying. But before she died, the queen, who had always thought first of the king's happiness, gathered up all her strength, and said to him:

"I know for the good of your people, as well as for yourself, that you must marry again. But do not set about it in a hurry. Wait until you have found a woman more beautiful and better formed than myself."

Years go by, but the king's efforts come to naught. There is no one in the kingdom whose beauty surpasses that of the dead queen. One day he realizes there is indeed someone in the land more beautiful than his late wife. That person is none other than his daughter. The princess has blossomed into a beautiful young maiden and now is of marriageable age. The king sets out to take her for his bride.

The princess was horrified when she learned of her father's plans. She ran to her godmother, a wise and powerful fairy, who counseled her to put off her father by requesting wedding gifts which the king could not possibly deliver. Following her godmother's advice, the princess asked first for a dress that sparkled like the stars; the next morning she found a star-studded dress lying outside her door. She next asked for a dress made of moonbeams; once again her wish was fulfilled. Finally she insisted on a dress that shone as bright as the sun. The next morning she woke to discover a golden gown of unimaginable brilliance by her door. One by one, her father managed to fill all her requests.

In desperation, the princess returned to her fairy godmother to ask what to do. The old woman advised the frightened princess to demand the skin of the king's prized donkey. The child's godmother was positive the king would never kill the animal for the donkey was the source of all his wealth. "It is from that donkey he obtains his vast riches," the fairy godmother told the royal princess, "and I am sure he will never grant your wish."

To the princess's dismay, the king killed the magic donkey and presented the hide to his daughter as a wedding gift. The godmother, sensing the hopelessness of the situation, told the child she must escape. She instructed her to smear her face and hands with soot, wrap herself in the donkey skin, and leave the palace under cover of darkness.

"Go as far as you can," she told her. "Your dresses and jewels will follow you underground, and if you strike the earth three times, you will immediately have anything you need."

The adventures of a beleaguered young girl who flees her father by adopting an animal disguise is a common theme in fairy tales. In an Italian fairy tale titled *L'Orsa* (The She Bear), the princess places a magic stick in her mouth that temporarily turns her into a bear so that she can escape the castle and her father. In *Allereiruh* (Many Furs), a German folk tale, a maiden demands that her father, the king, manufacture a dress made of the pelts of a thousand different animals. When he delivers the fur dress, thereby fulfilling her "impossible" request, she disguises herself by putting it on and escapes into the countryside.

The frightened princess in *Donkeyskin* also flees into the countryside, where she comes across a prince's castle. She secures work as a washerwoman in the castle laundry and keeps to herself, hoping no one will recognize her. But she is ridiculed by her coworkers, who dub her "Donkeyskin" because of the foul-smelling animal hide she wears. The princess endures their taunts in silence, not wanting to reveal her identity.

One day, weary of her slovenly appearance, the princess strikes the ground and retrieves her dresses. She tries on the one made of moonbeams and for a few moments relives her former glory. The prince, who happens to be inspecting the inner courtyard of the castle at the time, spies her in her finery and is dazzled by her beauty. He instantly falls in love with the mysterious maiden but is too love-stricken to approach her. He retires to his chambers and falls into a royal funk.

Eventually, though, true love wins out. The prince gets his mother to invite the maiden to the palace and devises a clever ruse involving a ring that will fit only the finger of a princess. Donkeyskin arrives at the great hall clad in the filthy donkey skin.

"Are you the girl who has a room in the furthest corner of the inner courtyard?" the prince asked.

"Yes, my lord, I am," answered she.

"Hold out your hand then," continued the prince, and, to the astonishment of everyone present, a little hand, white and delicate, emerged from beneath the black and dirty skin. The ring slipped on with the utmost ease, and, as it did, the skin fell to the ground, disclosing a figure of such beauty that the prince fell to his knees before her, while the king and queen rejoiced.

Donkeyskin concludes with the prince asking the princess for her hand in marriage, which she gladly gives. Her father—who by now has conveniently remarried and been cleansed of his unholy passion—is invited to the wedding and everyone lives happily ever after.

The reason *Donkeyskin* is deleted from children's storybooks has less to do with the donkey's unique talent—children delight in anything related to excretory functions—than with the king's unnatural longing. Incestuous desire is something one doesn't expect to find in a fairy tale. In some versions of the story, the princess is changed to an adopted daughter to play down the story's incestuous theme. Still, a fairy tale that describes a father lusting after his daughter—adopted or otherwise—is not the kind of story most parents would choose to read to their children.

Then why does it appear in Perrault's collection? For the simple reason that fairy tales were never meant for children. Originally conceived of as adult entertainment, fairy tales were told at social gatherings, in spinning rooms, in the fields, and in other settings where adults congregated—not in the nursery.

This is why many early fairy tales include exhibitionism, rape, and voyeurism. One version of *Little Red Riding Hood* has the heroine do a striptease for the wolf before jumping into bed with him. In an early rendering of *The Sleeping Beauty*, the prince ravages the princess in her sleep and then departs, leaving her pregnant. And in *The Princess Who Couldn't Laugh*, the heroine is doomed to a life of spinsterhood because she inadvertently views the private parts of a witch. As late as the eighteenth century, fairy tales were dramatized in exclusive Parisian salons where they were considered *divertissements* for the culturally elite.

It was not until the nineteenth century that fairy tales came into their own as children's literature. This happened, in part, through the activities of itinerant peddlers, known as "chapmen," who traveled from village to village selling household wares, sheet music, and affordable little volumes called chapbooks. Costing only a few pennies, chapbooks, or "cheap books," contained drastically edited folktales, legends, and fairy tales that had been simplified to appeal to less literate audiences. Though poorly written and crudely illustrated, they caught the fancy of young readers, who, in their quest for magic and adventure, took them to their hearts.

MYTH 2: FAIRY TALES WERE WRITTEN
BY THE BROTHERS GRIMM

In the early 1800s, Wilhelm and Jacob Grimm published their famous two-volume collection of fairy tales, *Children's and Household Tales*. Their intent was to create a definitive sourcebook of existing German stories and legends that would reflect the folk origins of the German *volk*. The result was an anthology that many consider the most comprehensive fairy-tale collection of all time.

But Wilhelm and Jacob never actually wrote any of the tales included in their volumes. They merely compiled them, relying on friends and relatives to supply them with stories that had been circulating throughout central Europe for centuries. A number of tales in their collection were contributed by Dorothea Wild, Wilhelm's mother-in-law, and others came from Jeannette and Amalie Hassenphlug, two sisters who later married into the Grimm family. Never mind that most of the stories had French and Italian origins; the Grimms considered them uniquely German and included them in their collection.

Thus, the Grimm brothers' *Aschenputtel* (Cinder Maid) turns out to be a close relative of Charles Perrault's *Cinderella*. In both stories, a mean stepmother and her selfish daughters collude to make the heroine's life miserable, denying her the simplest pleasures and making sure she doesn't come to the attention of the prince. But the Grimm version contains neither a fairy godmother nor a glass slipper; instead, it features a zealous stepmother who mutilates her daughters' oversized feet so that they will fit into a slipper made of embroidered silk.

Similarly, *Little Red Cap*, the Grimms' story of a little girl who dallies in the woods on the way to visit her grandmother, is a more elaborate version of Perrault's *Little Red Riding Hood*. The Grimm version features not one wolf but two and ends with one of the wolves drowned. And *Briar Rose*, the story of a slumbering princess, is a drastically revised version of Perrault's *The Sleeping Beauty in the Woods*.

Although the Grimm brothers did not, technically speaking, write any of the tales, they altered them to make them more suitable for young readers. Their alterations were prompted, in part, by Wilhelm's puritanical leanings. But commercial concerns also played a role. The children's market for fairy tales, fueled by a growing recognition that children had their own unique interests, was growing tremendously, and publishers were more willing to invest money in books that parents found acceptable.

Many of the tales "written" by the Grimms continued to be altered as they underwent translation. The preface to an English-language edition of their work published in the nineteenth century contains the following statement by the translators.

> We have omitted about a dozen short pieces to which English mothers
> might object, and for good and satisfactory reasons have altered, in a
> slight way, four other stories. The mixture of sacred subjects with
> profane, though frequent in Germany, would not meet with favor in an
> English book.

Tales saturated with blatant sexual references thus yielded to stories that catered more to childhood sensibilities. And in the process, people assumed the versions they were reading were authored by the Grimms.

MYTH 3:
FAIRY TALES TEACH LESSONS

The third common misconception has to do with the didactic value of fairy tales. Some folklorists believe that fairy tales offer "lessons" on correct behavior, advising young readers on how to succeed in life. *Little Red Riding Hood*, it is thought, exhorts children to listen to their mothers and to refrain from talking to strangers, especially while strolling through the woods. *Sleeping Beauty* allegedly cautions children not to venture into places where they don't belong; the heroine learns this lesson all too well when she wanders into a forbidden room and pricks her finger on a poison spindle.

The belief that fairy tales teach lessons can be traced, in part, to Perrault, whose stories came equipped with quaint morals, many of them delivered in rhyme. *Little Red Riding Hood* ends with the following caution:

> *Little girls, this seems to say*
> *Never stop upon your way.*
> *Never trust a stranger-friend;*
> *No one knows where it will end.*

Reasonable advice, except that *Little Red Riding Hood* has more to do with food and cannibalism than with avoiding strangers in the woods. It is doubtful that young women in New York refrain from chatting with strange men in Central Park because they read *Little Red Riding Hood* as children.

Some of Perrault's so-called lessons contain questionable advice and incline toward cynicism. Consider the caution he includes at the end of *Cinderella:*

> *Godmothers are useful things*
> *Even when without the wings.*
> *Wisdom may be yours and wit,*
> *Courage, industry, and grit—*
> *What's the use of these at all,*
> *If you lack a friend at call.*

Perrault seems to be preaching that intelligence, hard work, and courage count for little unless one has acquaintances in high places. It's not who you are but who you know; forget about native strengths and abilities if you don't have connections. Useful advice perhaps for someone entering politics, but not a laudable lesson for children barely out of the nursery.

If one wants to instill lessons in the young, it is better to look to Aesop's fables or other children's stories specifically meant to provide useful advice. *The Hare and the Tortoise* teaches children that slow and steady wins the race, that frivolous pursuits are to be avoided if one hopes to succeed. *The Wolf in Sheep's Clothing* teaches that you may end up paying a heavy price for pretending to be someone you're not.

And *The Little Engine That Could*—a testimony to perseverance—argues for the need to have faith in one's abilities ("I think I can, I think I can . . . "). Fairy tales have many appealing qualities, but teaching lessons is not one of them.

THE MEANING OF FAIRY TALES

So what is it about fairy tales that makes them so captivating? Why do *Jack and the Beanstalk*, *Snow White*, and *Cinderella* have such enormous appeal? The most obvious explanation is that fairy tales are an unparalleled source of adventure. Few children's stories contain death-defying chase sequences such as one finds in *Jack and the Beanstalk*. There is nothing that focuses one's attention as much as a cannibalistic ogre breathing down one's neck. And then there is *Hansel and Gretel*. How many tales from childhood can boast a sequence in which an innocent child is rescued from certain death at the very last moment? Stories like *The Velveteen Rabbit* and *The Little Engine That Could*, though delightful in their own right, do not provide the hair-raising thrills that fairy tales do.

But fairy tales are more than suspense-filled adventures that excite the imagination, more than mere entertainment. Beyond the chase scenes and last-minute rescues are serious dramas that reflect events taking place in the child's inner world. Whereas the initial attraction of a fairy tale may lie in its ability to enchant and entertain, its lasting value lies in its power to help children deal with the internal conflicts they face in the course of growing up.

This is why fairy tales endure. It is the reason anniversary editions of Disney classics sell out year after year and movies such as *The Little Mermaid* and *Aladdin* break box office records. How else can one explain the appeal of a story like *Hansel and Gretel* in which innocent children are sent into the woods to die of starvation? How can one justify a story like *The Little Mermaid*, in which the heroine's tongue is cut from her mouth merely to seal a bargain? Fairy tales, in addition to being magical adventures, help children deal with struggles that are a part of their day-to-day lives.

The Psychoanalytic View: Cinderella Meets Oedipus

What precisely is the nature of these struggles? Followers of Sigmund Freud contend that they are sexual by and large, rooted, as it were, in oedipal concerns. Bruno Bettelheim, a psychoanalyst and author of *The Uses of Enchantment*, maintained that the hidden text in fairy tales revolves about such matters as penis envy, castration anxiety, and unconscious incestuous longings. According to Bettelheim, hidden psychosexual conflicts are the driving force in a whole host of fairy tales ranging from *Little Red Riding Hood* to *Rumpelstiltskin*.

The Freudian emphasis on sexuality leads to a number of fanciful, if somewhat far-fetched interpretations. The struggle between Snow White and her stepmother, for example, supposedly derives from Snow White's oedipal longing for her father. The older woman embarks on her murderous quest because she believes that the seven-year-old poses a sexual threat. Her incessant query, "Mirror, mirror, on the wall, who is the fairest of them all?" literally reflects her fear that the king will find Snow White more appealing than her. It thus is the implicit sexual struggle between the young girl and the queen, rather than the queen's preoccupation with her looks, that fuels the plot.

Snow White's relationship to the seven dwarfs inspires a similarly inventive interpretation. Referring to the dwarfs as "stunted penises," Bettelheim writes, "These 'little men' with their stunted bodies and their mining occupation—they skillfully penetrate into dark holes—all suggest phallic connotations." It is because of their diminished sexual capacities that the dwarfs pose no threat to the pubescent Snow White. Since they are unable to perform, they provide the child with a safe haven at a time in life when she is sexually vulnerable.

Even *Cinderella* does not escape the swath of the psychoanalytic brush. In the Grimm brothers' version, the stepmother's wish to have the prince take one of her daughters as his bride is so intense that she orders them to cut off their heels and toes so their feet will fit into the slipper. When the prince notices blood flowing from the shoe, he naturally becomes distraught. But his distress, according to psychoanalytic doctrine, is prompted not so much by the stepmother's wanton brutality—or her efforts to deceive him—but by the castration anxiety aroused by the sight of the blood. In one fairy tale after another, sexuality is heralded as the propelling force behind anything and everything in the plot.

Is it reasonable to expect young children to respond to the sexual undertones in the narrative even if they do indeed exist? Folklorist and fairy-tale scholar Maria Tatar thinks not. She charges that using fairy tales to warn children about the dangers of sexuality stretches matters. Commenting on Bettelheim's psychosexual interpretation of *The Sleeping Beauty*, she writes: "It may be that parents will have sex on their minds when they read about a princess who pricks her finger on a spindle, then falls into a deep sleep, but children are unlikely to free-associate from the blood on the princess's finger to intercourse and menstruation, as Bettelheim believes they will." By the same token, it requires an imaginative leap to get from the parting of the thorny hedge that surrounds the castle to a symbolic opening of the vagina.

While no one will deny that children are sexual beings, and that some fairy tales may tap sexual longings, sex is far from the most pressing concern in the lives of the very young. Children worry more about pleasing their parents, making and keeping friends, and doing well in school than they do about sex. Children worry about their standing in the family, and about whether they are loved as much as their siblings. They wonder whether there is anything they might say or do that could lead to their being abandoned. Many of the concerns that occupy the minds of the very young have less to do with sex than with thoughts and impulses that affect their relationships with significant figures in their lives.

The Self Perspective: Pursuing Goodness

A psychological perspective that provides a powerful alternative to the psychoanalytic point of view focuses on the child's burgeoning sense of self. Instead of emphasizing sexual matters, self theory focuses on aspects of the personality that threaten to undermine a child's intimate connection to others, particularly parents and peers. Much of what takes place in a fairy tale, accordingly, mirrors the struggles that children wage against forces in the self that hamper their ability to establish and sustain meaningful relationships.

Within this perspective, *Hansel and Gretel*, for instance, is thought to address age-old issues having to do with *gluttony*. Even after Hansel and his sister descend on the witch's house and eat their fill, they continue to devour greedily what's left of the cottage: "Hansel, who liked the taste of the roof, tore down a great piece of it, and Gretel pushed out the whole of a sugar window pane." One of the great challenges of childhood is knowing when enough is enough.

Consider *Snow White*, the ultimate paean to *vanity*. The story graphically demonstrates what happens when concerns over appearances interfere with more important matters. Not only is the evil queen preoccupied with her looks, but Snow White almost loses her life when she lusts after the pretty laces offered to her by her disguised stepmother. And *Cinderella*, when one looks beyond the pretty gown and the prince, is essentially a story about *envy*.

Every major fairy tale is unique in that it addresses a specific failing or unhealthy predisposition in the self. As soon as we move beyond "Once upon a time," we discover that fairy tales are about vanity, gluttony, envy, lust, deceit, greed, or sloth—the "seven deadly sins of childhood." Though a particular fairy tale may address more than one "sin," one typically occupies center stage.

So even though *Hansel and Gretel* contains elements of deceit, it is primarily a story about food and overeating. It is true that the parents lie to the children, telling them that they will return to fetch them after leaving them in the woods, but food and sustenance are the themes that drive the plot. The children are abandoned because the family is out of food; they devour the candy cottage because they are hungry; and the witch fattens Hansel in order to turn him into a more savory meal.

The "sinful" underpinnings of fairy tales help explain why children respond to them with such emotional fervor, and why certain fairy tales become personal favorites. A story like *Snow White* can have special meaning for a child dealing with issues of looks and desirability, matters about which children are intimately concerned. The evil stepmother's obsessive preoccupation with her appearance literally mirrors this concern. In a similar vein, children in families where there is intense sibling rivalry are apt to be drawn to stories like *Cinderella* in which envy is an ongoing preoccupation.

The deeper significance of the so-called deadly sins is that they arouse what is perhaps the most dreaded fear of childhood: abandonment. To be abandoned, to be left on your own when you cannot fend for yourself, is a terrifying prospect for the very young. And it can affect adults as well. This was brought home some years ago in an episode involving a friend of mine named Virginia.

Ginnie and her husband were spending the afternoon with my wife and me at an outdoor antique fair on Cape Cod when she became separated from the group. The four of us had been wandering through the stalls, each engrossed in items of personal interest, but also keeping an eye out for each other. At some point, we realized we had lost Ginnie. We searched for her without success—the crowd was too large—so we continued meandering through the stalls, assuming that we would all meet up at some later time.

We eventually did, but when we found Ginnie, she was sitting on a stool near a security station sobbing like a child. The incident had rekindled memories of the time when her mother, lacking the means to care for her, had placed her in an orphanage. Though Ginnie had over the years become intellectually reconciled to her mother's decision, and though her mother eventually reclaimed her, she could not stem the tide of feelings that welled up within her when she found herself stranded once again.

Parents often unwittingly—and sometimes even intentionally—play on children's fears of abandonment to force them to behave. We all have witnessed a parent threatening a dawdling child with, "If you don't come this very minute, I'm going to leave you right here," or, "I'm going now and I'm not coming back." Very young children also worry that their parents will sell them or give them away if they are bad.

The fantasy of abandonment—or other dire consequence—as punishment for acting out "sinful" tendencies is a constant threat. But it is hard being good, and youngsters often find themselves at the mercy of tendencies they cannot fully control or understand. This is why reading fairy tales to children is reassuring. Not only does the parent's presence help the child manage scary passages, but it communicates that untoward thoughts and impulses will not bring about rejection.

A parent's sensitivity to the sin featured in a particular fairy tale can help enrich these stories for children. Youngsters invariably ask questions when they listen to a fairy tale: Why does Jack steal the harp? Why does Snow White let the old woman in the house? Why does the witch die? By subtly calling the child's attention to the underlying sin in the story, parents—and teachers—can make listening to a fairy tale a richer, more meaningful experience.

This doesn't mean that one should try to explain fairy tales to children; the meaning of these stories is best come upon intuitively. But knowledge of a story's featured "sin" can, in the context of children's natural curiosity, help make the answers to their questions more meaningful. When conducted in a context of playful exploration rather than explanation, feedback of this sort can enhance a fairy tale's psychological mission: resolving struggles between positive and negative forces in the self.

BALCONIES OF THE MIND

The way fairy tales resolve these struggles is by offering children a stage upon which they can play out inner conflicts. Children, in listening to a fairy tale, unconsciously project parts of themselves into various characters in the story, using them as psychological repositories for competing elements in the self. The evil queen in *Snow White*, for example, embodies narcissism, and the young princess, with whom readers identify, embodies parts of the child struggling to overcome this tendency. Vanquishing the queen represents a triumph of positive forces in the self over vain impulses. By couching struggles between different parts of the self as struggles between the characters in the story, fairy tales give children a way of resolving tensions that affect the way they feel about themselves.

In this way, fairy tales are akin to psychodrama, a therapeutic technique that blends theatrical concepts with psychotherapeutic principles. Introduced in Vienna in the late 1920s as *Stehgreiftheater* (the Theater of Spontaneity), psychodrama was later imported into the United States by Jacob Moreno. A pioneering psychiatrist in the field of group therapy, Moreno believed that dramatic reenactments were invaluable in exploring hidden psychological conflicts.

I was originally exposed to psychodrama as a psychology student in college. The professor of my abnormal psychology course took our class on a field trip to a small auditorium in Manhattan to see a demonstration of the technique by the master himself. After some introductory remarks, Moreno asked for a volunteer from the audience to participate in the presentation. A student in the class, Jack, climbed onto the stage and responded to some brief questions of Moreno's by telling him a little about his family, including the fact that he had a younger brother. Another student in the audience was recruited to play the brother, and Moreno and his wife took the parts of Jack's mother and father.

Moreno then asked Jack to recall an incident that characterized the kind of things that went on between him and his younger sibling. The incident Jack recounted started off innocently enough. He described how his mother made him and his brother take baths after they came in from play, and how he faithfully cleaned the bathtub to ready it for his brother once he had finished. His brother, he complained, never reciprocated, always leaving a dirty tub when he was the first to bathe. The "quarrel" that ensued drew laughter from the audience as well as from the participants onstage, centering as it did on the seemingly trivial matters of wet washcloths and bathtub rings.

But then the mood turned dark. Jack began to protest more vehemently to his "mother" and "father" about his brother's insensitivity. Neither Moreno nor his wife was very sympathetic, and both suggested that the brothers work things out between themselves. The ensuing interchanges became increasingly heated as Jack, fighting to hold back tears, insisted that his "parents" hardly ever took his side. At one point, he blurted out that they loved his brother more than him. The audience became hushed as Jack's long-standing resentment toward his brother—and anger toward his parents—filled the air. What started off as seemingly innocuous play-acting had turned into a heart-rending family drama.

Fairy tales are the psychodramas of childhood. Beneath the surface of these fanciful excursions into fantasy are real-life dramas that mirror real-life struggles. The rivalry between Cinderella and her sisters is not that far removed from the rivalry between Jack and his brother. This is why fairy tales are so captivating. Not only do they entertain, they tap into powerful feelings that might otherwise remain hidden. Although the characters in these miniature dramas—like Jack's brother and parents—are not "real," the intensity of their interchanges creates an emotional reality as powerful as anything in a child's life.

A major player in these dramas is the witch. Whether she's a black-hearted queen, an evil sorceress, or a vindictive stepmother, she is easily identified by the lethal threat she poses to the hero or heroine. The witch in *Hansel and Gretel* is not satisfied merely to scold Hansel for nibbling on her house—she plans to make a meal of him. The evil queen in *Snow White* will not rest until she sees Snow White dead. And the Wicked Witch of the West has one goal in mind: destroying Dorothy and her three companions.

At the same time that the witch poses an external threat to the hero or heroine, she magnifies inner flaws and frailties in the reader. The witch in *Hansel and Gretel* takes gluttony to its extreme: she is not only insatiable but a cannibal. The Sea Witch in Disney's *The Little Mermaid* is overtly lustful: she tells Ariel that the only way to get a man is to seduce him. In one fairy tale after another, the witch embodies unwholesome aspects of the self that all children struggle against.

Very often the witch in these stories takes the form of a malevolent stepmother. The Grimm brothers' *Children's and Household Tales* contains over a dozen stories, *Snow White* and *Cinderella* being two notable examples, in which a stepmother makes the heroine's life miserable by taunting her, withholding food from her, or forcing her to perform impossible tasks. The witchlike nature of the stepmother is compounded by her use of magic to perform her evil deeds. In one English fairy tale, the stepmother changes her stepdaughter into an enormous worm; in an Irish tale, she transforms her stepchildren into wolves.

Modern critics claim that negative portrayal of the stepmother is part of a misogynistic streak in fairy tales. There is a grain of truth to the notion that fairy tales often depict some women as cruel and malicious, but there is danger in attributing too much significance to this notion since it implies that fairy tales are faithful representations of reality; they are not. Though there certainly are historical instances in which stepmothers favored their own children and may have been mean to their stepchildren, there is no evidence that stepmothers are as cruel as they are made out to be in fairy tales. Indeed, the word *step* in *stepmother* derives from the Middle English *steif*, which means "bereaved," a term used to describe an orphaned child. Rather than being cruel, stepmothers historically were mother surrogates who provided comfort for orphaned children.

We consequently must not take the figure of the witch too literally. She is less an actual person than a representation of psychological forces operating in the child's psyche. Author Linda Gray Sexton, daughter of poet Anne Sexton, underscores this in her memoir describing her early relationship with her mother. In recounting the role of fairy tales in her childhood, she writes, "I see just how the stepmother operates in my mind—perhaps in every reader's mind—as a surrogate for my own mother's undesirable aspects."

THE STEPPING-STONES OF CHILDHOOD

Fairy tales are a part of not only children's lives but our adult lives as well. Images and themes from fairy tales regularly insinuate themselves into our thoughts and conversations, functioning as metaphors for our most fervent desires and deepest hopes. We long for a prince—or princess—to come into our lives and make us complete ("someday my prince will come"). We hope that our business ventures and other important endeavors will have a "fairy tale ending." We wonder whether it is possible in the face of environmental threats and global conflicts to "live happily ever after."

But fairy tales are more than convenient metaphors for describing adult aspirations. They can, under certain circumstances, address pragmatic concerns. An acquaintance of mine, the president of a management consulting firm, uses fairy tales to help troubled corporations increase productivity and improve the corporate culture. One of her interventions takes the form of early morning meetings with CEOs and middle managers in which a fairy tale is recounted, after which participants are asked to apply themes in the story to company dynamics. Because fairy tales include many of the same dynamics found in the workplace—power, control, envy—they offer a meaningful way of providing fresh insights into company conflicts. She tells me these early morning sessions are among the most effective interventions in the firm's consulting repertoire; rarely does anyone miss such a meeting or arrive late.

Fairy tales, finally, help illuminate what goes on in psychotherapy, especially as it relates to patients' efforts to reconcile childhood feelings—and failings. On more than one occasion, I have drawn on fairy tales to help a patient gain insight into conflicts that derive from envy, greed, vanity, or other childhood "sins." People take these stories very seriously and apply them to their lives. One of my patients who was mean to her sister reconsidered her behavior after we contrasted the Grimm brothers' version of *Cinderella* with the Perrault version. In the Grimm brothers' story, the heroine's emissaries, two white pigeons, peck out the eyes of the sisters at the end. The Perrault version ends with the sisters embraced by the heroine and invited to live in the palace with her and the prince.

Just as the queen in *Snow White* is obsessed with her looks, so we too get overly caught up at times with appearances. We may not kill to guarantee our status as the fairest in the land, but we certainly spend enough time and money making sure we don't go unnoticed. And who among us has not coveted the possessions—or position—of someone else? Only rarely does an individual usurp another person's identity—as does the evil servant woman in *The Goose Girl*—but that doesn't mean we don't occasionally entertain fantasies about taking another person's place.

Ultimately, the impact that fairy tales have on us as adults stems from the influence they had on us when we were young, for it is in childhood that the seeds of virtue are sown. In the pages that follow, we revisit many of the familiar tales of childhood—as well as some that are less well known—to illustrate how fairy tales help children combat sloth, envy, greed, and other troublesome tendencies. We'll learn why mothers in fairy tales die prematurely, and why fathers are so often depicted as weak and ineffectual. Why, for example, is Cinderella's father never around when she needs him? We will accompany Dorothy on her journey to the Emerald City to discover how modern fairy tales like *The Wizard of Oz* address sins in the twentieth century. And we'll consider the most fundamental question of all: Must the witch *always* die? The answer to this last question has far-reaching implications, for the witch lives not only in the pages of a fairy tale but in the deepest reaches of our minds.

2
The Witch Within
The Sleeping Beauties

$\mathfrak{T}$he prince approached the sleeping princess, who lay draped upon a velvet throne under a dais of brocade. He called out to her, but she seemed insensible, as if in a trance. As he contemplated her many charms, he suddenly felt his blood course hotly through his veins. The prince lifted her in his arms and carried her to a bed, whereon he gathered the first fruits of love while she slept on. When he was through, he left the princess, and returned to his own kingdom, where, in the pressing business of his realm, he thought no more of the incident.

An incident? Rape? Is this the *Sleeping Beauty* from our childhood? What happened to the tender kiss on the lips, the enchanted reawakening, the gala wedding celebration? Instead of a grateful princess welcoming her rescuer with open arms, we are presented with a vision of a defenseless maiden ravished in her sleep by a wandering prince. And that is only the beginning.

> The princess slept on for nine months, and when the nine months were up she gave birth to two beautiful infants, a boy and a girl. Throughout her pregnancy, the princess, whose name was Talia, had been attended by two fairies who now placed the infants at their sleeping mother's breasts. One of the children, unable to find the mother's nipple, sucked on Talia's finger, loosening the poison splinter that had lodged there when she pricked it on the forbidden spindle. The princess waked and christened the babies Sun and Moon. Some time later, the prince returned to claim Talia and the children.

There is only one problem. The prince is already married. His wife—an evil woman with cannibalistic tendencies—learns of her husband's infidelity and conspires to kill Talia and the infants. She invites the princess to her castle and secretly instructs the cook to slay the children, telling him to chop them up and serve them to her husband in a stew. But the cook cannot bring himself to do such a terrible deed. He hides the children and substitutes a lamb dish in their stead.

Convinced that the children have been disposed of, the wife turns her attention to Talia. While her husband is off on a journey, she orders her servants to build a bonfire in the castle courtyard and to throw Talia into the flames. Just as the heroine is about to be put to death, the prince returns to discover his wife's sinister plan. He is overjoyed to find Talia still alive and rescues her from the flames, but is horrified to learn that he has unwittingly devoured his own children.

> "Alas!" the heartbroken prince moaned. "Then I, myself, am the wolf of my own sweet lambs." He turned to his wicked wife and said, "Ah, thou

renegade bitch, what evil deed hast thou done? Begone, thou shall get thy just dessert." And thus saying, he commanded the wife to be thrust into the flames which had been prepared for Talia.

As the evil woman twisted in the fire, the cook told the stricken prince that his children were still alive. "They have been spared," the cook informed him, hurrying off to retrieve Sun and Moon from their hiding place. The two children rushed to their parents and clung to them in a joyful reunion. The prince took Talia to be his wife, and everyone lived happily ever after.

This story of an enchanted sleeping maiden, first recorded by the Neapolitan storyteller Giambattista Basile in 1634, is one of the earliest written versions of the sleeping beauty saga. Titled *Talia, Sun, and Moon*, the story contains all the ingredients of tales that feature a sleeping maiden: an enchanted princess under a deathlike spell, a long interment in a castle tower, and deliverance by a handsome prince. And in the manner of classic fairy tales, the story ends with the death of the witch—in this case, the evil wife.

Three hundred years later, another wicked woman suffers an equally horrible death. This time the witch's demise is brought about by the actions of an innocent child:

Dorothy picked up the bucket of water that stood near and dashed it over the Witch, wetting her from head to foot.

Instantly the wicked woman gave a loud cry of fear, and then, as Dorothy looked at her in wonder, the Witch began to shrink and fall away.

"See what you have done!" she screamed. "In a minute, I shall melt away."

Dorothy watches in astonishment as the witch dissolves into a shapeless mass. In what is perhaps the most popular children's story of the twentieth century, the Wicked Witch of the West melts away, never to be heard from again.

WHY THE WITCH MUST DIE

In the three centuries that elapsed between the publication of Giambattista Basile's *Talia, Sun, and Moon* and L. Frank Baum's *The Wizard of Oz*, hundreds of fairy-tale witches and their counterparts—sorceresses, ogresses, vengeful queens, and evil stepmothers—have met similar fates. In *The Juniper Tree*, a fairy tale recorded by the Brothers Grimm, the evil stepmother is crushed to death by a giant millstone. Her counterparts in *Snow White* and *Hansel and Gretel* fare no better. In one tale after another, the witch not only dies, but dies violently.

Charles Perrault's *The Sleeping Beauty in the Woods* bears striking similarities to Basile's tale except that the prince is single and considerate enough to marry the princess before getting her pregnant. But the prince isn't home free—instead of a jealous wife, he has an over-possessive mother.

To keep his mother at bay, the prince keeps his marriage a secret and shuttles between his home and the home of his new bride. He explains his lengthy absences by telling his mother he is off on hunting trips. Two years elapse, during which the prince and princess become the proud parents of a daughter and son. The prince does not dare tell his parents about his wife and children because his mother not only is possessive but, like the wife in Basile's tale, tends toward cannibalism: "It was whispered at court that she had the greatest difficulty keeping herself from pouncing on little children when they were near."

The prince's secret life is exposed when he is called home to assume the throne of his father, who has passed away. He returns with his wife and the children, confident that no harm will come to them now that he is monarch. But he has underestimated his mother. Like her counterpart in Basile's tale, she too plots to do away with the children and her daughter-in-law. The evil woman waits until her son is off conducting business in a distant land, and then swings into action. Her plan is to dispose of the children first, then throw her daughter-in-law into a vat filled with toads, poisonous snakes, and other vile creatures.

The prince, fortunately, returns home just in time to stop his mother from implementing her evil scheme. He rides onto the palace grounds just as his wife is about to be thrust into the cauldron.

Nobody had expected him so soon, but he had traveled posthaste. Filled with amazement, he demanded to know what the horrible spectacle meant. None dared tell him, and at that moment the ogress, enraged at what confronted her, threw herself headlong into the vat, and was devoured on the spot by the hideous creatures within.

Perrault, whose stories were enthusiastically received by members of Louis XIV's court, eliminated the more controversial ingredients from Basile's tale, no doubt to avoid ruffling feathers at Versailles. One would imagine that members of the royal entourage might not take kindly to a tale in which adultery and rape were prominently featured. By substituting a vindictive mother for a vengeful wife, Perrault conveniently eradicated the "dangerous liaisons" in the story with one bold stroke, thereby sparing royal sensibilities and potential discontent. The witch nevertheless remained the focus of the story.

In the Grimm brothers' story, *The Sleeping Beauty*, the one with which most readers are familiar, the witch is spared the fate of her predecessors for the simple reason that she doesn't exist. The story instead features a benevolent fairy who reverses a death curse by changing it into an extended sleep. One might argue that the uninvited thirteenth fairy, the one who issued the death curse, is the witch. But she disappears early in the narrative. Once she arrives at the ball celebrating the infant Rosamund's birth and delivers her pronouncement, she is never heard from again. There consequently is no enduring malevolent presence in the story, and no penultimate struggle between the forces of good and evil.

The Grimm version focuses instead on the fateful prophecy, the accidental pricking of the finger, and the hundred-year sleep. It thus ends where the other stories begin, with the princess roused from her enchanted slumber by the prince.

And when he saw her looking so lovely in her sleep, he could not turn away his eyes; presently he stooped and kissed her, and she awaked. The princess opened her eyes, and looked very kindly on him. And she rose, and they went forth together, and the king and the queen and whole court waked up, and gazed on each other with wonderment.

Then the wedding of the prince and Rosamund was held with all splendor, and they lived very happily together until their lives' end.

No sex, no babies, no vengeful wife, no jealous mother-in-law—in other words, no witch.

The exclusion of the witch from the Grimm brothers' *Sleeping Beauty* tends to be an exception in fairy-tale lore. She occupies a central position not only in other tales involving a sleeping princess but in most major fairy tales. The witch is an indispensable part of *Hansel and Gretel*, as she is in *Rapunzel* and *The Little Mermaid*. And she plays a pivotal role in *The Wizard of Oz*. Without the Wicked Witch of the West, the story would be reduced to little more than a fanciful travelogue through a land filled with sound but very little fury.

But why must the witch die? And why must she die such a horrible death? The answers to these questions lie not in the stories themselves but in the reader. Fairy tales may be enchanted adventures, but they also deal with a universal struggle—the battle between good and bad forces in the self. Born of a primitive psychological dynamic called "splitting," the battle has its origins in the earliest interactions between mother and child. To appreciate the psychological significance of fairy tales, we therefore need to travel back to a time in life when witches, wizards, and fairy tales were but mere specks on the psychological horizon.

THE ORIGINS OF GOODNESS:
SPLITTING AND THE SELF

Much of human existence entails reconciling basic divisions in the self that govern our relationships with others: lovable versus unlovable, loyal versus disloyal, worthwhile versus worthless. These divisions have their beginnings in the infant's crude separation of the world into satisfying (good) sensations and unsatisfying (bad) sensations: fullness is good, emptiness bad; warmth is good, cold bad; to be held is good, to be deprived of contact bad. Long before children are able to assign verbal labels to what is good or bad, a primitive sensory intelligence enables them to recognize that the world—or whatever is out there—is divided into good and bad.

As the infant matures, unconnected images, sounds, and sensations coalesce in the figure of the mother or the primary caretaker. Since the mother is the child's main source of sustenance, it is only natural that the child looks to her to fulfill its every need. For the infant, the mother is all-giving and all-loving, the source of all that is good in the world.

But mothers are only human. They cannot always satisfy the immediate needs of their infant charges. Mothers aren't always around to provide nourishment precisely when the infant suffers hunger pangs; they cannot drop everything at a moment's notice to soothe the infant when the infant is irritable. The demands of everyday life prevent the mother from being all the child wants and expects her to be.

This doesn't prevent children from clinging to the fantasy of a maternal Nirvana. But over time the realities of infant life force the child to face the unsettling realization that the person responsible for its survival is both consistent and inconsistent, both gratifying and frustrating—both good and bad. The problem is that the infant, hampered by limited conceptual resources, finds this idea difficult if not impossible to absorb. The result is confusion and anxiety.

The way young children deal with this distressing state of affairs is by mentally "splitting" the mother into two psychic entities: a gratifying "good mother" and a frustrating "bad mother." The child then responds to each image as if it were a separate and distinct entity so as to inject some semblance of order into what otherwise would be a highly unpredictable world. This allows children to respond internally to their maternal caretakers as "good mommies" one moment and as "horrible mommies" the next without having to deal with the inherent inconsistency.

Over time the two maternal representations—the good mother and the bad mother—are psychologically "metabolized" and become transformed into good and bad parts of the child's developing sense of self. Much of this comes about through language, and the increasing appearance of "I" in the child's vocabulary. As children mature, they stop referring to themselves in the third person ("Susie go potty") and begin to refer to themselves in the first ("*I* go potty"). Maternal directives ("Don't stuff your mouth") are increasingly replaced by self-directives ("*I* shouldn't overeat"). As a result, control by others becomes increasingly replaced by self-control. These changes herald the development of an autonomous self and a sense of "I-ness."

As a result, the internalized good mother comes to be experienced less as an inner figure and more as a part of the self (the "good me"), while the bad mother is experienced as a negative part of the self (the "bad me"). We are not speaking here about bad mothers per se, although there certainly are mothers who neglect and abuse their children. Rather, we are talking about naturally occurring splits in the self that evolve from attempts on the part of young children to reconcile conflicting maternal experiences early in life.

This is why female characters figure so prominently in fairy tales, and why there are many more witches than ogres, and appreciably more fairy godmothers than fairy godfathers. Fairy tales are essentially maternal dramas in which witches, godmothers, and other female figures function as the fantasy derivatives of early childhood splitting. By transforming splits in the self into an adventure that pits the forces of good against the forces of evil, not only do fairy tales help children deal with negative tendencies in the self, they pay homage to the pivotal role that mothers play in the genesis of the self.

In contrast, male figures are relatively minor figures in most fairy tales. The prince tends to be a cardboard character, almost an afterthought, who materializes at the end of the story to ensure a happy ending. In many instances, the intervention of the prince is incidental to the heroine's survival. Snow White reawakens not because of any action on the prince's part, but because a servant accidentally drops the glass coffin in which she is entombed. In the Grimm brothers' version of *Little Red Riding Hood*, the heroine and the grandmother join forces to destroy the wolf; only in the Perrault version does the huntsman figure in the story.

Fathers do not fare much better in these tales. They are either off hunting or otherwise oblivious to their children's distress. Cinderella's father is nowhere about when the young girl is tormented by her stepmother. For some reason, he is ignorant of the fact that his only daughter is forced to wear filthy clothes and made to sleep on the kitchen floor. In Basile's Cinderella story, titled *Cat Cinderella*, the father forgets about the promise he made his daughter when he left home on a voyage—to bring her the first twig that strikes his cap. Only when his boat is becalmed—a reminder that he has overlooked his vow—does he remember her request.

Hansel and Gretel's father similarly fails to distinguish himself. When his wife announces that she is going to send the children into the woods to their death, he hardly protests. A weak-willed excuse for a father, he abandons his love for his children by meekly going along with his wife's plan. Unlike Greek myths and legends, in which most of the dynamics in the narratives flow from the actions of male characters—Zeus, Poseidon, Agamemnon, and the like—fairy tales are about women and the important role they play in the child's emerging sense of self. It isn't the Wizard who ultimately helps Dorothy find her way back to Kansas, but Glinda.

SOMETHING WICKED THIS WAY COMES

To ensure that a fairy tale fulfills its psychological mission—combating sinful tendencies in the self—the reader or listener must be drawn into the story on a personal level. Fairy tales accomplish this by casting the protagonists as ordinary children with whom young audiences can easily identify. The children in the story are impulsive and easily succumb to temptation. Hansel and Gretel greedily devour the gingerbread house, even though a voice repeatedly cautions them to keep their distance; Snow White invites the disguised queen into the cottage—not once but three times—in spite of repeated warnings by the dwarfs; and Sleeping Beauty wanders about the castle, opening doors to rooms she has been forbidden to enter. Youngsters have little trouble identifying with characters who fail to heed the voice of authority.

Identification rules the day even if the hero or heroine comes from a titled background, as in stories that feature princes and princesses. Most children harbor fantasies about leading privileged lives and enjoying the liberties associated with such an existence. But the royal children in fairy tales possess neither extraordinary powers nor special skills. They are just like other children, except for their titles. It thus is not difficult for young readers to share in the emotional travails of their royal counterparts.

A dramatic illustration of the bond between the reader and the figures in a fairy tale is provided by Gina Higgins, author of *Resilient Adults: Overcoming a Cruel Past*. Recounting the case of two terribly abused brothers, she describes how identification with Dorothy in *The Wizard of Oz* allowed them to compensate for the trauma in their lives. One of the brothers told the author: "Watching the movie was a profound experience for me and my brother. The Wicked Witch was just like our mother. To see that there was a good witch as well as a bad witch was a healing experience."

As a result of viewing the film, the two brothers crept up on their mother one night while she was sleeping and doused her with a pail of water. Though this resulted in a severe beating, the brothers drew strength from their mutinous act, for it convinced them that they did not have to travel through life as passive victims. They told Higgins that the incident allowed them to take "infrequent but fierce and definitive stands" against the bullies in their lives. Whereas most youngsters usually do not act out fairy tales, the experience of the brothers demonstrates how fairy tales can in some instances provide an outlet for children who cannot express their feelings in other ways.

Of the many figures who make their presence felt in a fairy tale, the witch is the most compelling. She is the diva of the piece, the dominant character who frames the battle between good and evil. The witch has the ability to place people in deathlike trances—and just as easily bring them back to life. Conjurer of spells and concocter of deadly potions, she has the power to alter people's lives. Few figures in a fairy tale are as powerful or commanding as the witch.

For a fairy tale to succeed—for it to accomplish its psychological purpose—the witch must die because it is the witch who embodies the sinful parts of the self. In some fairy tales, her death comes about through the use of brute force; in the film version of *The Little Mermaid*, Prince Eric impales the Sea Witch on the splintered bow of his sailing ship. In other fairy tales, cunning wins the day: Gretel saves

Hansel by luring the witch into the oven. If a witch proves too formidable or elusive, a fairy godmother or some other benevolent figure is always waiting in the wings to lend a helping hand.

In the end, the child in the story emerges victorious: Jack vanquishes the giant, Snow White defeats the evil queen, and Dorothy kills the Wicked Witch of the West. Fairy tales are renowned for their happy endings. There are no tragic finishes in these stories, no frightening finales, no apocalyptic conclusions. Unlike Wagnerian operas and Greek tragedies, fairy tales do not end with the sky crashing down or in a firestorm. Rather, they are tales of transcendence. Once the witch dies, everyone lives happily ever after.

JOURNEY TO THE CENTER OF THE SELF

The events that make up a fairy tale typically are played out in a four-part journey, with each leg of the journey a way station on the road to self-discovery. The first part of the journey, the *crossing*, leads the hero or heroine into an alien land marked by magical occurrences and strange creatures. This is followed by an *encounter* with an evil presence—a malevolent stepmother, a murderous ogre, a treacherous wizard, or some other witchlike figure. In the third part of the journey, the *conquest*, the hero or heroine enters into a life-and-death struggle with the witch, one that inevitably leads to the witch's demise. The voyage concludes with a *celebration:* a gala wedding feast or a family reunion in which the victory over the witch is heralded and everyone lives happily ever after.

The fairy-tale journey into unexplored worlds is paralleled by an inward journey. As the protagonist travels deeper and deeper into forbidden territory, so the reader is transported into unexplored regions of the self. And just as the hero or heroine is forced to face conflicts and dangers in the narrative—cannibalism, torture, or exile—so the reader is forced to confront struggles and threats in the psyche. In this way, fairy tales provide children with an opportunity to confront internal forces that threaten their sense of who they are and their place in the world.

Part 1: The Crossing

Practically every fairy tale begins with a step across an invisible frontier that leads straight into uncharted territory. This initial step is precipitated by some sort of dilemma. Hansel and Gretel find themselves in the wood not because they are curious or in search of adventure, but because they have been abandoned by their parents: the family has run out of food, and the children must find something to eat if they hope to survive. Snow White flees into the woods because of a life-threatening situation: her evil stepmother is bent on her destruction. And Dorothy's adventure in the land of Oz is fueled by a desire to get back to Kansas.

The search for a solution to the dilemma delivers the child into an unfamiliar landscape, an environment filled with strange figures and strange occurrences. The passage into the unknown, or "threshold crossing," as Joseph Campbell calls it, deposits the protagonist in a world that is almost the complete opposite of the world with which the child is familiar. This is the world Alice enters when she passes *Through the Looking Glass;* it is the land at the top of the beanstalk; it is *Where the Wild Things Are.*

Every crossover contains an implicit message for young readers: in order to grow, one needs to explore, to examine, to take chances. Childhood is a time of apprehension about the unknown: fear of the dark, worries about school, anxiety over making new friends. For psychological growth to occur, children have to take risks. Every step Hansel and Gretel take into the forest, every step Dorothy takes down the yellow brick road, represents a step along the path to self-realization.

In many fairy tales, the unknown is symbolized by a forest, or simply "the wood." The wood is where fierce animals reside, where sorcerers and witches make their home. Baba Yaga, the great witch of Russian folklore, lives in the wood, as does the wolf in *Little Red Riding Hood.* The wood is where the witch in *Hansel and Gretel* and the ogre in *Hop o' My Thumb* lurk. But whereas the wood contains unimaginable dangers, it also offers protection. When Snow White wanders through the wood alone and exhausted, the wild beasts of the forest allow her to pass in safety. Just as she is about to abandon hope, the house of the seven dwarfs looms in the distance.

In some fairy tales, the crossover leads to unexpected pleasures. The king's daughters in *The Twelve Dancing Princesses* descend into a passageway hidden beneath their bedroom floor that leads to an underground lake. There, twelve handsome princes wait in boats to escort them across the water to an enchanted castle where they dance the night away. It is hard to imagine a more enchanting scenario. But looks can deceive. There is as much danger across the lake as there is in the wood.

The danger is forbidden desire. The motif of a staircase leading to a subterranean lake symbolizes a crossover into the unconscious, a descent into the unexplored and potentially perilous regions of the inner world. The maidens in the story are not twelve mature princesses, but rather twelve innocent maidens on the verge of entering unfamiliar territory—the world of sexual temptation. It is not an accident that the passageway lies beneath their bedroom floor, or that the excursions take place in the dead of night. Their surreptitious excursions reveal a side of the princesses of which they themselves are unaware.

The image of a descent signifies communication not only with lustful parts of the self but with other "sins" as well. In *Mother Hulda*, a Grimm fairy tale about avarice, the heroine falls into a well that lands her in a world populated by talking loaves of bread and other strange objects. This particular underworld also is inhabited by a witchlike figure who teaches wayward children the consequences of greed. Whether through a well, a secret staircase, or a dark forest, fairy tales transport the protagonist—and the reader—into a universe very different from the world to which they are accustomed.

Part 2: The Encounter

Once the hero or heroine crosses to the other side, strange shapes begin to materialize: mysterious animals, enchanted objects, benevolent helpers, and, ultimately, the witch. Whether she appears in the guise of an evil queen, a malevolent stepmother, or a cannibalistic mother-in-law, the witch is the obstacle the child must overcome if the journey is to succeed. There are no shortcuts, no secret passages, no back alleys. If Dorothy hopes to get back to Kansas, she must travel to the kingdom ruled over by the Wicked Witch of the West and confront her in her lair.

The encounter with the witch often involves challenges that take the form of trials or "impossible" tasks. Because agriculture was a dominant economic and social force when folktales and storytelling were an important part of village life, the tasks in these stories tend to have a distinctly farmlike flavor. In *Cinderella*, the heroine is forced by her stepmother to draw water, tend the fire, and separate lentils from ashes. In *Vasilisa the Beautiful*, a Russian fairy tale that has much in common with *Cinderella*, the heroine is required to clean the corn bin and sort bushels of wheat. In other fairy tales, heroines are forced to unravel tangles of yarn or spin endless baskets of flax.

What makes these tasks difficult, if not impossible, is that they come with time limits. *Cinderella* has to separate the lentils from the ashes in two hours, a next-to-impossible task. She succeeds only because animal helpers come to her aid. The miller's daughter in *Rumpelstiltskin* not only has to spin a roomful of gold out of straw but must complete the task before dawn. After she completes the task, through the timely intervention of Rumpelstiltskin, she is told that she must spin two more rooms of straw by the following morning—or die.

Joseph Campbell, in *The Hero with a Thousand Faces*, notes that tasks and trials are a defining characteristic of legends and myths. The protagonists in the narrative are required to undergo an ordeal, the successful completion of which results in praise, admiration, and exalted status. Jason assumes the mantle of conquering hero when he subdues the fire-breathing bulls of King Aetes and returns home with the Golden Fleece.

But fairy tales are not myths; the heroes and heroines in these miniature dramas are not the larger-than-life figures described in legends. Nor are the tasks in fairy tales great feats of derring-do. There is a difference between harnessing fire-breathing bulls and sorting lentils from ashes. The purpose of these assignments is merely to accentuate the witch's evil nature. Forced to perform unreasonable chores, the child in the story—and the reader—comes to appreciate how bad the witch really is.

The child's encounter with the witch brings to the fore the negative trait the witch personifies. Though all witches are bad, the precise shape of their badness varies from story to story. The evil stepmother in *Snow White* is conspicuously vain; she devotes a significant portion of her day contemplating her image in a mirror. The witch in *Hansel and Gretel* spends her day setting traps for little children in order to satisfy her ravenous appetite. And the evil wife in *Talia, Sun, and Moon* is consumed by envy.

The encounter with the evil presence in the story forces children to come face to face with unwholesome tendencies in themselves by casting these tendencies as concrete characteristics of the witch. Confronting the witch thus becomes an act of self-recognition, a means by which children are forced to acknowledge parts of themselves that might otherwise be denied or ignored. In the words of Pogo, a popular cartoon character of the 1960s, "We have met the enemy, and it is us."

Part 3: The Conquest

Destruction of the witch is the third, and quintessential, portion of the fairy-tale cycle. If children hope to overcome bothersome thoughts and unwholesome impulses, the witch must die. Her death constitutes the emotional core of the tale. Only by destroying the witch can one ensure that bad parts of the self are eradicated and that good parts of the self prevail.

Justice in a fairy tale is swift and sure. There is no jury to decide guilt, and no judge to pass sentence. In *Born Black: Memories of Girlhood*, feminist theorist and critic bell hooks writes that fairy tales provided a refuge during difficult parts of her life by championing justice: "The evocation of a just world, where right would prevail over wrong, was a balm to my wounded spirits during my childhood. It was a source of hope. In the end I could believe that no matter the injustice I suffered, truth would come to light and I would be redeemed."

It therefore is fitting that the vengeful wife in *Talia, Sun, and Moon* is thrown into the funeral pyre intended for Talia. In *The Adroit Princess*, a fairy tale by Marie-Jeanne L'Héritier, the evil prince, a male witch, is rolled down a precipice in a barrel spiked with nails previously prepared for the heroine. And in *Hansel and Gretel*, the witch ends up in the oven reserved for the children. In one fairy tale after another, the punishment fits the crime.

Whereas in most stories the witch dies at the hands of the hero or heroine, the witch in Perrault's *The Sleeping Beauty in the Woods* dies by her own hand. Frustrated by her failure to execute her evil plan, the mother-in-law commits suicide by jumping into the vat filled with "toads, vipers, snakes, and serpents." Perrault's story thus is one of the few fairy tales in which the witch takes her own life.

There is a reason for this. A cardinal rule in fairy tales mandates that children are not permitted to destroy their own flesh and blood. Heroes and heroines are allowed to kill witches, ogres, and sorceresses, even stepmothers, but never their own parents. Such an act would hit too close to home. If the prince destroyed the witch in Perrault's story, he would be committing matricide. By having the ogress-mother take her own life, Perrault avoids an ending that might prove overly disturbing to young readers.

The death of the witch signals a victory of virtue over vice, a sign that positive forces in the self have prevailed. Dorothy is halfway home once the Wicked Witch of the West is dead, even though she still must make a detour to visit the Wizard a final time. But why does the Wicked Witch have to die such a horrible death? Why must the evil queen in *Snow White* be forced to dance to her death in red-hot shoes? Why does the wicked servant woman in *The Goose Girl* have to be dragged through the street in a barrel studded with nails and razor-sharp knives? Wouldn't it suffice to place the witch in chains or lock her in a dungeon? Why not banish her to a distant land where she could do no harm? Is it really necessary to resort to such extreme measures to get rid of the witch?

The answer is an unequivocal yes. If the underlying intent of a fairy tale is to cleanse the reader of sinful feelings and shameful thoughts, only an extreme act of ritual purification will do. If the psychological purpose of the story is to scourge every last bit of badness from the self, the reader needs to know that the death of the witch is thorough and complete, even if it means exposing young readers to acts of violence that are extreme by contemporary standards.

But there is another reason such drastic steps need to be taken, and it has to do with the way death is understood by children. Young children have difficulty grasping the finality of death, and adults often confuse matters by telling them that loved ones are asleep or have gone away on a long trip. The apparent rationale is to spare the child pain and provide a ray of hope for an eventual return. But if the child does not construe death as final, the witch could conceivably reappear. It makes no sense to get rid of the witch only to have her suddenly show up on your doorstep. If the witch is to die—and remain dead—she must die in a way that makes her return highly unlikely.

Part 4: The Celebration

The final step in the fairy-tale voyage is the happy ending. In some stories, this takes the form of a joyous reconciliation with family members; in other stories, it is a gala wedding ceremony. Happy endings are so much a part of these dramas that one wonders whether stories without them really deserve to be called fairy tales. Some of Hans Christian Andersen's stories, for example, end on a tragic and depressing note. *The Little Match Girl* freezes to death, and *The Little Mermaid* dissolves into sea foam. The Disney studio was astute enough to recognize that a faithful retelling of *The Little Mermaid* would disappoint moviegoers, and that a happy ending was necessary if the movie was to succeed at the box office. The film version consequently ends with Ariel marrying Prince Eric, followed by a festive wedding reception.

From a psychological vantage point, a happy ending signifies that positive forces in the self have gained the upper hand. Once the witch is disposed of, and the parts of the self she embodies are vanquished, the child no longer is plagued by self-recriminations and self-doubts. The self is transformed—purified, so to speak—leaving the young reader feeling more secure and self-assured.

But fairy-tale endings are ephemeral. The feelings and tendencies that are vanquished through the death of the witch undoubtedly will return, one hopes with less urgency but still possessing power. When they do, fairy tales will be waiting in the wings to work their special brand of magic anew. This is why children return to these stories over and over again. Every time the witch dies, the child's faith in his or her ability to conquer self-doubts and troublesome tendencies is magically restored.

Fairy tales are ultimately journeys of triumph and transformation. By making sure the witch dies, they empower positive parts of the self, thus freeing children to exploit their latent potential for good. But if elimination of the witch were the only consideration, the stories themselves would be simple and straightforward: a battle between the forces of good and evil, with good prevailing in the end. Fairy tales, however, contain not only witches and fairy godmothers but mothers and fathers, princes and kings, and an amazing array of enchanted objects, including blood-stained handkerchiefs, magic distaffs, and talking mirrors. A full appreciation of the meaning fairy tales have for children therefore requires us to explore the significance of these various figures and objects.

To do this, we need to join the heroes and heroines on their magical journeys: we must travel with Snow White into the forest primeval, swim with the Little Mermaid to the top of the sea, and jump into bed with the wolf. We must join hands with Dorothy as she heads down the yellow brick road. Only by accompanying the children on their trek into the unknown can we make sense of the sins they hope to eradicate and the parts played by the various characters in the story. The journey can be daunting, but we push on, knowing we will encounter ourselves at journey's end.

3

Vanity

Mirror, Mirror, on the Wall

"Oh, heavens, where am I?" cried Snow White.

The king's son answered, full of joy, "You are with me." He went on to tell the princess all that had happened, and said, "I love you more than anything in the world. Come with me to my father's palace and you shall be my bride." And Snow White went with the prince, and their wedding was held with pomp and great splendor.

This joyful scene might never have taken place had not one of the prince's servants stumbled over a tree stump and dropped his end of the glass coffin. If he hadn't been so clumsy, the poisonous piece of apple lodged in Snow White's throat might never have fallen out and the princess would still be on display somewhere in the king's palace.

Fortunately for all concerned, he did lose his footing, and the prince and princess were able to live happily ever after.

Snow White, with its dramatic portrayal of resurrection and love reborn, ranks as one of the most memorable fairy tales of all time. Not only is the story the centerpiece of the Grimm collection, it also marks the beginning of Walt Disney's career as an animator of feature-length cartoons. Though Disney had produced a number of shorter cartoons earlier in his career, some also based on fairy tales, his transformation of the familiar Grimm story into a full-length feature film was a groundbreaking achievement. More than any other film, *Snow White and the Seven Dwarfs* heralded an era of fairy-tale animation that changed the public's view of fairy tales forever.

Snow White includes all the ingredients that make up the fairy-tale cycle: a threshold crossing, an encounter with a witch (the evil stepmother), the defeat of the witch, and a happy ending. Since the Disney version is loosely based on the Grimm brothers' story, the film more or less conforms to the original story line. In both Disney and Grimm, a child is pursued by an evil stepmother; in both, her life is spared by a kindly huntsman; and in both she is given refuge by a group of benevolent dwarfs. There nevertheless are some telling differences between the two versions, one of which occurs at the very start. Whereas the Disney version begins with Snow White's mother already dead, the Grimm version begins with her very much alive.

> Once upon a time in the middle of the winter, when snowflakes were falling like feathers from the sky, a queen sat at her window sewing, and the frame of the window was made of ebony. While she was sewing and gazing out the window, she pricked her finger with the needle, and three drops of blood fell upon the snow. When she saw how pretty the red looked upon the snow, she thought to herself, "Would that I had a child as white as snow, as red as blood, and as black as the ebony window frame."
>
> Soon thereafter, the queen gave birth to a daughter whose skin was as white as snow, whose lips were red as blood, and whose hair was as black as ebony. She named the child Snow White. And when the child was born, the queen died.

This poetic opening sets the tenor of the story by reflecting the deep emotional tie that binds the queen to Snow White. The three drops of blood that fall from the queen's finger underscore the biological blood bond between the two, graphically portraying the immutable connection between mother and child. They remind the reader that a mother's lifeblood continues to flow in her offspring even if she is no longer able to physically care for her child.

A HAND FROM BEYOND THE GRAVE

The death of the mother is a common occurrence in fairy tales: *Snow White*, *Donkeyskin*, and *Cinderella* all begin with the mother's demise. Other children's stories—*Bambi*, for example—also feature this traumatic and transforming event, but its occurrence in fairy tales is especially poignant: the dying mother usually attempts to protect the child after she is gone. In some fairy tales, a blessing or benediction is used to cement the spiritual connection between the two. Moments before Cinderella's mother dies, she says to her daughter: "Dear child, be pious and good, and God will take care of you; I will look down upon you from heaven, and will be with you."

Sometimes the connection between mother and child is sealed by a talisman or some other magical object. In *Vasilisa the Beautiful*, a Russian fairy tale, the heroine's mother gives her a doll and tells her: "I am dying, and together with my maternal blessing I leave you this doll. Always keep it with you, and do not show it to anyone; if you get into trouble, give the doll food and ask its advice." Though the death of a parent obviously is a traumatic occurrence, even in "make-believe," the mother's promise to reach beyond the grave assures children that there always will be a force to guide and care for them even if they are all alone in the world.

In some fairy tales, the mother is already dead by the time the story begins—or is simply missing. The miller's wife in *Rumpelstiltskin*, for example, is nowhere about. The story begins: "There once was a miller who was poor, but who had one beautiful daughter." No clue exists as to the mother's whereabouts or what might have happened to her. Even the fate of Dorothy's mother is a mystery. Aunt Em and Uncle Henry seem to be Dorothy's only living relatives.

One explanation for the mother's absence in fairy tales is rooted in historical reality. Before the nineteenth century, childbirth was one of the major causes of death, and repeated pregnancies constantly placed a woman's life in jeopardy. Common infections and disease also took their toll. It thus was not unusual for children to find themselves motherless before they were able to fend for themselves.

The replacement of the birth mother by a stepmother, a common occurrence in fairy tales, also has a basis in historical fact. The demands of agricultural life forced men to replace their deceased wives quickly with women who could care for the children and tend to the hearth. Love and extended romantic involvements lost out to practical considerations. Fairy tales are historical documents of a sort and provide a rough picture of what life was like during periods in history when every day was a struggle for survival.

Psychologically, the death or absence of the mother in fairy tales has its roots, paradoxically, in the child's need to protect positive elements in the self. The mother in the story, the symbolic representative of all that is good in the world, might be injured, even annihilated, if forced into a face-to-face confrontation with a powerful and dangerous witch. If conflict arose between the two—if the mother, for example, directly challenged the witch's authority—she would find herself in mortal danger.

One way to protect, or insulate, the mother from potentially lethal onslaughts is to simply leave her out of the story. Another is to make sure she dies a natural death early on. Accordingly, many fairy tales, *Snow White* being just one of them, start off with the mother either dying or simply missing. Though her absence makes the child highly vulnerable, her peaceful departure is preferable to a scenario in which she dies a violent death.

The mother's exit, paradoxically, is empowering in that it forces the children in the story to confront a cruel and dangerous world on their own. Lacking a mother or protector, the hero or heroine must draw on inner resources that might not have been tested were the mother still around. It is the mother's death that sets the stage for the later confrontation with the witch.

Snow White contains other potent themes in addition to loss of the mother. There is compassion (the huntsman's last-minute reprieve), security (the dwarfs' offer of sanctuary), and ultimate redemption (the death of the witch). But the dynamic that drives the story and guides it to its inexorable conclusion is vanity. Vanity is the thread that weaves itself throughout, making its presence felt soon after the king selects a new wife.

After a year had gone by, the king took another wife, a beautiful woman, but proud and overbearing, and she could not be surpassed in beauty by anyone. She had a magic looking glass, and she used to stand before it, and look in it, and say,

> *Mirror, mirror, on the wall*
> *Who is fairest of us all?*

And the looking glass would answer,

> *You are fairest of them all.*

And she was contented, for she knew the looking glass told the truth.

Now Snow White was growing prettier and prettier, and when she was seven years old, she was as beautiful as the day, far more so than the queen herself. So when the queen went to her mirror and said,

> *Looking glass upon the wall,*
> *Who is fairest of us all?*

The mirror answered,

> *Queen, you are full fair, 'tis true,*
> *but Snow White fairer is than you.*

This gave the queen a great shock, and she became yellow and green with envy, and from that hour her heart turned against Snow White, and she hated her.

HELL HATH NO FURY

Vanity as a fairy-tale dynamic is almost as old as fairy tales themselves. It makes an early appearance in *Cupid and Psyche*, a tale told by Aupelius in the second century A.D. Considered by many to be the first fairy tale, *Cupid and Psyche* tells how Venus, the Greek goddess of beauty, becomes jealous of a mortal princess named Psyche when she learns that the young girl's beauty surpasses her own. Realizing her positon as the most beautiful woman in the world is threatened, Venus initiates a campaign to retain her title.

The story begins with Venus abandoned by her supplicants, who now scatter roses at the feet of Psyche, a beautiful mortal. Venus is so enraged at this affront that she summons her son Cupid and orders him to destroy the maiden. "I implore you to use your arrows against that impudent girl," Venus tells him. "If you have any respect for your mother, you will give me revenge."

Cupid intends to carry out his mother's orders but becomes smitten by Psyche the moment he lays eyes on her. Instead of obeying his mother's edict, he puts down his bow and declares his love for Psyche. When Venus learns that Cupid has fallen for her rival, she not only becomes furious at her son but decides to take vengeance against Psyche.

Venus's efforts to punish the young girl take the form of familiar fairy-tale chores. The first requires Psyche to perform an impossible sorting task. She is led to a storehouse filled with piles of wheat, barley, millet, and lentils and told to place each grain in a separate bag. "You must finish the task by nightfall," Venus tells her. Psyche is overwhelmed but manages to complete the task with the aid of an army of industrious ants, which, unbeknownst to her, have been sent by Cupid.

Irritated by Psyche's ability to complete the task, Venus next orders her to secure a piece of golden fleece from a flock of angry and dangerous rams grazing on the other side of a raging river. Psyche crosses the treacherous stream safely with the help of a river god and reaches the pasture where the rams are feeding. She is about to venture into the field, but the river god advises her to wait until the animals have tired themselves out before approaching them. She follows his instructions and retrieves the wool, which she dutifully delivers to Venus.

But Venus is not to be denied. She conjures up an even more dangerous task, one that requires Psyche to undertake a perilous journey into the underworld. Her mission is to find Proserpine, the wife of Pluto, and retrieve a "golden jar of beauty" that Proserpine has in her possession. Psyche is told to deliver the jar to Venus, and under no circumstances may she open it on the journey home.

Venus knows full well that Psyche will find it difficult to resist temptation. And she is right. The maiden disobeys orders and foolishly opens the jar, hoping to sample its contents for herself. You would think that someone whose beauty is so great as to challenge the likes of Venus would not need to improve upon her appearance. But that is the way of vanity: one can never be beautiful enough. Psyche removes the lid and is immediately overcome by a cloud of lethal fumes that rises from the jar.

Cupid, fortunately, is nearby and observes what has happened. He collects the deadly fumes, returns them to the jar, and wakes Psyche, admonishing her about the dangers of foolish curiosity. Wiser for having survived her close brush with death, Psyche continues on her journey and delivers the jar to Venus. The story concludes with Psyche elevated to goddess status for having fulfilled her mission. She is allowed to ascend to Olympus, where she and Cupid are blissfully united. Venus even forgives her wayward son and confers her blessing on the young couple, who live happily ever after.

Though *Cupid and Psyche* is not, strictly speaking, a fairy tale (the major players are gods rather than mortals), it contains many of the features commonly found in fairy tales. More important, it dramatizes the complications that ensue when vanity takes precedence over more important considerations. This becomes evident with Snow White's stepmother, whose vanity is all-consuming. More than just a harmless preoccupation, it affects everything she says and does, ranging from how she spends her time (peering into a mirror) to contemplating murder.

When the queen realized Snow White was fairer than she, envy and pride grew like ill weeds in her heart. Finally she could stand it no longer and sent for a huntsman, saying,

"Take the child out into the woods, so that I may set eyes on her no more. You must put her to death, and bring me her heart as a token."

The huntsman consented and led the child away; but when he drew his cutlass to pierce Snow White's innocent breast, she began to weep, and cried out,

"Oh, dear huntsman, do not take my life; I will go away into the wild wood, and never come home again."

And as she was so lovely, the huntsman had pity on her, and said,

"Away with you, then, poor child"; for he thought the wild animals would be sure to devour her, and it was as if a stone had been rolled away from his heart when he spared to put her to death. Just at that moment, a young wild boar came running by, so he caught and killed it, and taking out its heart, he brought it to the queen as proof that the child was dead. And it was salted and cooked, and the wicked woman ate it up, thinking that there was the end of Snow White.

WHO'S FOR SUPPER?

Cannibalism is a frightening concept for most people, especially children. Yet the consumption of human flesh—or even its prospect—occurs fairly regularly in fairy tales. Cannibalism plays a role not only in *Snow White* but in *Talia, Sun, and Moon* and Perrault's *The Sleeping Beauty in the Wood*. Both the wife in Basile's tale and the mother-in-law in Perrault's are intent on killing the children to satisfy their cannibalistic urges. Even though the witch in Perrault's tale does not intend to eat the children herself, she clearly is cannibalistically inclined.

Another fairy tale in which cannibalism figures prominently is *Hop o' My Thumb*, a story by Perrault in which a flesh-eating ogre schemes to eat the diminutive Hop and his six brothers. Then, of course, there is *Hansel and Gretel*. Perhaps the best-known tale of a cannibalistic undertaking, the story details the witch's attempt to fatten Hansel so he will make a more savory meal.

Why does cannibalism appear as frequently as it does, and why is it described in such excruciating detail? The reason is clear in light of a fairy tale's psychological intent. Flesh eating is an altogether reprehensible act that identifies its practitioner as a thoroughly repugnant human being. If the witch is to perish, as she must, the reader must be convinced that she deserves to die. Whereas killing another person can be understood, even condoned if there are mitigating circumstances, cutting them up into little pieces and consuming them extends beyond the pale. The appetite of Snow White's stepmother for human flesh classifies her as a thoroughly despicable creature who deserves the worst conceivable punishment.

Fortunately for Snow White, the huntsman feels compassion for her and spares her life. But what is the nature of his compassion for the young princess? Does he spare the girl because she is innocent of wrongdoing? Does he allow her to live because he is repelled by the queen's bloodthirsty habits? Not exactly. He allows Snow White to live because of her beauty. The story explains: "And as she was so lovely, the huntsman had pity on her." The queen would destroy Snow White for her looks; the huntsman spares her because of them.

Preoccupation with appearances is featured not only in children's fairy tales but in adult tales of splitting as well. An example is Oscar Wilde's *The Picture of Dorian Gray*. In Wilde's novel, Dorian Gray, a young man blessed with unusually good looks, is disturbed that time will erase his boyish appearance and wreak havoc on his handsome features. He voices this concern while sitting for a portrait by his artist friend Basil Hallward.

"How sad it is," Dorian murmured, with his eyes still fixed upon his own portrait. "How sad it is! I shall grow old and horrible and dreadful. But this picture will remain always young. It will never be older than this particular day of June. If it were only the other way! If it were I who was to be always young, and the picture that was to grow old! For that—for that—I would give everything! Yes, there is nothing in the whole world I would not give! I would give my soul for that!"

While the wish to retain one's looks and preserve one's youthful appearance is understandable, the desire to stay beautiful *forever* is unnatural. Dorian's wish flies against the natural order and clearly reflects elements in the self that are less than healthy.

Dorian's wish comes true, but it is accompanied by a subtle but significant change in his personality. Soon after the painting is completed, he callously rejects Sybil Vane, a young actress with whom he is involved, driving her to suicide. He subsequently engages a series of young women and young men in scandalous relationships with as little regard for their feelings as for Sybil's. As Dorian's behavior deteriorates, so does the split-off part of his self as represented by the portrait.

The years pass, and Dorian's behavior becomes more and more decadent. He remains as handsome as the day he made his wish, while the figure in the painting becomes increasingly ugly and deformed. Dorian is aware that the portrait is the visual counterpart of his dissolute self, but he cannot part with it. Unlike children who struggle against the witch, he protects the witchlike creation that is his evil self.

The portrait eventually poses a threat to Dorian in the same way that vain tendencies pose a threat to children. Fearing that someone will learn his secret and expose him, he decides to hide the painting in an obscure part of his mansion. Dorian settles on his old nursery, a room hidden away on an upper story of his house away from the prying eyes of servants.

It is telling that Dorian chooses the nursery to hide the portrait, for nurseries symbolize the period in life when splitting first occurs, a time when fairy tales reign supreme. But fairy tales are able to separate the good from the bad by depositing sinful tendencies in the witch. Splitting tales for adults recognize that life is more complex: good and bad are intertwined, and it is not that easy to disentangle the two.

The nursery hiding place fails to solve Dorian's dilemma. Tormented by the painting's ability to give him away, he decides to destroy it. He climbs the stairs to his childhood sanctuary and examines the portrait one last time. Then he picks up a knife and slashes the canvas. The servants hear a piercing scream and rush into the room only to find their master on the floor, a knife in his chest. Standing nearby on an easel is the portrait, as pure and unsullied as the day it was painted.

THE GREATEST FEAR OF ALL

Although Snow White's life has been spared, her problems have only begun. She is alone in a great forest with no place to hide, and no one to whom she can turn for help. The emotional abandonment experienced by the loss of her mother has suddenly turned into a frightening reality.

The young child's predicament triggers normal apprehensions about abandonment that all children experience at different times in their lives. To fend off fears of being left on their own, children seek out what child psychoanalyst Margaret Mahler refers to as "safe-bases," people who provide the child with a sense of safety and security. Before children can strike out on their own, before they are able to function independently, they need to know there are people in their world on whom they can rely. Without safe-bases, without human anchors, the world is a frightening and unpredictable place, as Snow White quickly finds out.

> Now the child was all alone in the great forest, and so terrified she did not know what to do. She began to run, and ran over sharp stones and through thorns, and the wild beasts ran past her, but did her no harm.
>
> She ran as long as her feet would go until it was almost evening; then she saw a little cottage and went into it to rest herself. Everything in the cottage was small, but neater and cleaner than can be told. There was a table on which was a white cover and seven little plates, along with seven little spoons and seven little knives. Next to each was a little cup. Against the wall stood seven little beds side by side covered with snow-white coverlets.

Snow White eats a little food from each plate and sips a little wine from each cup, for she doesn't want to consume all of one portion. Then she lies down on one of the beds and falls asleep. When she wakes in the morning, she finds herself surrounded by seven little dwarfs. At first she is frightened, but then she realizes that the little men are friendly. They ask her what her name is.

"My name is Snow White," she answered.

"How have you come to our house?" asked the dwarfs.

She told them her stepmother had wished to have her killed, but that the huntsman had spared her life, and she had run for the whole day, until at last she had found their dwelling.

The dwarfs said, "Will you take care of our house, cook, make the beds, wash, sew, and knit, and keep everything neat and clean? If you do, you can stay with us and you shall want for nothing."

"Yes," said Snow White, "with all my heart." And she stayed with them and kept the house in order.

Though the hospitality of the little men indicates that Snow White has indeed found a safe-base, feminist critics tend to cast the dwarfs' proposal in a somewhat different light. They contend that the dwarfs' offer of sanctuary symbolizes a more widespread attempt of society to force women into domestic roles, thus relegating them to a position of subservience. There is some validity to this observation, which I came to appreciate in the course of doing psychotherapy with a client named Vivian. During our sessions, Vivian, whose husband had deserted her, began to question her role as devoted wife and dedicated housekeeper. She wondered where it had gotten her. Not only had her husband forsaken her for another woman, but she realized that the time spent tending to his needs might have been better spent on establishing a career.

One day while she was musing on this and other matters, she spontaneously remarked, "You know, I think I have a different take on *Snow White* than I did when I was a child."

I asked her what she meant, and she replied, "Cleaning and cooking for the dwarfs all those years was a lot to give up for security. In the end, the dwarfs really didn't protect her from anything, did they?"

Vivian's associations to the story had changed now that she was a grown woman. When she was small, the dwarfs signified security, and the cottage was a haven in the storm. All the items in the cottage—the tiny chairs, the miniature eating utensils, the little beds—symbolized a secure home life. But as an adult going through a painful divorce, she viewed her favorite childhood story in a different light.

For Vivian, *Snow White* had become a parable of sexual oppression and opportunities squandered. The princess, in her adult eyes, was a gullible naif, a foolish child who was all too willing to sacrifice her future and self-respect for a security that was at best illusory. Just as the two brothers who doused their mother with a pail of water were able to see parallels between their lives and Dorothy's, so Vivian was able to gain insight into her circumstances by looking at her life through the eyes of a fairy-tale figure.

WHERE MAGIC DWELLS

However one views Snow White's relation to the dwarfs, there is little question that the little men provide the heroine with a refuge from the storm. And not a moment too soon. Though the stepmother has been temporarily appeased, she will come hunting for Snow White once she learns the child is alive. But for the time being, the princess can rest easy knowing she can rely on the dwarfs for food and shelter.

The dwarfs, however, are more than just benevolent little innkeepers who happen to be at the right place at the right time. Consider the warnings they give Snow White before they leave for work. "Don't talk to strangers," they tell the child. "Don't let anyone you don't know into the house." These are precisely the kinds of things mothers tell their children when they leave them alone. It doesn't take much of a stretch of the imagination to see that the dwarfs are maternal icons, symbols, as it were, of the good mother.

Proof that the dwarfs are, in fact, a part of Snow White is revealed in the objects that make up their household. Not only is the table spread with a *white* cloth, but the beds are covered with *snow-white* coverlets. It is as if Snow White has stumbled across a manifestation of herself in the little house. The dwarfs' maternal origins, additionally, are mirrored by the interior makeup of the cottage. Described by the Grimm brothers as "pretty and clean as possible," even the beds are made. It is hard to conceive of seven adult males—no matter how tiny—living in close quarters and maintaining a tidy, uncluttered household. Magic has its limits.

Disney obscures the maternal nature of the dwarfs by turning the inside of the cottage into a shambles. In the film, the dishes are unwashed, clothes are strewn about, and the furniture is in disarray. Whatever maternal inclinations the dwarfs possess are overshadowed by their raucous behavior: they dance, sing, and carry on like a bunch of drunken sailors. With names like Sneezy, Sleepy, Grumpy, and Dopey, they are transformed from maternal icons into miniature clowns.

The dwarfs' maternal nature nevertheless shines through as they endeavor to shield Snow White from the dangers that lurk without. But like most children in fairy tales, she ignores their advice. The moment she hears a voice outside the cottage call out, "Pretty things to sell, very cheap, very cheap," she throws caution to the wind and opens the window. Little does she know she is about to embark on the most harrowing leg of her journey.

> Snow White looked out the window and called out, "Good day, my good woman, what have you to sell?"
>
> "Good things, pretty things," she answered, "stay-laces of all colors," and she pulled out a ribbon woven of bright-colored silk.
>
> "I will let the worthy old woman in," thought Snow White, and she unbolted the door and bought the pretty lace.

The figure standing outside the cottage is none other than Snow White's evil stepmother cleverly disguised as a peddler woman. The question is, why does Snow White allow the old woman to enter the cottage? Why, after all the dwarfs have told her, does she subject herself to such terrible danger? Is it merely a matter of curiosity? Is she trying to test the limits of adult authority? The answer is in the laces.

The laces Snow White covets are not the ribbons that children might use today to decorate their hair. Rather, they are stay-laces, gaily colored ribbons used by young women in mountain villages to tie the fronts of their bustiers. Wrapped tightly in criss-cross fashion to exaggerate the bosom, the laces are designed to make the wearer more alluring. Snow White lusts after them not merely because they are intrinsically attractive, but because they make her more desirable.

If we pay close attention to the business being conducted, we see that Snow White allows the queen into the cottage for precisely the same reason that fuels the wicked queen's murderous quest. Like the queen, Snow White wants to be pretty, to be elegant, to be admired. The young child also is driven by vain impulses. Perhaps she doesn't aspire to be the fairest in the land, but there is no doubt she would like to be alluring and voluptuous, perhaps more than her tender years warrant.

One of the ways fairy tales heighten their psychological impact is by locating the sin in the story in both the witch *and* the protagonist. For a fairy tale to have a lasting effect on young readers, the hero and heroine must experience the same failings as the witch: they must be tempted by the same temptations. Otherwise, the sin in the story can be construed as alien to the child, as something only the witch suffers. By fostering the reader's identification with Snow White, and calling attention to her concern with external appearances, *Snow White* entices readers to confront their own vain proclivities. A similar dynamic occupies center stage in Hans Christian Andersen's *The Emperor's New Clothes*.

Keeping up appearances

Like Snow White, the ruler in Andersen's story also is obsessed with appearances, so much so that he ignores affairs of state and spends his time parading like a peacock before his subjects. Andersen writes, "He took no interest in his army or the theater or in driving through the country unless it was to show off his new clothes." It thus is not surprising that the emperor falls prey to two swindlers who claim they have the ability to weave unusually attractive garments. They declare that their outfits are invisible to anyone who is undeserving of his or her position—or very stupid.

The emperor, unable to see beyond his own vain nose, falls for their ruse and marches naked before his subjects, all of whom are also reluctant to admit that the king is parading about without clothes.

There marched the emperor in the procession under the beautiful canopy, and everyone in the streets and at the windows said: "Goodness! The emperor's new clothes are the finest he has ever had. What a wonderful train! What a perfect fit." No one would let it be thought that he could not see anything because that would have meant he was not fit for his job, or he was very stupid.

The charade at first succeeds, but the emperor is ultimately exposed by a small child who cries out, "But he hasn't got anything on!"

"Well, but he hasn't got anything on!" the people all shouted at last. And the emperor felt most uncomfortable, for it seemed to him that the people were right. But somehow he thought to himself: "I must go through with it now, procession and all." And he drew himself up still more proudly while his chamberlains walked after him carrying the train that wasn't there.

In much the same way as the emperor falls prey to his vain inclinations, so Snow White falls victim to hers. The young princess, however, will suffer a greater price for her excesses than the emperor. It is one thing to pay for one's sins with shame and mortification. It is quite another to pay with one's life.

"Child," said the old woman, "what a sight you are; I will lace you properly for once."

Snow White made no objection and placed herself before the old woman to let her lace her with the new lace. But the old woman laced so quickly and tightly that she took away Snow White's breath, and she fell down as though dead.

Fortunately for Snow White, the dwarfs return from work moments after the queen departs. They enter the cottage to find the princess lying lifeless on the floor. Quickly assessing what has taken place, they cut the stay-laces and revive her.

The Disney version of *Snow White* omits this episode entirely, as well as the comb sequence that follows. In the film, the witch pays only one visit to Snow White, during which she tempts her with a tainted apple. The reason for omitting the stay-laces sequence is unclear unless the purpose was to shorten the story or, as is more likely, to mute its sensual connotations. Whatever the reason, the omission of the sequence weakens the psychological underpinnings of the story by minimizing the motivational significance of vanity in the plot.

Once Snow White comes to and tells the dwarfs of the old woman's visit, the little men become increasingly alarmed. They explain that the old peddler woman was none other than the wicked queen, and they again admonish Snow White to take care. "You must beware of letting anyone in when we are not here," they tell her.

While the dwarfs are doing their best to convince Snow White of the danger that surrounds her, the evil queen has received news by way of the magic mirror that her stepdaughter is still alive. When she asks the mirror who is the fairest in the land, the mirror replies,

> *Queen, thou art of beauty rare,*
> *But Snow White living in the glen*
> *With the seven little men*
> *Is a thousand times more fair.*

The queen is now more determined than ever to dispose of Snow White. Hurrying to her magic storeroom, she fashions a poison comb capable of killing her rival the moment it touches her scalp. The evil woman dresses herself up in a new disguise and sets out across the mountains that separate her castle from the dwarfs' cottage.

The old woman knocked at the door, again crying out, "Good things to sell, cheap, cheap!"

"Go away; I cannot let anyone in," Snow White answered.

"But you are not forbidden to look," said the old woman, pulling out the poisoned comb, and holding it up.

It pleased the poor girl so much that she let herself be beguiled and opened the door.

When they had made a bargain, the old woman said, "Now I will comb your hair properly for you."

Poor Snow White had no suspicion, and let the old woman do as she pleased, but no sooner was the comb put in her hair than the poison took effect, and the poor girl fell down senseless.

"You paragon of beauty," said the wicked woman, "you are done for now," and she went away.

The comb constitutes the second symbol of vanity in the story. Snow White is seduced again, not by a toy or trinket, but by an object she feels will enhance her looks. The evil that threatens the princess exists not only outside the cottage but as an inner propensity that allows vain considerations to cloud her better judgment. Fortunately for Snow White, the dwarfs again return in time to save her life. They pull the poison comb from her hair and lecture her anew about the evil that surrounds her.

One would think that Snow White would have learned her lesson by now, but fate is about to tempt her a third and final time when the queen, now clothed as a peasant woman, arrives at the cottage with a basket of apples, one of which is poisoned. She offers Snow White the tainted apple, but the princess turns her down. To allay the child's suspicions, the old woman cuts the apple in two and proceeds to eat the green half. Snow White falls for the deception, not realizing that the apple has been cunningly prepared so that only the red half contains poison.

What lies beneath the surface . . .

The return of the witch places the existential dilemma posed by vanity in sharp focus. What is more important, that which is on the surface or that which lies within? The distinction between the pretty red skin and the poison tangibly highlights the difference between the two. Most parents, accordingly, counsel their offspring not to get caught up in appearances. Beauty, we teach children, is only skin-deep. You cannot tell a book by its cover. It's what's inside that counts.

But what are children to think when television elevates the pursuit of beauty into high art? The media saturates the airways with messages extolling the virtues of physical attractiveness. The pervasiveness of the vanity industry is mind-boggling when one counts up the face lotions, hair preparations, and makeup products sold every year. Youngsters hardly out of kindergarten compete against one another in national beauty contests. And Mattel has joined forces with Avon to come up with a makeup kit for girls age three and up. Called "The Barbie Glamour Cosmetic Kit," it contains cream eye shadow and strawberry lip gloss.

Stories like *Snow White* and *The Emperor's New Clothes* teach that overinvestment in appearances has harmful repercussions. Relying on looks to make one's way in the world, using image as a substitute for character, leads only to heartache. But is it reasonable to expect fairy tales to counteract the powerful messages about appearance that bombard young children every day? Perhaps not. On the other hand, children are exposed to fairy tales relatively early in life, at a time when vivid emotional experiences have a lasting impact. By fostering identification with figures similar in age to themselves, and showing how these figures confront their own vain tendencies, fairy tales provide children with an opportunity to combat forces within themselves that are difficult to counter by other means.

To ensure that the heroine's vain predilections—as well as those of the reader—are vanquished, the witch must die. But before this happens, Snow White must face one more challenge. Just as she faced death at the hands of the huntsman earlier in the story, she now comes face to face with death in a final encounter with the witch.

> No sooner had the child taken a morsel of the apple into her mouth than she fell to the earth as dead. And the queen, casting on her a terrible glance, laughed aloud and cried, "As white as snow, as red as blood, as

black as ebony! This time the dwarfs will not be able to bring you to life again."

The words the stepmother-witch utters are the same words Snow White's mother spoke years earlier as she sat by her window longing for a child. The witch's use of precisely the same expression—"as white as snow, as red as blood, as black as ebony"—is more than a coincidence. It demonstrates that the witch, like the good mother, is also a part of Snow White. As such, each is privy to the other's innermost thoughts. The words invoked by Snow White's mother to bring the child into the world are now summoned by the witch to drive her out of it.

When the dwarfs return to find Snow White lying motionless on the ground, they loosen the child's clothing and bathe her with water and wine in a desperate attempt to revive her. But this time they are too late. The young maiden they sheltered and counseled is no more.

The dwarfs grieve over their loss. They consider burying Snow White, but they cannot bear to put her beneath the earth. The child is too precious, too beautiful, to be hidden from the world. She looks as if she were still alive.

> "We cannot hide her away in the black ground," the dwarfs said. And they made a coffin of clear glass, so as to be looked into from all sides. They laid her in it, and wrote in golden letters upon it that she was a king's daughter. Then they set the coffin out upon the mountain, and one of them always remained to watch over it.

The glass coffin echoes the vanity motif one last time. Even though Snow White no longer is alive, her looks ensure that she will continue to be valued and cherished. Keeping her on display in the crystal casket for all to admire seems to indicate that vain considerations have won the day. But there is hope. Snow White and the reader can still overcome their sinful tendencies if the princess somehow is resurrected. Enter the prince.

> It happened that one day a king's son rode through the wood and up to the dwarfs' house, which was nearby. He saw on the mountain the coffin,

and beautiful Snow White within it, and he read what was written in golden letters upon it. Then he said to the dwarfs,

"Let me have the coffin, and I will give you whatever you like."

But the dwarfs told him that they could not part with it for all the gold in the world. But he said,

"I beseech you to give it to me, for I cannot live without Snow White."

Bedazzled by Snow White's beauty, the prince wants to marry her and apparently is willing to overlook the fact that she is dead. He suspects that his parents will not be overjoyed at the prospect of a lifeless daughter-in-law, but that does not deter him. All he wants is to possess Snow White, or, more accurately, her beauty. He persuades the dwarfs to give him the princess and sets out for his father's palace, where he intends to place her on display.

To everyone's lasting relief, one of the servants stumbles on the way to the palace and drops the coffin. The poison apple flies from Snow White's throat, and she wakens. The story could easily end here. Snow White is resurrected, and the prince to his utter delight is blessed with a live princess. But there is one detail that needs to be resolved. The wicked queen is still alive. Her continued existence means not only that Snow White's life remains in jeopardy, but that the princess is apt to be plagued by vain temptations for the rest of her days. Unless the evil woman is eliminated once and for all, Snow White will never be free.

SAVE THE LAST DANCE FOR ME

Snow White and the prince by now have arrived back at his father's palace and are in the midst of planning their upcoming wedding. Invitations have been sent throughout the land announcing the happy event and the gala wedding feast that is to follow the nuptials. Everyone is invited—even the queen, who has no inkling that Snow White is still alive.

Snow White's wicked stepmother was bidden to the feast, and when she had dressed herself in beautiful clothes, she went to her looking glass and said,

> *Looking glass upon the wall,*
> *Who is the fairest of us all?*

The looking glass answered,

> *O Queen, although you are of beauty rare,*
> *The young bride is a thousand times more fair.*

The wicked woman uttered a curse, and was so utterly wretched that she knew not what to do. At first, she thought she would not go to the wedding at all, but she had no peace. She had to go to see the young queen.

When she arrived, she recognized Snow White; the wicked woman was filled with rage and fear, and could not stir. But iron slippers had already been put upon the fire, and they were brought in with tongs, and set before her. Then she was commanded to put on the red-hot shoes, and forced to dance until she dropped down dead.

In the Disney version of *Snow White*, the witch meets a different end. When the dwarfs return from work, she is still in the cottage hovering over Snow White's lifeless form. She tries to escape, but the dwarfs give chase and pursue her up a dangerous mountain path where they corner her on a high precipice. The witch attempts to push a large boulder onto the dwarfs, but the ground beneath her gives way and she plummets to her death. The film version thus softens the story's psychological impact by transforming the witch's death into an accident.

In most fairy tales, the witch dies as a result of action taken by the hero or heroine. The Sea Witch in the Disney version of *The Little Mermaid* doesn't drown in a freak accident; the prince impales her on the prow of his ship. In the original version of *The Wizard of Oz*, Dorothy melts the Wicked Witch of the West by *intentionally* dousing her with water. The active involvement of the hero or heroine in the witch's demise communicates to readers that they must take an active role in overcoming their own errant tendencies.

This is the hidden message of *Snow White:* children need to combat their vain inclinations if they want to live productive lives. These tendencies do not go away on their own. By vanquishing the evil presence in the story, thereby overcoming bad elements within the self, Snow White masters her own vain tendencies as well as those of the reader.

4
Gluttony
Where Bread Crumbs Lead

Nibble, nibble, like a mouse
Who is nibbling at my house?

Who indeed?

Everywhere you look in fairy tales, someone is either looking for a meal or trying desperately not to become one. The search for food and all that is associated with it—hunger, starvation, and simply making sure there is enough to go around—forms the basis for some of the most riveting stories in fairy-tale literature. Jack's journey in *Jack and the Beanstalk*, for example, begins innocently enough with Jack's effort to trade the family cow for money with which to buy food. Instead, Jack's exchange of Milky-White for a handful of beans marks the beginning of a harrowing journey to "the land beyond the sky." But it is the lack of food that prompts the sale of Milky-White in the first place and leads to Jack's fateful encounter with a cannibalistic giant.

The search for food, and indeed eating itself, is a cardinal concern not only in traditional fairy tales but in contemporary ones as well. In Maurice Sendak's *Where the Wild Things Are*, Max is sent to his room without dinner for threatening to devour his mother after she scolds him for refusing to eat. While alone in his room, Max crosses into the kingdom of the wild things, a fantastic collection of ferocious creatures that threaten to eat *him* in much the same way as he threatened to eat his mother. Max's adventure highlights the not-so-secure position humans occupy in the food chain, as well as the central importance of food and feeding in children's lives.

What gets eaten, who gets eaten, and how it gets eaten vary tremendously from story to story; fairy tales include everything from minor instances of snacking to outright cannibalism. At one end of the spectrum is Snow White's innocent sampling from each of the dwarfs' plates. At the other end is the wicked queen's desire to partake of the heroine's vital organs. Then there is the wolf's wholesale consumption of Red Riding Hood and her grandmother, not to mention the whale's ingestion of Pinocchio. Fortunately, both Red Riding Hood and Pinocchio make it through their gastrointestinal adventures in one piece.

The fear of being eaten reaches its most graphic expression in *Hansel and Gretel*, the popular tale of a hapless brother and sister who happen across a gingerbread cottage in the woods and greedily proceed to devour it. The story depicts the potential dangers of gluttony in clear, unambiguous terms, but it begins with a family suffering from a scarcity of food.

At the edge of a great forest there lived a poor woodcutter and his wife, and his two children; the boy's name was Hansel and the girl's Gretel. They had very little to bite or to sup, and once, when there was great dearth in the land, the man could not even gain the daily bread. As he lay in bed one night thinking of this, and turning and tossing, the man sighed heavily, and said to his wife,

"What will become of us? How are we to feed our poor children when we no longer have anything for ourselves?"

"I will tell you what, husband," answered the wife, "we will take the children early in the morning into the forest where it is thickest; there we will make a fire for them, and we will give them each a piece of bread, then we will go to our work and leave them alone. They will never find the way home again, and we shall be quit of them."

"No, my wife," said the man, "I cannot do that; I cannot find it in my heart to take the children into the forest and to leave them there alone. The wild animals would soon come and devour them."

"Oh, you fool," said she, "then we will all starve. You had better plane the planks for our coffins." And she left him no peace until he consented.

The thought of two parents lying in bed planning the deaths of their children is too horrendous to contemplate. We have become all too accustomed to reading about parents who abuse their children, even abandon them, but only rarely do we hear of parents who plot the death of their offspring. The familial implications of this dread deed are reduced somewhat by the fact that the woman in *Hansel and Gretel* is not the children's real mother, but rather their stepmother. Still, the prospect of abandonment and starvation is a child's worse nightmare.

The architect of this nightmare is, of course, a witch, or at least as close as one can come to being a witch. Who else but a witch would put her own selfish needs before those of her children? Who but a witch would deprive children of what little food they need to survive? And who but a witch would contemplate child murder? There is, of course, another witch who shows up a little later on, but for the moment, the evil in the story resides in the stepmother.

When there's not enough to go around

As dreadful as it is to contemplate that parents might want to rid themselves of their children solely for the sake of expedience—or, as the story puts it, because "there was great dearth in the land"—the abandonment of young children was not unheard of when fairy tales circulated among the peasantry. The historian Robert Darnton points out that the seventeenth and eighteenth centuries saw widespread famines on the European continent, and it was common to see corpses by the roadside with straw stuffed in the mouths. In this context, families often were forced to take drastic measures to survive. Not only did parents turn their children out in the streets to beg and steal, they left infants in the woods to die of exposure or starvation.

The scarcity of food and the search for a meal is a central dynamic in a number of fairy tales. Charles Perrault's *Hop o' My Thumb* features a family on the verge of starvation; their food needs are even graver than those suffered in *Hansel and Gretel*. In Perrault's story, the parents, along with their seven sons, must cope with a catastrophic famine that has swept the countryside. By far the smallest is the youngest of the brothers, Hop o' My Thumb, so named because he was "very, very tiny when he came into the world, and hardly bigger than your thumb." Although the most intelligent of the lot, Hop is belittled by the rest of his family because of his size. It nevertheless falls on the boy's shoulders to rescue the family from their unfortunate circumstances.

As in *Hansel and Gretel*, the parents in *Hop o' My Thumb* come to the realization that they can no longer provide for their offspring. They decide to leave the seven boys in the forest, in full knowledge of the fate that awaits them. But unlike Hansel and Gretel's parents, Hop's father and mother are racked with guilt; they abandon the children only because they do not have the heart to watch them starve to death.

> "You know we've got nothing to give our children to eat," said the husband to his wife with a breaking heart. "I can't bear to see them die of hunger in front of my very eyes. Better a quick end to it," he said to his wife. Then he told her of his plans to leave them in the woods.

"Oh!" cried his wife. "How could you think of abandoning your own children?"

The husband reiterated the grisly predicament the family was in, but the wife refused to go along with his scheme. She was poor, but she was their mother.

But when finally she became convinced that the children would, in fact, die, and that watching them starve to death would be too heart-wrenching, she consented to her husband's plan. Then she went to bed and cried herself to sleep.

Perrault's description of the circumstances leading up to the abandonment of Hop and his siblings is very different from that depicted by the Grimm brothers in *Hansel and Gretel*. Perrault tended to imbue his stories with noble sentiments and lofty ideals so as to make them more palatable for the delicate sensibilities of upper-class audiences. Ruthless behavior was not altogether absent from Perrault's tales, but it was reserved for witches, ogres, and other villainous characters, not for children or their parents. The Grimms' *Hansel and Gretel*, on the other hand, conforms to the peasantry's view of the world: the lower classes were intimately acquainted with the cruel decisions parents were forced to make in times of famine and disease.

HOME IS WHERE THE HEART IS

Once Hansel realizes the fate in store for him and his sister, he concocts a scheme that will enable the two to find their way home. He gathers up some flints, planning to use them as markers. As his parents lead him and his sister into the forest, he carefully deposits the flints along the path. Later that night the light of the moon illuminates the flints, thus allowing Hansel and his sister to retrace their steps.

The following morning the stepmother is shocked to find the two children standing in the doorway. She masks her involvement in arranging their absence by feigning annoyance: "You naughty children, why did you sleep so long in the wood? We thought you were never coming home again." But even as she speaks, she is plotting to return the children to the forest.

A scenario of a different sort takes place in *Hop o' My Thumb*. Hop also collects pebbles to line the path so that he and his brothers can find their way home. But unlike the reception accorded Hansel and Gretel, the brothers' arrival is met with genuine rejoicing. While they were gone, a local squire repaid a debt of ten sovereigns to the parents, and the family now has more than enough money for food. Unfortunately, the money soon runs out, and the parents are faced with the same dilemma. They decide to abandon their children a second time.

Though the plots of *Hansel and Gretel* and *Hop o' My Thumb* revolve about food—more accurately, the lack thereof—the theme of abandonment runs through both stories, as it does in many other fairy tales. As always, the fear of being left alone is a terrifying proposition, something that always looms as a potential threat for children. Instead of trying to deny it, fairy tales make the threat explicit, thus forcing children to confront their anxieties about abandonment. Hansel and Gretel's parents are about to turn the threat into a reality a second time.

Not very long after that, there was again great dearth throughout the land, and the children heard their mother say at night in bed to their father,

"Everything is finished up; we have only half a loaf left, and that is the end. The children must go; we will take them farther into the wood this time so that they shall not be able to find the way back again. There is no other way to save ourselves."

The man felt sad at heart, and he thought,

"It would be better to share one's last morsel with one's children."

But the wife would listen to nothing that he said, but scolded and reproached him. He who says A must say B, too, and when a man has given in once he has to do it a second time.

The parents' interchange signifies how difficult it is to take the high ground once one has made questionable compromises. Young children often will align themselves with a school bully, for example, and pick on a weaker child though they know it is wrong. Once having done so, it becomes difficult to refuse to go along with the bully the next time. The implicit message to young readers is that they should stick to their guns if they think right is on their side. Once you betray your principles, it is more and more difficult to turn back.

Hansel again tries to gather flints to line the path, but his stepmother locks him in the house before he is able to collect any. The next morning she gives Hansel a piece of bread and leads him and his sister into the woods. Hansel crumbles the bread in his pocket and scatters the crumbs along the way while his parents aren't looking.

The parents once again leave the children in a clearing, promising to return after they collect branches for a fire. They, of course, do not intend to return, and the children find themselves entirely on their own. This time they cannot make their way home, for birds have eaten all the bread crumbs Hansel has strewn along the way. He and Gretel are hopelessly lost.

The two children wander for three days until finally they come upon a little cottage. They approach the house and, to their delight, find that it is made of confectioneries and bread: the roof is covered with cakes, and the window panes are fashioned from transparent sugar. The two descend on the cottage and begin to devour it. Hansel tells Gretel, "I will eat a piece of the roof, and you can have some of the window."

One cannot fault the children for indulging themselves after wandering about for days with nothing to eat. But their appetites get the best of them, and they continue to consume the cottage even after they have had their fill. Dissatisfied with just a small portion of the roof, Hansel takes down "a *great* piece of it," and Gretel follows his lead by pulling out "a *large* window pane." The children know what they are doing is wrong, that it is sinful, but they cannot control themselves. What started off as "nibbling" has turned into a feeding frenzy. Ordinary hunger has given way to gluttony.

The feasting does not end there. Once the owner of the cottage invites them to come in, they continue to stuff themselves. Inside the cottage, the two find "a good meal laid out, of milk and pancakes, with sugar, apples, and nuts." The children gorge themselves, and then go to sleep. The story tells us, "Hansel and Gretel laid themselves down on the beds, and thought they were in heaven."

The owner of the cottage is, of course, a witch. Not only does she prey on young children, she lives in a house that is a monument to temptation. The witch knows that most children, if not all, are gluttonous creatures and uses this knowledge to trap them.

How does the witch know? Because she is the children; she is the sinful or bad part of Hansel and Gretel, the part driven by gluttony. This is not lost on the children. At a deep intuitive level, they know the witch is a part of them, and that the voice that calls from within the house is their own. But they cannot resist. And who can blame them? How often do we as adults ignore the voice of reason and succumb to temptation?

Early in the morning, before the children were awake, the witch rose to look at them as they lay sleeping so peacefully with round rosy cheeks, and said to herself,

"What a fine feast I shall have!"

Then she grasped Hansel with her withered hand, led him into a little stable, and shut him up behind a grating. Then she went back to Gretel and shook her until she woke.

"Get up, you lazy bone; fetch water, and cook something nice for your brother; he is outside in the stable, and must be fattened up. And when he is fat enough, I will eat him."

Gretel began to weep bitterly, but it was of no use, she had to do what the wicked witch bade her. She cooked the best of the victuals for poor Hansel, while she got nothing for herself but crab shells. Each morning the old woman visited the little stable and cried,

"Hansel, stretch out your finger, that I may tell if you will soon be fat enough."

Hansel, however, held out a little bone, and the old woman, who had weak eyes, could not see what it was. Supposing it to be Hansel's finger, she wondered very much that it was not getting fatter. When four weeks had passed and Hansel seemed to remain so thin, she lost patience and could wait no longer.

"Now then, Gretel," cried she to the little girl; "be quick and draw water; be Hansel fat or be he lean, tomorrow I must kill and cook him."

While the witch is preparing to make a meal of Hansel, Hop and his brothers aren't faring much better, having been unsuccessful in their attempts to find food or shelter. But suddenly they spy a cottage with a candle in the window. They knock on the door, and the woman who answers the door invites them in.

The woman informs the boys that they have arrived at the house of a flesh-eating ogre, and that she is the ogre's wife. Despite her poor choice in husbands, she is a kind woman and feels pity for the brothers. She hides them under a bed, hoping her husband will not find them when he returns. But her efforts come to naught.

When the ogre returned home, he smelled the brothers' presence and immediately located their hiding place. The ogre chastised his wife for trying to deceive him and ordered her to cook the brothers on the spot, planning to eat them for supper. Hop, terrified, looked on as the ogre proceeded to sharpen an enormous knife on a grindstone. All seemed lost when, at the last moment, the wife prevailed upon her husband to hold off until the next day.

"Oh, very well then," said the ogre. "Give them some supper to fatten them up and put them to bed." His wife was overjoyed and brought them plenty of food, but the brothers were too frightened to eat. So she gave them nightcaps and sent them to their room, where they lay in the dark shivering over the fate that awaited them in the morning.

The excesses of eating, captured symbolically by the ogre's cannibalistic nature, are magnified by his gluttony. He is not content merely to eat the brothers, he must fatten them up before devouring them. The same is true of the witch in *Hansel and Gretel*. She puts off eating Hansel for four whole weeks, patiently waiting for him to put on weight before indulging her ravenous appetite. Like Mr. Creosote in the Monty Python film *The Meaning of Life*, who literally explodes while gorging himself at a restaurant, the ogre and the witch both find it impossible to deny their cravings.

EATING AND THE ORIGINS OF SELF

Why is it that so many fairy tales revolve about food and feeding? Why does danger to the hero or heroine so often boil down to either having food withheld or being eaten? Because food and feeding is the conduit through which early forms of caring—and noncaring—are communicated. Some of the most intense emotional experiences of infancy take place at the breast, involving a complex commingling of tactile sensations and feelings of satiation. It is through the act of feeding that children are soothed, comforted, and made to feel secure.

The converse holds true as well. Allowing a child to go hungry can lead to overwhelming feelings of insecurity, if not severe psychopathology. A young boy I treated when I worked at a children's psychiatric hospital was admitted to the facility because he suffered from pica, a disorder in which children ingest chalk, crayons, and other inedible objects. The onset of the disorder occurred soon after the child was deserted by his parents and literally left to starve in a cold-water flat. Only through the quick response of neighbors who heard the boy's moans and summoned police was he rescued and spared serious physical damage or death. The experience nevertheless left its mark, as evidenced by the boy's feelings of emptiness and the belief that he was bad and utterly worthless.

We therefore should not be surprised to find food and feeding featured so prominently in fairy tales. Since fairy tales are essentially tales of splitting, they necessarily center on experiences that presage divisions in the self. To be fed, to go to sleep with a full belly, is tantamount to feeling good about yourself. To not be fed, to be deprived of food, signifies just the opposite. Eating has symbolic ramifications that transcend biology. Before children begin to experience the primitive beginnings of selfhood, the foundations of self are set down in the act of being fed.

But increased intake of food does not necessarily mean increased goodness. While a good meal can be physically fulfilling and psychologically soothing, overindulging oneself has negative implications. Gluttony is associated with slovenliness, with selfishness, and with obesity. The goodness-badness food nexus even extends to the way people with healthy and unhealthy eating habits are perceived. A study at the University of Arizona indicated that people identified as "healthy eaters" were rated as more attractive and likable than "bad eaters." In the study, bad eaters were defined as people who indulged in French fries, ice cream, and other fattening foods. The raters considered bad eaters as bad as the food they consumed.

BED, BULIMIA, AND THE WAY OF DIETS

One arena where the intimate connection between food and the goodness-badness dynamic is most conspicuous is in BED (binge eating disorder), or bulimia, a secretive and intense form of behavior in which eating sprees are followed by self-induced vomiting or laxative abuse. Isabel, a thirty-two-year-old patient of mine who suffered from BED, related that her binges typically began with the urge to have a single cookie or a piece of cake. Her "snacking" then progressed to the point where she was so bloated that she literally was unable to force another piece of food down her throat. At this point in the binging cycle, she typically would gag herself and force herself to throw up.

A typical episode for Isabel usually was triggered by feelings that she was a bad wife and bad mother. Such feelings resulted in intense anxiety, which she would try to allay by indulging in her favorite snack, Vienna Fingers. The first couple of cookies calmed her down and led to what she described as "a warm, smooth feeling" inside of her. This acted as a stimulus for more eating. She downed a few more cookies and continued until she had emptied an entire package of Fingers, finishing up by picking at the crumbs in the bottom of the cellophane wrapper. Then she would start on another package.

Before long, feelings of shame would begin to overwhelm her, and her stomach would begin to ache. Isabel would feel even worse about herself, compounding the bad feelings that had initiated the binging in the first place. She was bad for being so weak, for giving in to her compulsion, for not being able to change. The only solution was to purge herself of the offending substance, which she accomplished by forcing herself to throw up. Purging functioned as a psychological purification ceremony for Isabel, a symbolic way of expelling the bad parts of her self.

The *New York Times* food columnist Jane Brody, who grappled with a weight problem for long periods in her life, describes how "bad" foods relate to bad feelings about the self, and how the two form a vicious cycle: "Too often, [overeating] results in what I call the 'falling off the cliff' syndrome. You eat one bad food, conclude that you are hopelessly bad and then proceed to eat every bad thing in sight." The dynamics of bulimia are not that different from the dieting regimens subscribed to by millions of people who struggle to lose weight in that it represents a physical way of addressing tensions between good and bad parts of the self.

The use of terms such as "bad" and "sinful" to describe different foods—and different eating patterns—not only reflects the emotional connotations of food but shows how deeply attitudes about eating are embedded in the self. People who struggle unsuccessfully to change undesirable parts of their personalities speak about being "fed up with themselves." We talk of being "filled with envy" or "consumed with shame." On the positive side of the ledger, we "feast on compliments" and "feel full of ourselves" when we succeed in what we set out to do.

The overarching significance of food in people's lives helps explain why food and feeding play such a prominent role in fairy tales, and why ravenous witches are so central to these stories. The witch is the hungry self, the gluttonous part of the personality that craves fulfillment. We therefore must confront her if we hope to address the sinful tendencies associated with food. The problem is that the witch is a formidable foe when it comes to anything having to do with culinary matters.

Gretel, accordingly, is not going to talk the witch out of eating Hansel; there is very little chance she is going to sell the evil woman on the merits of vegetarianism. Nor will Gretel be able to convince the witch that there are tastier morsels in the forest, yet plumper children to be captured and consumed. If she hopes to save her brother, she must figure out a way to destroy the witch.

Early next morning Gretel was wakened by the witch and told to make the fire and fill the kettle.

"First we will do the baking," said the old woman; "I have heated the oven already, and kneaded the dough."

She pushed poor Gretel toward the oven, out of which the flames were already shining.

"Creep in," said the witch, "and see if it is properly hot, so that the bread will be baked."

Once Gretel crawled inside, the witch meant to shut the door upon her and let her be baked, and then she would have eaten her, too. But Gretel saw what she had in mind and said,

"I do not know how to do it: how shall I get in?"

"Stupid goose," said the old woman, "the opening is big enough, don't you see? I can get in myself!" and she stooped down and put her head into the oven. Then Gretel gave her a push, so that she went in farther, and she shut the iron door upon her, and fastened the bolt.

The witch must die, and Gretel is the instrument of her death. Thrusting the evil woman into a fiery furnace—dispatching her in the same way she planned to dispose of the children—both saves Hansel and Gretel from death and liberates them from their own voracious tendencies. "Hansel, we're free!" Gretel calls out to her brother, "The old witch is dead."

Though the witch has been eliminated, Hansel and Gretel are not completely out of the woods. Their journey will not be over until they arrive home. The children make their way through the forest but find their path blocked by a body of water soon after they emerge from the woods. The two search for a bridge or perhaps some stepping-stones to help them cross, but there is nothing in sight. Suddenly Gretel spies a duck swimming in the distance.

Gretel summoned the duck and asked it to ferry them across the water. The duck approached the shore, and Hansel hopped on the animal's back, instructing Gretel to get on behind him. Gretel declined, realizing that both of them would surely drown if they attempted the crossing together.

She warned Hansel, "No, that would be too hard upon the duck; we can go separately, one after the other."

Hansel followed his sister's advice, and the two made it safely across.

In the course of growing up, children discover that the world is fraught with pitfalls, and that they must learn to keep their wits about them if they hope to avoid major disasters. Fairy tales, in addition to everything else they represent, offer children an opportunity to engage in problem-solving. The dilemmas faced by the hero and heroine teach children they can succeed in the world if they draw on their inner resources.

This is one of the important messages in *Hansel and Gretel*, as well as the chief message in *The Wizard of Oz*. Dorothy and her three companions learn that they must reach deep within themselves if they hope to discover what they are searching for. The solution to their problems ultimately lies within themselves. The same message also is found in *Hop o' My Thumb*.

We left Hop and his brothers shivering in the dark, knowing the ogre will be coming for them at the break of dawn. As Hop's eyes become accustomed to the dark, he senses that there is another bed in the room. In it are seven little girls, the ogre's daughters, each with a golden crown on her head. Baby ogresses, they possess enormous mouths filled with long sharp teeth with which they have already taken to biting defenseless babies.

Hop is fearful that the ogre will wake in the night and butcher him and his brothers before dawn. He decides to take action and silently creeps across the room, removing the crowns from the heads of the baby ogresses and exchanging them for his brothers' caps.

Soon after midnight struck, the ogre woke up. Seized with regret that he had left till the morrow a task he might have performed during the day, he jumped out of bed, picked up a big knife, and tiptoed into the bedroom where his daughters and the little boys were sleeping. He approached the bed where the boys slept soundly—except for Hop o' My Thumb—and groped at their faces. Hop was very frightened, but he lay still. The ogre, feeling the golden crown on Hop's head, went to the other bed and felt for the boys' caps.

"Here they are, the little lambs!" he cried. "Let's fall to work." And with those words, he slit the throats of his seven daughters. Then he went back to bed, well content with the night's work.

As soon as Hop o' My Thumb heard the ogre start to snore, he woke up his brothers and told them to put on their clothes and follow him.

Enraged by the inadvertent slaughter of his brood, the ogre gives chase to Hop and his brothers. Hop manages to elude him and guides his brothers safely home. But not before he circles back to the ogre's house and steals his treasure. The parents are overjoyed to see their offspring and delighted to receive the riches little Hop presents to them.

Perrault ends his story with a moral, as he does all his fairy tales:

> It is no affliction to have a large family if they are all handsome, strong, and clever. But if one of them is a puny weakling, he will be despised, jeered at, and mocked. However, often the runt of the litter ends up by making the family fortune.

Young readers are once again reminded that resourcefulness is a useful virtue, and that children can be valuable family members even though they do not compare favorably to their siblings. This is a reassuring message, for all children feel unloved and passed over at some point in their lives. A story in which the smallest of the brood not only emerges victorious over a powerful adversary but wins the love and appreciation of his parents and siblings can be comforting as well as uplifting.

In the end, Hop and his brothers manage to return home in one piece, as do Hansel and Gretel. Hansel and his sister, however, are faced with an unpleasant prospect: they must confront the woman who tried to arrange their deaths. Whereas Hop's parents are basically well-meaning people, the same cannot be said for Hansel and Gretel's stepmother. In many ways, she is just as evil as the witch they only recently dispatched.

Fortunately for the children, the stepmother has mysteriously disappeared by the time they arrive home. There is no indication of what happened to her; we learn only that she is no longer around. The Grimms explain: "The father had not had a quiet hour since he left his children in the woods; but the wife was dead."

It is just as well. If she were still alive, the children would again have to match wits with someone who only a few weeks earlier had decreed their deaths. From a psychological standpoint, the stepmother's death is perfectly understandable. She and the witch in the forest are two sides of the same evil coin. In Engelbert Humperdinck's 1893 children's opera *Hansel and Gretel*, the same actress typically plays the part of both the stepmother and the witch. Though Gretel did not know it at the time, she conveniently managed to kill two witches with one stone when she shoved the evil hag into the oven.

IN THE COMPANY OF WOLVES

Of all the animals that appear in fairy tales and other forms of folklore, wolves are depicted as having the most voracious appetites. When one thinks of wolves descending upon their prey, one almost automatically thinks of uncontrolled cravings. Wolfishness is synonymous with gluttony, something echoed in the familiar warning directed at us by our parents when we were young: "Don't wolf down your food!"

Little Red Riding Hood, like *Hansel and Gretel*, also is a story about gluttony, only the witch in the story is replaced by the wolf. In this tale of an innocent child who unwittingly courts disaster on her way to visit her grandmother, a ravenous wolf eats not only one human being but two. Or does he? It depends on the version one reads.

One of the earliest versions of *Little Red Riding Hood* tells of a young girl sent by her mother to deliver a basket of bread and fruits to her grandmother. The story, widely circulated among the peasantry in eighteenth-century France, describes how the wolf intercepts Red Riding Hood in the woods, tricks her into revealing her destination, and hurries off to the grandmother's house to get there before she does. But there the story departs sharply from the familiar Perrault version.

When the wolf arrived at the grandmother's house, he killed her, poured her blood into a bottle, and sliced her flesh onto a platter. Then he got into her nightclothes and waited in bed. Soon there was a knock on the door.

"Come in, my dear," said the wolf.

"Hello, Grandmother. I've brought you some bread and milk."

"Have something yourself, my dear. There is meat and wine in the pantry."

So the little girl ate what was offered, unaware of what she was consuming.

Then the wolf said, "Undress and get into bed with me."

"Where shall I put my apron?" asked the child.

"Throw it on the fire for you won't need it anymore," replied the wolf.

For each garment—bodice, skirt, petticoat, and stockings—the child asked the same question, and each time the wolf told her: "Throw it on the fire for you won't need it anymore."

When the girl got into bed, she said, "Oh, Grandmother, what hairy legs you have."

"The better to keep me warm, my dear," said the wolf.

"Oh, Grandmother, what big shoulders you have!"

"The better to carry firewood, my dear."

"Oh, Grandmother, what long nails you have."

"The better to scratch myself."

"Oh, Grandmother, what big teeth you have."

"The better to eat you with," said the wolf.

And he leaped out of bed and swallowed her up.

In some versions, Red Riding Hood escapes the wolf's clutches by insisting that she has to go outside the cottage to relieve herself. He grants her request but ties a rope around her leg to make sure she doesn't get away. The child cleverly ties her end of the rope to a tree and escapes by running off into the woods.

Charles Perrault, in what is perhaps the most well-known rendering of the tale, deals with the more blatantly aggressive and sexual elements in the story by conveniently dropping them from the narrative. There is no flesh eating or drinking of the grandmother's blood in the Perrault version, nor does Red Riding Hood strip off her clothes and hop into bed with the wolf.

The emphasis instead is on Red Riding Hood's irresponsible behavior—the fact that she dawdles along the way to her grandmother's house and talks to strangers instead of following her mother's advice. The story, consequently, has more to do with failure to follow parental instructions than with eating and its perversions. The moral at the end of Perrault's tale warns young readers:

> Children, especially pretty, nicely brought up young ladies, ought never
> to talk to strangers; if they are foolish enough to do so, they should not
> be surprised if some greedy wolf consumes them, red riding hood and all.

The same theme of parental obedience is echoed in a contemporary retelling of Perrault's tale that ends with Little Red Riding Hood remarking to herself, "I will never wander off the forest path again as long as I live. I should have kept my promise to my mother."

ANOTHER WAY TO GO

The Grimm version of *Little Red Riding Hood*, in contrast, exploits the sinful nature of gluttony to much greater advantage. Titled *Little Red Cap*, the story not only makes sure the wolf is punished for his unseemly behavior but features a second wolf who also is punished for gluttony. In both instances, overeating, not irresponsible behavior, is the focus of the story.

Like the Perrault version, and the earlier peasant tale from which it is derived, *Little Red Cap* begins with an innocent child's encounter with a wolf on her way to visit her grandmother. The wolf calls the child's attention to all the pretty flowers growing in the woods and, having distracted her, heads for the grandmother's house. The moment he gets to the old woman's house, the wolf swallows her and waits for Red Cap to arrive. When she does, he swallows her whole as well.

The Grimm version, however, doesn't end there. A huntsman passes by the cottage shortly after the double murder and, hearing snores, decides to investigate. He discovers the wolf sleeping in the grandmother's bed and confronts the beast.

> "At last I've found you, you old sinner!" said the huntsman. "I've been looking for you a long time."
>
> The huntsman decided the wolf had swallowed the grandmother whole, and that she might yet be saved. So he did not shoot the wolf, but instead took a pair of shears and began to slit up the wolf's body. When he made a few snips, Little Red Cap appeared.
>
> The little girl jumped out and cried, "Oh, dear, how frightened I have been! It is so dark inside the wolf." Then the grandmother came out, still living and breathing.
>
> Then Little Red Cap went out and fetched some large stones with which she filled the wolf's body. The stones were so heavy that when the wolf woke up and prepared to run away, he sank down and fell dead.

The story is not quite over. A few days later Little Red Cap once again sets off to visit her grandmother. Another wolf intercepts her and, like the first wolf, tempts her to leave the path. This time the child ignores the wolf and heads straight to her grandmother's house to warn her of the danger. She and the grandmother, both wiser for their earlier brush with death, bolt the door and refuse to open it. The wolf then climbs onto the roof to wait for one of them to venture out.

> But the grandmother sensed what the wolf had in mind, and devised a plan. There was a great stone trough beside the house, and the grandmother said to the child, "Little Red Cap, I was boiling sausages yesterday, so take the bucket and carry the water in which I boiled them to the trough and pour it in. Be careful not to make noise or the wolf will hear you."
>
> Little Red Cap did what her grandmother said, and filled the trough until it was quite full. When the smell of the sausages reached the nose

of the wolf, he snuffed it up, and looked round, and stretched his neck out so far that he lost his balance and began to slip. When he could no longer keep his footing, he slipped down off the roof straight into the trough, and drowned. Then Little Red Cap went cheerfully home, and came to no harm.

Little Red Cap presents a richer and more complex vision of the Red Riding Hood saga than either the Perrault version or the peasant version that antedates it. The Grimm rendering, for one, notifies the reader that sinful impulses (gluttony in this case) are ubiquitous and not easily disposed of. Just as there are two evil presences in *The Wizard of Oz*—the Wicked Witch of the East and the Wicked Witch of the West—so there are two wolves in *Little Red Cap*. Kill one and another springs up to take its place.

The story, moreover, takes the wolf's penchant for gluttony seriously. It does not cloak it in a tale stressing obedience to parents. Not only does the first wolf die because of his ravenous appetite, but so does the second in a manner that matches his depravity. When the sin is gluttony, what more fitting end than to die lusting after sausages? The death of the two wolves—essentially witches in wolf's clothing— guarantees a truly happy ending.

But not as happy an ending as in Japan. In the Japanese version of *Little Red Riding Hood*, the wolf survives. Furthermore, the heroine puts only enough stones in the wolf's stomach to give him a stomachache, not enough to kill him. Then she sews him up again. The wolf staggers off, muttering, "I must have eaten too much; my stomach feels so heavy." Since the wolf presumably has learned his lesson, he is allowed to live. In a variant of this, the wolf apologizes to Red Riding Hood and promises to be good in the future.

Cultural variations on basic fairy-tale themes confirm the interplay between fairy tales and the mores and concerns of the societies of which they are a part. Educators in Japan believe it is important to teach children very early on to be forgiving members of society. In modern Japan, social harmony is stressed as a fundamental value, and fairy tales are expected to transmit this value. It thus would not do for Red Riding Hood to exact vengeance on the wolf or to behave vindictively. A happy ending in Japan requires the perpetrator—be it a witch or a wolf—to offer apologies to the victim for transgressing.

Western fairy tales, particularly those of the Grimm brothers, subscribe more to the biblical principle of an eye for an eye, a tooth for a tooth. One must, in the last analysis, pay for one's sins. Only by destroying the evil in the story can justice be served and undesirable tendencies in the reader mastered. By mounting a frontal attack on gluttony and making sure the wolf dies, Little Red Cap joins Hansel, Gretel, and Hop o' My Thumb in providing children with an opportunity to combat one of the more consuming seven deadly sins of childhood.

5

Envy

If the Slipper Fits . . .

○nce upon a time there was a nobleman who took as his
second wife the proudest and haughtiest woman there ever
was. The husband, by his first wife, had a young daughter
who was exceptionally sweet and gentle. His second wife
had two daughters who had their mother's temper and
resembled her in every way. No sooner was the wedding
over than the stepmother began to display her bad temper.

—**Charles Perrault**

There once was a rich man whose wife lay sick, and when she felt her end drawing near she called to her only daughter to come near her bed, and said, "Dear child, be pious and good, and God will take care of you; I will look down upon you from heaven, and will be with you." And then she closed her eyes and died. When the early spring came and melted the snow, the man took another wife. The new wife brought two daughters with her, and they were beautiful and fair in appearance, but at heart were black and ugly. And then began very evil times for the poor stepdaughter.

—Jacob and Wilhelm Grimm

Once upon a time, there lived a widower who possessed an only daughter. The girl had a governess for whom she cared greatly and the governess felt equal affection for her. Eventually, the girl's father remarried, and took a wife who had an evil temperament. She treated the charming daughter with such coldness and contempt that the young girl would complain to her governess, "O God, would that thou hath been my darling mother, thou who lovest me and art always caressing me."

—Giambattista Basile

So begin three very different versions of *Cinderella*. All feature an innocent child, a malevolent stepmother, and her ill-tempered daughters. All include a great feast or a festive ball and a lost slipper. There the similarity ends. In one of the stories, a fairy godmother changes a pumpkin into a coach; in another, the stepmother orders her own daughters to mutilate themselves; and in a third, the heroine enters into a plot with her nanny to murder her stepmother!

The three are only a small sample of the many *Cinderella* stories in existence. Over seven hundred have been documented, and new versions are constantly cropping up. "Maid to Order," a Hollywood retelling of the tale, describes a pampered adolescent from a rich family forced to work as a maid in the home of a well-to-do California couple. In a twist on the traditional plot, the film describes how Cinderella's hip fairy godmother arranges things so that the heroine learns the value of an honest day's work.

Although the story of Cinderella is believed to be over a thousand years old, the earliest written version, titled *Cat Cinderella*, made its debut in Giambattista Basile's *La Pentamerone* (The Tale of Tales), published in 1634. Basile begins his tale by proclaiming, "Envy is ever a sea of malignancy." He goes on to say that extreme jealousy can even cause one's bladder to burst. It is obvious that the author does not take the subject of envy lightly, and that his story probably will reflect this sentiment.

Basile's story starts off, as do most Cinderella stories, with a widower taking a new wife. The woman moves in with two of her daughters from a previous marriage and proceeds to take over the household, treating the heroine, Zezolla, with contempt. The young girl runs to her governess, whom she adores, and complains, "O God, would that thou hath been my darling mother, thou who lovest me and art always caressing me."

One day, after being constantly approached in this manner by Zezolla, the governess said to her, "If thou wilt do as I bid, I will become thy mother." She told her to wait until her father was off hunting, and then to ask her stepmother to fetch some of Zezolla's old clothes from a chest in the attic.

"She will tell you to hold up the lid," said the governess. "When she is searching within, creep up behind her and let the lid fall, and thus her neck will be broken." Zezolla followed the governess's instructions and crept up behind her stepmother and slammed the lid on her stepmother's neck, killing her instantly.

The father, believing his wife's death an accident, turned to Zezolla for consolation. After a decent mourning period, Zezolla praised the virtues of her governess and urged her father to marry her. The father was reluctant at first but eventually yielded to his daughter's request.

Zezolla's new stepmother initially lavishes attention on her, but before long she trots out six daughters of her own whom she has managed to keep hidden. Forsaking Zezolla, she ingratiates her own daughters in the father's eyes until he withdraws all his love and affection from his daughter. From then on, the young girl's status in the household plummets precipitously: "Zezolla was sent from the chamber to the kitchen, from the dais to the fireplace, from the silken and golden raiment to the coarse cloth, and from the scepter to the spit." Curled up at night by the hearth like a household pet, the forsaken child is dubbed "Cat Cinderella" by her stepmother and stepsisters.

Bruno Bettelheim, predictably, attributes Zezolla's fall from grace to repressed oedipal wishes, indicating that Zezolla's incestuous longing for her father is responsible for her downfall. Hidden sexual desires, he claims, are the reason the girl decides to join with the governess in carrying out the murder.

But this explanation makes little sense. If Zezolla wanted her father for herself, she would not have pleaded the governess's case so vigorously. It is unlikely that her father would have married the nanny had Zezolla not been so zealous on her behalf. What the child really longs for is the love of her dead mother; this is what motivates her to pursue the governess and to participate in the stepmother's death. It is the governess who covets the father, and the power that accrues from her new position. She is the one driven by envy.

RETURN OF THE GOOD MOTHER

One day Zezolla's father announces he is off to Sardinia on business and asks his stepdaughters what they would like as gifts. One asks for fine clothing, another requests jewels for her hair, and yet another wants playthings to pass the time of day. Almost as an afterthought, he inquires of his own daughter what she would like. Zezolla answers, "I want nought, but that thou recommend me to the queen of the fairies, bidding her that she might send me something."

The father transacts his business in Sardinia and, before sailing for home, delivers Zezolla's request to the fairy queen. She gives him a date tree in a container, a golden bucket, and a silken napkin. On his return, Zezolla replants the tree, lovingly waters it with the golden bucket, and uses the napkin to soak up the excess moisture. Before long the tree grows to full height and from its branches emerges a fairy who promises to fulfill all the child's wishes.

The tree, with its life-giving properties and connection to the earth, is a common ingredient in Cinderella stories, symbolizing, as it were, the spirit of the good mother. Reaching from beyond the grave, she offers comfort and protection to the beleaguered child, letting her know she is not alone. Her appearance represents both the fulfillment of a fantasy and a projection of the positive side of the self. As a symbol of an essential life force, she represents all that is good in the heroine.

Different fairy tales describe the emotionally sustaining character of the mother in their own unique way, each reflecting aspects of the culture of which they are a part. Before she dies, the mother in *Rashin Coatie*, a Scottish variant of *Cinderella*, tells the heroine, "After I am gone, a little red calf will come to you and give you whatever you want." In Scotland, long-haired red cattle (the Highland "koos") are an important source of sustenance, providing farmers with a means of earning a livelihood. In this tale, the calf materializes to provide for the needs of Rashin Coatie, the impoverished heroine.

When the wicked stepmother learns that the calf is helping to keep the daughter alive, she becomes enraged and orders the animal butchered. Rashin Coatie, so named because she is forced to wear a coat of rushes, buries the animal's bones beneath a stone and prays to the dead calf for help. The bones supply the child with fine clothes that capture the attention of a young prince who ultimately falls in love with her. Indian variants of *Cinderella* substitute other animals since killing a cow violates the Hindu belief of *aghnya*, which prohibits the slaughter of cattle.

In *Yeh-hsien*, a Chinese rendering of the tale recorded in the ninth century A.D., the heroine is befriended by a golden fish—a highly revered animal in Chinese folklore. As in *Rashin Coatie*, the stepmother destroys the animal, in this case by eating it, and hides the bones under a dunghill. A wise man tells Yeh-hsien where the bones are hidden and advises her to conceal them in her room, promising that the bones will supply her with whatever she needs when the time comes. Later on, when Yeh-hsien needs proper clothing to meet the warlord who ultimately takes her as his bride, the bones supply her with gold shoes and a cloak made of kingfisher feathers.

All three stories—*Cat Cinderella, Rashin Coatie, and Yeh-hsien*—fulfill a universal need in children to feel they are loved and cherished, to know someone will be there for them at the end of the day. Listening to or reading any of a number of Cinderella tales fulfills this need and helps assuage fears of maternal loss.

One day Zezolla learns that the prince plans to throw a ball in order to choose a bride.

Zezolla wanted desperately to attend, but she did not have the proper clothes. She waited for her stepsisters to depart, and then ran to the tree, where she recited a magic incantation given to her by the tree fairy. The tree threw down a golden gown and a necklace made of pearls and precious stones. So that she would be able to get to the ball, the tree also provided Zezolla with a handsome steed and twelve pages.

When Zezolla arrived at the king's palace, she met her sisters, who regarded her with envy but failed to recognize who she was. She made her way into the ballroom, where she immediately captured the prince's attention. Smitten by her beauty and regal bearing, he proposed to her. But Zezolla fled the palace, fearing the prince would reject her once he learned of her lowly circumstances.

Like most Cinderella tales, the plot turns on the prince's attempt to find the mysterious princess, who, in making her escape, loses one of her slippers. The monarch retrieves the shoe and, holding the dainty slipper in his hand, proclaims,

"O beauteous candlestick, which holdeth the candle that consumeth me! O trivet of the beauteous kettle where boileth my life! O fine cloth, to which is tied the net of love wherewith thou hast caught this soul. I embrace thee and hold thee to my bosom."

This prince obviously has a way with words. He orders a great banquet to be held and decrees that all the women in the kingdom must attend. No expense will be spared to find the maiden whose foot fits the slipper.

The use of a banquet or some other grand event to conduct a competition excites the imagination because it conjures up some of the most primitive feelings about being chosen. Only one maiden will get the prize, only one lucky person will reap the benefits associated with being number one. Though the competition is basically a glorified beauty contest, it taps into complex feelings that children harbor about parental preference, about what it means to be the golden child, the son or daughter valued above all other children in the family.

The competition, of course, stirs up feelings of envy. But if Zezolla wins, so does the reader, for she is the figure in the story with whom the reader identifies. Unlike the stepsisters, who mistreat the heroine and thus represent reprehensible parts of the self, Zezolla is well-meaning and virtuous. The outcome of the competition will determine whether good parts of the self will prevail.

Oh, what a banquet that was, and what joyance and amusements were there, and what food: pastry and pies, and roast, and balls of mincemeat, and macaroni, and ravioli, enough to feed an army.

There is no doubt this is an Italian fairy tale, and that no one will go hungry. All the women in the kingdom are invited—rich and poor, young and old, titled and untitled—but none of their feet fit the slipper. The prince wonders whether someone may have been missed. Zezolla's father confesses that he has a daughter who makes her home by the kitchen fireplace but insists that she is not worthy of notice. The prince extends the feast another day, this time decreeing that *every* woman must attend.

When all had eaten their fill the following day, the prince again ordered that all the women in the banquet room try on the slipper. One by one, they tried on the shoe. No sooner came he to Zezolla than her foot was caught by love like a moth to the flame. Taking Zezolla by the arm, the prince bid her sit beside him on the dais and placed a crown on her head, commanding all his subjects to do her obeisance as their queen.

The story ends with the prince and Zezolla living happily ever after. The sisters are punished for their jealous nature by being forced to return to their stepmother empty-handed, or more correctly, empty-footed. Bitter and resentful, they learn the hard way the price of envy. Good elements in the self—unselfish tendencies—emerge triumphant, and Zezolla comes out on top even though the path she traveled to achieve her goal was less than commendable.

Why did the story of *Cat Cinderella*, with its powerful and poignant imagery, fall by the wayside and become superseded by the Grimm and Perrault versions? For one, it portrays a child killing another human being. Gretel also commits murder in *Hansel and Gretel* but only to save her brother's (and her own) life. There is a difference between killing in self-defense and killing to advance selfish ends.

The murder of the stepmother also produces a morally ambiguous ending. Zezolla not only goes unpunished but gets to marry the prince. One might argue that Zezolla's betrayal by the governess is, in fact, her punishment. But the end of a fairy tale is what counts, and in the end the heroine gets off scot-free. Fairy tales are renowned for presenting children with an uncluttered, black-and-white depiction of good and evil, and *Cat Cinderella*, which is lacking in this regard, leaves readers with unanswered questions and nagging doubts.

WILL THE REAL CINDERELLA PLEASE STAND UP?

Basile's *Cat Cinderella* nonetheless forms the basis for dozens of subsequent Cinderella tales, the most notable being those of the Grimm brothers and Charles Perrault. Children nowadays tend to be more familiar with the Perrault version, not only because it has been reproduced countless times in storybooks, but because it formed the inspiration for Walt Disney's full-length feature film. The pumpkin-coach and glass slipper—invented by Perrault—have become cultural icons, largely owing to the film's popularity. The Grimm version, however, titled *Aschenputtel*, is infinitely richer and delves into matters the Perrault version barely touches upon.

The Grimms' *Cinderella* takes as its point of departure a dying mother's promise to keep watch over her daughter. Just before the mother succumbs, she admonishes the girl to be good and assures her that she will look after her from heaven. After the mother dies, the father soon remarries.

The introduction of a new wife into the household signals the beginning of "very evil times for the poor stepdaughter." As in most Cinderella stories, the woman not only favors her own daughters but forces her stepdaughter to labor endlessly in the kitchen. To compound matters, the stepsisters saddle Cinderella with meaningless tasks: they strew peas and lentils on the floor and make her pick them up in order to amuse themselves. They also make the child draw heavy buckets of water from the well and force her to slave by a hot stove all day. While the sisters in the Perrault version are self-centered, the sisters in the Grimm version are sadistic.

One day Cinderella's father announces that he is going to the fair. As he heads out the door, he asks his daughters what they would like him to bring back as gifts. As in *Cat Cinderella*, the stepdaughters' demands far outstrip the more modest request of his daughter.

"Fine clothes!" said one of the stepdaughters.

"Pearls and jewels!" said the other.

"But what will you have, Cinderella?" said the father.

"The first twig, father, that strikes against your hat on the way home; that is what I should like you to bring me."

Psychoanalytic writers tend to attribute sexual significance to Cinderella's request. In *Cinderella: A Folklore Casebook*, psychoanalyst Ben Rubenstein poses the rhetorical question, "Can not the twig be related, in part, to the penis envy and phallic aspirations of the little girl?" Perhaps. But if the child's oedipal strivings are so all-consuming, why only a twig? Why not a branch or even the whole tree? Cinderella's subsequent actions make it clear that her request is motivated not so much by sex as by other concerns.

So the father brought for the two stepdaughters fine clothes, pearls and jewels, and on his way back, as he rode through a green lane, a hazel twig struck against his hat; and he broke it off and carried it home with him. And when he reached home he gave to the stepdaughters what they had wished for, and to Cinderella he gave the hazel twig.

Cinderella thanked her father, and went to her mother's grave, and planted this twig there, weeping so bitterly that the tears fell upon it and watered it, and it flourished and became a fine tree. Cinderella went to see it three times a day, and wept and prayed, and each time a white bird rose up from the tree, and if she uttered any wish, the bird brought Cinderella whatever she had wished for.

The graveside scene once again reiterates the deep immutable bond that exists between mother and child. Sitting beneath the hazel tree, the child longs for the love she once knew, for the mother who nurtured and protected her. The dove, the symbolic embodiment of the mother, rises up to assure the child that she is not forgotten, and that she will be looked after.

Prior to this point in the story, there has been no indication that anyone, living or dead, is particularly concerned about Cinderella's welfare. Her father, the one person who might shelter her from harm, is blind to her situation—or simply self-absorbed. He is either off hunting, attending to business, or engaged in other pursuits.

As in *Snow White, Hansel and Gretel*, and now *Cinderella*, male figures in fairy tales tend to be portrayed as weak or unavailable. This does not mean that fathers are unfeeling. It is just that fairy tales are maternal documents and so place greater emphasis on the relationship between mother and child, particularly as it relates to the development of the self. As a result, the role of fathers tends to be devalued or given short shrift.

The hazel tree, by means of the doves, signals to Cinderella that someone cares for her. It communicates that there is a maternal presence in the universe concerned about her welfare, a presence that was once part of her life and is still a part of it. The idea that people who die can be an ongoing source of comfort and nurturance is a difficult concept for young children to absorb. Fairy tales like *Cinderella* use concrete images to advance the notion that a psychological continuity exists with those we cherish even after they are no longer around.

Both Perrault's Cinderella and the Disney film omit the mother's deathbed vow and the graveside scene and take as a starting point a motherless Cinderella. This conveniently does away with the pain of separation brought about by the mother's death. But it also deletes an important psychological dimension from the story: the child's experience of loss and desire to reclaim the missing mother. The psychological import of *Cinderella* thus is diminished in favor of an opening sequence that purportedly is less disturbing.

The Perrault version further detracts from the psychological meaning of the story by depicting Cinderella as cheerful and good-natured, in spite of the abuse heaped upon her by her sisters. In Perrault's tale, Cinderella makes light of their taunts when they refer to her derisively as "Cinder-britches" and "Cinder-slut." She even volunteers to do her stepsisters' hair in the face of endless ridicule: "Anyone else would have tangled their hair, but Cinderella was good and she coiffed it to perfection." The sentimentalized vision of an impossibly loving Cinderella all but erases envy from the story. We instead are presented with a goody-goody heroine who seems to be willing to put up with any affront. This perverts the story's original intent.

Jane Yolen, a noted author of children stories, points out that Cinderella is a three-dimensional figure, a stalwart heroine who harbors strong feelings about the way she is treated and wants to change her life for the better. She writes: "To make *Cinderella* less than she is, then, is a heresy of the worst kind. It cheapens our most cherished dreams, and it makes a mockery of the true magic inside us all—the ability to change our own lives, the ability to control our own destinies."

The Grimm version, accordingly, portrays Cinderella as embittered and jealous. In one instance after another, we are told how truly miserable she is. Cinderella's bitter tears, in fact, feed the tree that represents the spirit of her dead mother. The child's circumstances deteriorate even further once the ball is announced. When Cinderella asks her stepmother whether she can attend, the woman becomes cruel and vindictive, saddling the child with a series of impossible tasks. "I have strewn a dish-full of lentils in the ashes," she tells her, "and you may go with us only if you can pick them all up in two hours."

The wicked woman obviously has no intention of letting Cinderella attend the ball since the task cannot be completed in the allotted time. Cinderella, however, calls upon the doves in the enchanted tree to help her. They execute the "impossible" task by picking the lentils from the ashes in less than an hour.

The stepmother is undaunted. She responds by telling Cinderella she cannot attend the ball because she lacks the proper clothes. Besides, she does not know how to dance. "You would only be laughed at," she declares in a derisive tone. She nevertheless promises the child she can go if she can pick two dishes full of lentils from the ashes in one hour, a task she is certain the young girl can never perform.

Cinderella again summons her helpmates, who separate the lentils from the ashes, once again completing the task in half the time. But when Cinderella presents her stepmother with the two dishes of lentils, she refuses to honor her promise and marches out the door with her two daughters. Disappointed and totally disheartened, Cinderella watches them leave.

> As there was no one left in the house, Cinderella went to her mother's grave under the hazel bush. Remembering what the little bird had told her, she cried out:
>
> > *Shiver and quake, my little tree,*
> > *Silver and gold throw down on me.*
>
> Then the bird who lived in the tree threw down a dress of silver and gold, and a pair of silk-embroidered gold slippers. All in haste, Cinderella put on the dress and went to the festival.

There is no bird in the Perrault version. Instead, a fairy godmother appears and, with a wave of her wand, summons up a beautiful gown for the heroine. To ensure that the child arrives at the ball in style, she fashions a coach out of a pumpkin and turns six mice into horses to draw the carriage. To complete the tableau, she transforms a rat into a coachman and changes six lizards into footmen.

While charming in its own right, Perrault's description places more emphasis on Cinderella's wardrobe and her means of getting to the ball than on the feelings raging inside of her. The child's longing for her lost mother and the emotional turmoil she experiences—portrayed so vividly by both Basile and Grimm—is completely missing in the Perrault version.

Disney, to his credit, compensates for Perrault's omission by including a small but significant detail in the screenplay. In the film, Cinderella retrieves one of her mother's old gowns from an attic chest. Making use of her mice-helpmates, she uses pieces of ribbon discarded by her stepsisters to decorate the dress, making it come to life, so to speak. Though this presents a marvelous opportunity to explore further the connection between Cinderella and her lost mother, Disney abandons the dress entirely in the next scene. The stepsisters reclaim the discarded pieces of cloth, and the dress is never mentioned again.

Ever a sea of malignancy

In the Grimm version, envy emerges as a conspicuous dynamic, surfacing both in the stepmother's envy of Cinderella's initial position in the family and in Cinderella's envy of the privileges usurped by her sisters. If the child's predicament is to be successfully resolved—if the story is to have a happy ending—envy must be addressed and destroyed or, at the very least, condemned. If allowed to go unchecked, envy can have serious consequences.

This is vividly portrayed in the real-life example of a mother who was so jealous of her daughter's rival that she plotted a murder to ensure her daughter's success. Wanda Webb Holloway, the mother of a junior high school student in Texas, apparently was so concerned that her daughter might be eclipsed by a rival cheerleader that she arranged to have the mother of the girl murdered. Dubbed the "Cheerleader Mom" by the media, Holloway hired a hit man to do the job, reasoning that the death of her mother would unnerve the rival. She hoped this would enhance her own daughter's chances of making the cheerleading squad. Fortunately, the individual she recruited reported the plot to the police, who promptly arrested Holloway, putting an end to her devious scheme.

It is not necessary to recount bizarre scenarios such as this to demonstrate the pervasive effects of envy. Joey, the ten-year-old boy I treated for pica, had a history of fire-setting and property destruction in addition to the eating disorder. By the time I saw him, he had been in and out of numerous foster homes and was deemed virtually unmanageable. He regularly flew into uncontrollable rages and was impossible to control.

Joey's destructive behavior, not surprisingly, persisted on the ward after he was admitted to the hospital. Not only did he set fires, but he regularly stole or smashed toys belonging to other children. His murderous outbursts were exacerbated on visiting days. Most of the other children were visited by parents and relatives, but no one ever came to see Joey.

The dynamics behind Joey's behavior were largely fueled by envy. It was not so much that he was jealous of the other children's toys or possessions—the hospital provided all the children with an ample number of playthings—but rather that they had parents who cared for them. To satisfy his frustration and resentment, he ravaged the belongings of the other children, symbolically destroying the one thing they possessed but he lacked: loving parents.

The stepmother in the Grimm version of *Cinderella* doesn't set fires or smash people's belongings, but she is as destructive as Joey. This becomes painfully evident toward the end of the tale when the prince begins his kingdomwide search for the mystery maiden. By this point in the story, Cinderella has already attended the ball on three successive nights, and on each occasion has managed to escape before the prince learns her true identity. On the third night, the prince spreads pitch on the palace steps hoping to catch her. Instead, he traps one of her slippers.

From this point on, the story departs drastically from the Perrault-Disney version. When the servants of the prince reach the house where Cinderella dwells, they are met at the door by her stepmother and stepsisters. The daughters are delighted to try on the slipper, for each is confident it will fit. The older of the two goes to her room to try on the shoe while her mother waits outside the door. A few moments pass, and it becomes obvious there is a problem.

> The elder daughter could not get her great toe into the slipper for the shoe was too small. So her mother handed her a knife and said,
> "Here, cut the toe off, for when you are queen, you will never have to go on foot."
> So the girl cut her toe off, squeezed her foot into the shoe, concealed the pain, and went down to the king's son.

The prince rides off with his bride-to-be. As they pass by the grave of the mother, two pigeons perched on the hazel bush cry out:

> *Turn and peep, turn and peep*
> *There's blood within the shoe,*
> *The shoe it is too small for her,*
> *The true bride waits for you.*

The prince looks down at the shoe and sees that there is indeed blood oozing from it. He wheels his horse around and heads back to the house, insisting that the other sister try on the slipper.

> The younger sister went into the house to try on the shoe. But though she was able to get her toes comfortably in, her heel was too large.
> Then her mother handed her the knife, saying, "Cut a piece off your heel; when you are queen you will never have to go on foot."
> So the other sister cut a piece off her heel, and thrust her bloody foot into the shoe. Then she went down to the prince, who placed his bride before him on his horse and rode off.

The stepmother's envious nature emerges full-blown in this passage. Here is a woman so determined to become queen-mother that she will stop at nothing to make sure one of her daughters marries the prince. Her ambition is so great, her envy of Cinderella so compelling, that she is willing to mutilate her daughters to make sure one of them ascends the throne. Her total disregard for her own flesh and blood marks her as one of the most wicked women in fairy tales, the quintessential bad mother.

When the prince rides by the hazel bush with the second sister, the birds once again call his attention to the deception by pointing out the blood dripping from the shoe. He turns around and brings the false bride home, expressing his strong displeasure to the father and the stepmother.

"This is not the right one," said he. "Have you no other daughter?"

"No," said the father, "only a stunted Cinderella left by my dead wife. She cannot possibly be the bride." The king's son ordered her to be sent for, but the stepmother said,

"Oh, no! she is much too dirty, I could not let her be seen."

But the prince would have her fetched, and so Cinderella had to appear.

Before she came down, Cinderella washed her face and hands quite clean. Then she went to the prince, who held out to her the golden shoe. Then she sat down on a stool, drew her foot out of the heavy wooden shoe, and slipped it into the golden one, which fitted it perfectly.

And when she stood up, and the prince looked in her face, he knew again the beautiful maiden that had danced with him, and he cried, "This is the right bride!"

The stepmother and the two sisters were thunderstruck, and grew pale with anger as the prince put Cinderella before him on his horse and rode off. And as they passed the hazel bush, the two white pigeons came flying after Cinderella and perched on her shoulders, one on the right, the other on the left, and so remained.

Another happy ending. Except that this story is not quite over. Justice has not yet been served.

When the wedding day arrives, the two stepsisters attend the festivities hoping to curry favor with the prince and his new bride. They join the bridal procession, each taking a place at Cinderella's side. Their stepsister's guardians, however, are not through with them.

As the bridal procession went to the church, the eldest walked on the right side and the younger on the left. When they passed by, the pigeons picked out an eye of each of them. And as they returned, the elder was on the left side and the younger on the right, and the pigeons picked out the other eye of each of them. And so they were condemned to go blind for the rest of their days because of their wickedness and falsehood.

It is the stepsisters who are punished at the end of the Grimm brothers' tale, rather than the stepmother who escapes unharmed. The question is, why? She certainly is nasty enough; she barely hesitates before ordering her daughters to mutilate their feet. Perhaps blinding the daughters is the story's way of punishing her. After all, they are her flesh and blood.

But there may be other reasons the stepmother's life is spared. For one, she never actually tried to kill Cinderella, even though the ill treatment she meted out came close to destroying the young girl's spirit. Furthermore, the stepmother is a real mother. Unlike witches who reside in dark corners of the forest and are childless, the stepmother in *Cinderella* has children of her own. So does the governess in Basile's *Cat Cinderella*; she too survives. The violent death of a bona fide mother—though she has all the characteristics of a witch—hits too close to home. This helps explain why the stepsisters are spared death. Though they are self-absorbed and mean-spirited, they nevertheless are real children, born of a real mother. In fairy tales, witches and ogres die, not children—unless, of course, they are pointy-toothed little cannibals like the ogre's daughters in *Hop o' My Thumb*.

But someone in the story has to pay the piper, and it is the sisters. Though they escape with their lives, they lose their sight. The price they pay, while draconian, is nevertheless consistent with the sin in the story. Envy often is dubbed "the green-eyed monster," and the word itself derives from the Latin *videre*, to see. By being deprived of their ability to see, the stepsisters are forever deprived of their ability to envy.

I SHOT AN ARROW THROUGH THE AIR

The Grimm version of *Cinderella* once again echoes the theme of retribution that is so common in fairy tales. There nevertheless are some fairy tales in which envy is dealt with less harshly. One of these is a Russian tale that relies on humor to characterize what happens when envy gains the upper hand. Titled *The Frog Princess*, the story begins with a king who is eager to have grandchildren. He summons his three sons and tells them he would like them to wed.

"Very well," they all replied. "Who do you want us to marry?"

"Each of you must take an arrow and shoot it into the sky," he told them. "Where the arrows fall, there shall be your destiny."

So the sons went into a meadow, drew their bows, and let their arrows fly.

The eldest son's arrow fell into the garden of a nobleman whose daughter retrieved it. The middle son's arrow fell into the garden of a merchant; she too picked the arrow up. The arrow of the youngest son, Prince Ivan, flew into a marsh. Ivan went looking for it and came upon a frog sitting on a leaf with the arrow in its mouth.

"Give me back my arrow," the prince said to the frog.

The frog replied, "Marry me!"

"How can I marry a frog?" the prince asked.

"Marry me, for it is your destiny," the frog answered.

Ivan is disappointed, but he nevertheless feels honor-bound to fulfill his father's request and carries the frog home. Soon thereafter the king celebrates three weddings: his eldest son to the nobleman's daughter, the middle son to the merchant's daughter, and poor Prince Ivan to the frog.

Sometime later the king calls his three sons to his side and tells them he would like to see which of their wives is most skilled with a needle. He wants each of his daughters-in-law to sew a shirt for him by the next morning.

Prince Ivan is worried, for he knows the frog cannot sew. When the frog sees him sitting in the corner of the room looking forlorn, it hops over and tries to console him.

"Why are you so sad, Prince Ivan? Are you in trouble?"

"My father wants you to sew him a shirt by morning."

"Don't be so downhearted," said the frog. "Go to bed; night is the mother of counsel."

When the prince was asleep, the frog hopped outside, cast off her frog skin, and turned into a maiden fair beyond compare.

She clapped her hands and servants suddenly appeared from out of nowhere. She told them, "Maids and nurses, get ready to work! By tomorrow morning, sew me a shirt like my own father used to wear."

The next morning the brothers appear before the king with the shirts their wives have sewn. When the first brother presents his shirt, the king looks at it with disdain and declares, "This shirt will only do for one of my servants." The king responds to the shirt presented by the second brother by exclaiming, "This one is only good for the bathhouse." But when Ivan displays the handsomely embroidered shirt the frog has sewn, the king takes one look and says, "This is a shirt indeed! I shall wear it on the best occasions."

Envy rears its ugly head the moment the news of what has happened reaches the sisters-in law. Upon hearing about the shirts, the two wives become extremely jealous. They are sure the frog is a sorceress. So when the king announces a competition to see which wife can bake the best bread, they send someone to spy on the frog, hoping to discover her secret. But the frog is clever. Realizing her sisters-in-law are up to no good, she breaks a hole in the top of the stove and throws the dough inside. The spy runs back and tells the other wives what she has seen, and they do the same.

Once the spy no longer is watching, the frog turns into the pretty maiden again and commands her servants to bake a perfect loaf. They plug up the hole, place the dough on a bread pan, and slide it into the oven the normal way. The next morning Prince Ivan delivers a perfect loaf to the king while the other brothers offer up burnt lumps of charred dough. The king discards the charred lumps and holds Ivan's bread up for all to see. "Now this is what I call bread!" he exclaims. "It is fit to be eaten only on holidays."

The other wives, of course, become even more jealous. Once again they have been outdone by a lowly frog! When the king invites his sons and their wives to a fancy feast the following day, the wives are determined to outshine their amphibian counterpart. They order their servants to lay out their loveliest dresses and to take out their dancing shoes.

The prince, upon receiving the invitation, is beside himself. How can he bring a frog to the banquet, much less one who is his wife? The frog tells him to go alone, and she will arrive later. "When you hear a loud knocking at the door, do not be afraid," she says. "Just tell everyone it is only your froggy riding in her box."

At the feast, the other daughters-in-law tease Prince Ivan about his wife. "Why didn't you bring her in a handkerchief?" they taunt him. "You must have had to search all the marshes for such a beauty."

Suddenly there is a loud knock at the door. The guests jump in fright, but Ivan calms them. "It is only my froggy riding in her box."

Just then a gilded carriage drawn by six white horses dashed up to the palace door and out of it stepped a beautiful princess in a dress of sky-blue silk strewn with stars and a shining moon upon her head—a maiden as fair as the sky at dawn. She took Prince Ivan by the hand and led him to the table where the others were feasting.

Although *The Frog Princess* is not a Cinderella story by any means, it contains elements in common with Cinderella tales. One is a character who is the lowest of the low—in this case, a frog—but is transformed into a beautiful princess. She arrives at a ball in a gilded carriage wearing a beautiful gown and immediately captures the attention of the court. Another common element, of course, is envy. Appearing initially in the shirt and bread episodes, it now makes its presence known in the wives' attempts to emulate and outdo the princess.

The guests began to eat, drink, and make merry. The princess drank from her glass and emptied the dregs into her left sleeve. Then she ate some swan meat and put the bones in her right sleeve. The wives of the elder princes saw her do this and they did the same.

When the eating and drinking were over, the time came for dancing. The princess took Prince Ivan and tripped off with him. She whirled and danced and everybody watched and marveled. She waved her left sleeve, and lo! a lake appeared. She waved her right sleeve, and white swans began to swim on the lake. The king and his guests were struck with wonder.

Then the other daughters went to dance. They waved one sleeve, but only swashed wine all over the guests; they waved the other, but only scattered bones through the room. One hit the king right in the middle of his forehead. The king flew into a rage and ordered both his daughters-in-law out of his sight.

The sisters-in-law thus are punished, perhaps not by death or mutilation, but by shame and mortification. By letting envy get the best of them, they become the laughingstock of the court and are banished from the palace.

Stories like *Rashin Coatie*, *Aschenputtel*, *The Frog Princess*, and particularly *Cinderella* target jealous tendencies and the interpersonal difficulties they create. This is one of the reasons *Cinderella* and its derivatives strike a universal chord in children. Children's lives are filled with envy, and stories that include it as a major dynamic help them find ways of dealing with their own jealous urges. Whereas the Grimm brothers' rendition of *Cinderella* drives messages about envy home in a more forceful and sober way than *The Frog Princess*, the two stories can be read in tandem to expose children to the different consequences of jealousy. Each in its own way communicates that conquering jealous urges is a laudable objective and holds out hope for more satisfactory relationships. Most people would agree that getting along with the Joneses is infinitely more satisfying than trying to keep up with them. We achieve this goal when we are satisfied not only with what we have—but with who we are.

6
Objects That Love

In a certain kingdom, there lived a merchant who had an only daughter named Vasilisa. When the girl was eight years old, her mother fell gravely ill, and called her daughter to her side. She took a doll from under her coverlet and gave it to the girl, saying, "Listen, Vasilisa, and heed my last words. I am dying, and together with my maternal blessing I leave you this doll. Always keep it with you, and do not show it to anyone; if you get into trouble, give the doll food and ask its advice. When it has eaten, it will tell you what to do." Then the mother kissed her child goodbye and died.

The Russian fairy tale *Vasilisa the Beautiful* is one of a number of stories in which magic objects play a major role. Like *Cinderella*, it begins with a young girl forced to put up with an overbearing stepmother and two selfish stepsisters. But unlike *Cinderella*, there is no prince, no fairy godmother, and no lost slipper. Instead, it features an enchanted doll with lifelike properties who comes to the aid of the heroine. Not only does the doll help Vasilisa deal with her vindictive stepmother, it sees her through a series of harrowing encounters with a ferocious witch.

After his wife's death, the merchant mourned as is proper, and then began to think of marrying again. He was a handsome man and had no difficulty finding a bride, but he liked best a certain widow. Because she was elderly and had two daughters of her own, of almost the same age as Vasilisa, he thought she was an experienced housewife and mother. He married her but was deceived, for she did not turn out to be as good a mother for Vasilisa as he hoped.

Vasilisa was the most beautiful girl in the village, so her stepmother and stepsisters were jealous of her beauty. They tormented her by giving her all kinds of work, hoping she would grow thin from toil and burned from exposure to the wind and sun. But Vasilisa bore all this without complaint and became lovelier and more buxom every day, while the stepmother and her daughters grew thin and ugly from spite.

Vasilisa was able to withstand the onslaughts of her stepmother for she was helped by her doll. Without its aid the girl could never have managed all that work. In return, Vasilisa sometimes did not eat, but kept the choicest morsels for her doll. And at night, when everyone was asleep, she would lock herself in her room, and give the doll a treat, saying: "Now, little doll, eat and listen to my troubles. I live in my father's house but I am deprived of all joy. A wicked stepmother is driving me from this world. Tell me how I should live and what I should do."

The doll ate the food, and afterwards offered Vasilisa advice and comfort. In the morning, it would perform all the chores for Vasilisa, who rested in the shade and picked flowers. The doll weeded the flower beds, sprayed the cabbage, and fired the stove. The doll even showed

Vasilisa an herb that would protect her from sunburn. Thanks to her doll, Vasilisa led an easy life.

The doll bequeathed to Vasilisa by her mother is a magic talisman. It allows Vasilisa to unburden her woes in the privacy of her room, and it performs all the household chores in exchange for a morsel of food. It even supplies her with an herbal sunscreen. Like the doves in *Cinderella*, the doll is an extension of the mother and looks after Vasilisa, making sure she survives her trials and tribulations.

Some years go by, and Vasilisa approaches marriageable age. She is wooed by the village men, none of whom pay the slightest attention to her stepsisters. The stepmother naturally is furious and vents her anger by raining blows on Vasilisa's head. As time passes, the stepmother becomes increasingly convinced that her daughters will never marry while Vasilisa is alive.

The stepmother waits for Vasilisa's father to leave on a journey to a far-off land, and then moves the family to a house on the edge of a thick forest. The forest is the home of Baba Yaga, a fearsome and ferocious witch. Every day the stepmother sends Vasilisa into the woods to perform errands, hoping the witch will devour the child. But each time the doll takes care to keep Vasilisa far from where the witch has her cottage, ensuring that the girl returns home safe and sound. The stepmother responds by hatching a plan to get rid of Vasilisa once and for all.

Every evening, the stepmother set the three maidens to work: the oldest had to make lace, the second was told to knit stockings, and Vasilisa's job was to spin. One night, she put out all the lights in the house, leaving only one candle in the room where the girls worked. Then she went to bed. Soon after she retired, the candle began to smoke. Instead of trimming it, one of the stepsisters snuffed it out according to her mother's instructions, making it look like an accident.

"What shall we do now?" said the girls. "There is no light in the house and our tasks are not finished. Someone must run to Baba Yaga and get some light."

"The pins on my lace give me light," said the one who was making lace. "I shall not go."

"I shall not go either," said the one who was knitting stockings. "My knitting needles give me light."

"Then you must go," both of them cried out, pointing to Vasilisa.

Vasilisa went to her bedroom, and put the supper she had prepared before her doll. Then she told the doll what had happened. The doll ate the supper and its eyes began to gleam like two candles.

"Fear not, Vasilisa," the doll said. "Go to Baba Yaga, only keep me with you all the time. With me in your pocket you will suffer no harm."

Dolls and other enchanted objects in fairy tales—pieces of clothing and animals with magical qualities—shelter the hero or heroine from evil and help them perform seemingly impossible tasks. Such objects not only introduce a supernatural element into the story but help redress the balance of power between the child and an all-powerful adversary. At the same time, they represent the child's natural desire to be connected to a loving force.

Magic objects typically make their appearance when the hero or heroine is in dire need of help. The doves in *Cinderella* come to the child's rescue when she is forced to perform the tasks dictated by her stepmother. The ruby red slippers fly onto Dorothy's feet just as the Wicked Witch of the West is about to attack her for killing her sister. And Vasilisa's little doll assists her in executing onerous chores. It also looks after her when she is sent into the woods.

The psychology of aloneness

The significance of these objects touches on the young child's early experience of abandonment. Because mothers are subject to innumerable demands, they cannot always be by the child's side. The mother may work outside the home, or her time may be occupied tending to other siblings, cleaning the house, or preparing meals. The mother may not stray far, but it might as well be another galaxy as far as the young child is concerned. Infants are bound by their sensory worlds, and the "disappearance" of the mother means that she ceases to exist. "Out of sight, out of mind" literally depicts the child's experience in early stages of development.

This can be particularly disconcerting before the age of two, when the child is still developing an autonomous sense of self. Before children begin to experience themselves as separate entities, they behave as if they and the mother were one and the same, a state of dependence Margaret Mahler refers to as "symbiosis." Under such circumstances, even brief separations can cause significant distress. This explains why young children make repeated efforts to maintain connection with the mother even when she is in the immediate vicinity. Infants, for example, will crawl back to the mother or maintain visual contact while playing to make sure she is around. Signs of panic may emerge even when she is gone for only short periods of time. The existential formula of infancy seems to be "Mother equals Me," so that even brief disappearances can trigger bouts of anxiety. If "Mother equals Me," then "No Mother equals No Me."

Over the course of development, children develop a mental image of the mother that acts as a substitute for her physical presence. The appearance of this maturational landmark tends to be facilitated by "disappearance games" such as peek-a-boo. At first, children will watch the mother cover her face with her hands, erupting in squeals of delight when she drops them to magically make herself "reappear." Later in development, children will re-create this scenario by covering their own faces, using an internal representation of the mother as reassurance that she has not totally vanished. By turning maternal disappearance into a game, young children gain mastery over the fleeting nature of their interpersonal worlds.

The problem is that the ability to sustain a maternal image doesn't develop overnight. Although developmental psychologists believe the capacity for "maternal imaging" is present as early as one or two months, it may be another five or six months before the first mental representation of the mother becomes relatively stable. It then can take as much as a year or two until the mother is fully internalized and transformed into a viable inner presence.

A year or two is a long time in the life of a child. In the meantime, these "mini-abandonments" can result in many worrisome moments. To deal with the anxiety associated with maternal separation, young children rely on favorite playthings—commonly known as "transitional objects"—to comfort them when the mother is gone for any length of time. Operating as mother surrogates, these playthings take the place of the mother until maternal imaging becomes automatic and instinctive.

The maternal significance of transitional objects can be seen in a number of fairy tales. In *The Goose Girl*, the mother, a queen, presents her daughter with a handkerchief tinged with three drops of blood just before the girl travels to a distant land to marry a prince. The blood, a concrete reminder of the blood tie that binds mother and child, is meant to protect the princess as long as she keeps the handkerchief in her possession. The red calf in *Rashin Coatie* is given to the heroine by her mother shortly before she dies, while in *Yeh-hsien*, the heroine is the recipient of a golden fish. Even though the witch in both stories destroys the animal, the bones survive. As embodiments of the mother's spirit, they function as transitional objects, ensuring that the maidens receive the garments they need to attract the king's attention.

The British pediatrician and psychologist D. W. Winnicott writes that a distinguishing characteristic of the transitional object is its irreplaceability. Once a toy is adopted as a transitional object, children develop an intense attachment to it, and it becomes difficult, if not impossible, to separate the child from it. Something along these lines occurred with Jeffrey, the child of one of my next-door neighbors.

A bright, precocious three-year-old, Jeffrey was deeply attached to a stuffed giraffe his parents had bought when he was an infant. The animal was Jeffrey's constant companion: it slept in his bed, went with him to the bathroom, and accompanied him to every meal. Occasionally Jeffrey would "share" a morsel of food with his giraffe, much as Vasilisa shared her food with her doll.

Over time the animal began to show signs of wear. One of its eyes had worked loose, an ear was gone, and its coat was coming apart at the seams. As a result of countless trips to the dinner table, the giraffe's outer covering was encrusted with peanut butter and stained with catsup. Jeffrey's mother, convinced that the toy had outlived its usefulness, decided it was time to replace it. She managed to find a stuffed giraffe practically identical to the original, had it wrapped in a pretty box, and presented it to Jeffrey the following day.

Did Jeffrey express delight over his new acquisition? Hardly. He showed absolutely no interest in the new giraffe and clung to the old one with renewed fervor. That night, after Jeffrey went to sleep, his mother replaced the old giraffe with the new one. When the boy awoke the next morning to find that his cherished friend was gone, he had a temper tantrum. His mother resigned herself to the likelihood that she would have to live with the giraffe until it completely fell apart—or disintegrated in the washing machine.

Making life bearable

Among the most beloved transitional objects are teddy bears, made popular at the turn of the century by Theodore Roosevelt when he refused to shoot a small, bedraggled black bear during a hunting trip. The incident was picked up by the press, which labeled the reprieved animal "Teddy's bear." Roosevelt's sportsmanship was subsequently lauded in a *Washington Star* cartoon that showed him refusing to kill the defenseless cub, thus stamping the incident in the public's consciousness.

Not long afterward, an enterprising toy manufacturer in Brooklyn decided to manufacture and market a stuffed version of the animal as a Christmas novelty. In the meantime, Margarete Steiff, who was manufacturing stuffed bears in Germany and labeling them "Fritz's Friends," jumped on the bandwagon and renamed her creations "Teddy Bears." The rest is history. Teddy's bear and his many "relations"—Rupert Bear, Paddington, and Winnie-the-Pooh—struck a chord in people's imaginations and spawned an industry of immense proportions that today includes teddy bear conventions and even magazines specifically devoted to teddy bears. A survey of over one thousand children some years back revealed that 60 percent regarded stuffed animals as the most popular comforting objects (after parents), and that the preferred animal was a teddy bear.

Although practically any plaything can function as a transitional object, children tend to gravitate toward dolls, stuffed animals, blankets, and pieces of clothing, possibly because they re-create the tactual experience of feeding and cuddling that occurs in the first few months of life. But a child's decision to imbue a toy with transitional significance often has less to do with its features than with its emotional meaning. A plaything often becomes a transitional object because it was given to the child during a particularly stressful time in the child's life—a parental divorce or the death of a loved one. Sometimes children develop attachments to objects—a blanket or pillow, for example—because they provided solace and comfort during an extended illness.

In Margery Williams's classic children's story *The Velveteen Rabbit*, a young boy has a strong attachment to one of his playthings, a stuffed rabbit. Cooped up in his room during the course of a protracted bout with scarlet fever, he turns to the Velveteen Rabbit for comfort and companionship but is forced to give up the toy for hygienic reasons: his doctor fears the Rabbit may harbor scarlet fever germs and orders it destroyed. The stuffed animal is relegated to the trash heap, but it continues to occupy a cherished position in the child's emotional life and is treasured long after he gets better.

One of the compelling features of *The Velveteen Rabbit* is that it is told from the perspective of the Rabbit, thus offering insight into the emotional significance that transitional objects have for their owners. Early in the story, the Rabbit engages another plaything in the nursery, the Skin Horse, in a discussion about what it means to be real.

> "What is REAL?" asked the Rabbit one day, when they were lying side by side near the nursery fender, before Nana came to tidy the room. "Does it mean having things that buzz inside you and a stick-out handle?"
>
> "Real isn't how you are made," said the Skin Horse. "It's a thing that happens to you. When a child loves you for a long, long time, not just to play with, but REALLY loves you, then you become REAL."

In reading Williams's story, it is obvious that "Real" has two meanings. On the one hand, it connotes being alive, being part of the world of living, breathing objects. The other meaning—the one the Skin Horse seems to have in mind—has to do with being cherished and valued. The Skin Horse confesses that he is "Real" because at one time in his life he was loved by the boy's uncle. The fact that he lives in a nursery rather than a pasture doesn't alter this. This is the meaning of "Real" that the Rabbit comes to realize is important.

> Weeks passed, and the little Rabbit grew very old and shabby, but the Boy loved him just as much. He loved him so hard that he loved all his whiskers off, and the pink lining to his ears turned grey, and his brown spots faded. He even began to lose his shape, and he scarcely looked like a rabbit any more, except to the Boy. To him he was always beautiful, and that was all that the little Rabbit cared about. He didn't mind how he looked to other people, because the nursery magic had made him Real, and when you are Real shabbiness doesn't matter.

The Rabbit's sentiments, a reflection of the boy's sentiments, are shared by all children: a desire to be loved and cared for no matter what. When there is no one who can provide the companionship and affection a child craves, when loneliness is a constant companion, transitional objects take up the slack.

The dynamics that make *The Velveteen Rabbit* resonate in the hearts of children are the same dynamics that drive the plot of *Toy Story*. Like *The Velveteen Rabbit*, the Disney film tells of a boy and his relationship to a transitional object, again told from the vantage point of the object. In this case, however, there are two transitional objects, a toy cowboy and a toy spaceman, each vying for a special place in the child's psychological world.

In the film, the cowboy, Woody, is the favored object. The protagonist's prized possession, he enjoys a preeminent position in the boy's collection of toys. Woody sleeps on his owner's bed while Little Bo Peep, Mr. Potato Head, a toy dinosaur, and other playthings are either scattered about the room or stashed away in a toy box. The other toys look up to Woody as their leader, recognizing that he holds a special place in their owner's affection.

Woody's position in this emotional hierarchy is challenged when his owner receives a brand-new toy as a birthday gift: a space figure named Buzz Lightyear. To his dismay, Woody is immediately displaced by Buzz. The little cowboy is relegated to the lower depths of the play kingdom (the floor) while Buzz takes his place in the heights of his owner's world (the bed). The movie describes the struggle between the two toys to achieve most-favored toy status in the boy's eyes.

What makes *Toy Story* more than just a story about toys is that it is set in the context of a family's move to a new neighborhood. All such moves raise apprehensions, especially in children, and the two toys reflect the conflicting feelings conjured up by the prospect of new surroundings. Woody represents the past, the comfort of sameness, the security and comfort of old haunts. Buzz embodies the unknown and the unexpected. Woody is conservative, while Buzz is adventuresome: the little spaceman is willing to jump out the window in the belief that he can fly. The conflict between the toys mirrors the inner conflict of the child.

Young children who find themselves in the throes of a move, whether it is prompted by a parent's job demands or by a divorce, can benefit from watching *Toy Story* and talking about it with their parents. The film teaches that toys can be a source of solace in traumatic times, and that it is all right to cling to the old even though the new looms large. At the end of the story, Woody and Buzz Lightyear join forces to make the move a positive and uplifting experience.

Children who read or listen to fairy tales intuitively recognize the connection between the magic objects in these stories and the transitional objects in their own lives. Articles made of cloth—a handkerchief, a dress, an embroidered slipper—are not that far removed from security blankets and similar artifacts to which children develop strong attachments. My own daughter for many years refused to go to bed without a stuffed reindeer named Rudolphene by her side. The Velveteen Rabbit, Woody, and Buzz Lightyear are merely part of a long line of transitional objects that children cherish and revere.

Perhaps the most recognizable transitional objects of the twentieth century are the ruby red shoes in *The Wizard of Oz*. Fashioned out of silver in Frank Baum's original story, the shoes not only protect Dorothy from the Wicked Witch but provide her with a ticket back to Kansas.

"The Silver Shoes," said the Good Witch, "have wonderful powers. And one of the most curious things about them is that they can carry you to any place in the world in three steps, and each step will be made in the wink of an eye. All you have to do is knock the heels together three times and command the shoes to carry you wherever you wish to go."

This is powerful magic. Three clicks of the heels, and Dorothy is back in Kansas, reunited with Aunt Em and Uncle Henry. Their major function in the story, however, is to shield Dorothy from the endless onslaughts of the Wicked Witch of the West. As transitional objects, they protect Dorothy from the evil in the world.

The doll in *Vasilisa the Beautiful* is equally powerful. It not only helps Vasilisa harvest the crops but assists her in completing the onerous chores assigned by her stepmother. Early in the story, it also keeps her from falling into the hands of Baba Yaga. But now the doll's power is about to be put to the test. If Vasilisa is to secure the light she has been sent to find, she will have to confront the witch. It will take all the skills the little doll possesses to make sure her mistress survives her adventure unscathed.

Wandering through the wood in search of the witch's den, Vasilisa is startled by a noise. A horseman dressed in white gallops past her mounted on a magnificent white horse. As he passes, daylight breaks. A little farther on, she encounters a second horseman mounted on a red horse; he is dressed entirely in red. As he rides past, the sun bursts on the horizon. Vasilisa presses on until she arrives in an open glade in the middle of which stands the house of Baba Yaga. A wave of fear comes over her as she beholds the spectacle in the clearing.

The fence around the hut was made of human bones, and on the spikes were human skulls with staring eyes; the doors had human legs for doorposts, human hands for bolts, and a mouth with sharp teeth in place of a lock. Vasilisa was numb with horror and stood rooted to the spot.

As Vasilisa stands transfixed, a third horseman rides by. This one is dressed in black; his horse is black as pitch, as are the animal's trappings. He gallops up to Baba Yaga's door and vanishes as if the earth had swallowed him up. The moment he disappears, night descends.

The darkness lasts but a moment; the eyes of all the skulls begin to gleam, and the glade suddenly becomes bright as day. From out of nowhere Baba Yaga appears. Flying through the air in a giant mortar, she sniffs the air about her and cries out, "Who is there?"

Vasilisa came up to the old witch and, trembling with fear, bowed low to her and said: "It is I, Vasilisa. My stepsisters sent me to get some light."

"Very well," said Baba Yaga. "I know them, but before I give you the light you must live with me and work for me; if not, I will eat you up."

Then she turned to the gate and cried: "Hey, my strong bolts, unlock! Open up, my wide gate!" The gate opened, and Baba Yaga drove in whistling. Vasilisa followed her, and then everything closed down behind them.

Baba Yaga is a celebrated witch in Russian folklore. Flying through the air in a gigantic mortar, using an oversized pestle to steer her way through the forest, she appears in dozens of Russian fairy tales, inspiring fear and awe wherever she goes. Her cottage, a testament to her ruthless nature, is an architectural house of horrors constructed out of the skull and bones of her victims. She is as fearsome a witch as any witch found in the stories of the Brothers Grimm.

Once inside the hut, Baba Yaga ordered Vasilisa to prepare dinner. "Serve me what is in the stove; I am hungry," she told the frightened child. After she finished, she informed the young girl that she would be away the next day, and that she expected Vasilisa to sweep the yard, clean the hut, cook dinner, and wash the linen while she was gone. On top of everything else, she ordered Vasilisa to sort out the chaff from a bushel of grain.

Vasilisa was overwhelmed. Weeping bitter tears, she turned to the doll for help. The doll told her not to be afraid: "Fear not, Vasilisa the Beautiful! Eat your supper, say your prayers, and go to sleep; the morning is wiser than the evening."

The next morning, Vasilisa awoke to find all the work was done; the little doll was picking up the last shreds of chaff from the wheat.

She thanked the doll. "You have delivered me from death," she said.

The doll crept into Vasilisa's pocket. "All you have to do," she answered, "is cook dinner, and then rest for your health's sake."

The doll once again rescues Vasilisa. When Baba Yaga returns later that evening, she is astounded to find all the work done. She summons up her magic helpers and says to them, "My faithful servants, my dear friends, grind my wheat!" Three pairs of hands magically appear out of thin air and carry the wheat away.

A similar scenario is played out the following day. This time Baba Yaga orders Vasilisa to separate a bushel of poppy seeds from dust in addition to performing all the household chores. When she returns to find the tasks completed, she summons up the disembodied hands once again, this time instructing them to press the oil from the poppy seeds. Then she sits down to eat the supper Vasilisa has prepared while the girl silently stands by.

"Why do you not speak to me?" said Baba Yaga. "You stand there as if you were dumb."

"I did not dare to speak," said Vasilisa, "but if you'll give me leave, I'd like to ask you a question."

"Go ahead. But not every question has a good answer; if you know too much, you will soon grow old."

"I only want to ask you about what I have seen. As I was on my way to you, a horseman on a white horse, all white himself, and dressed in white overtook me. Who is he?"

"He is my bright day," answered Baba Yaga.

"Then another horseman overtook me; he had a red horse, was red himself, and was dressed in red. Who is he?"

"He is my red sun."

"And who is the black horseman whom I met at your very gate?" Vasilisa asked.

"He is my dark night—and all are my faithful servants."

Baba Yaga's explanation reveals that she is more than just an evil witch who feeds on defenseless victims. She is a great earth mother who holds dominion over the universe. Not only does she control the bounty of the fields, as evidenced by her vast cache of wheat and poppy seeds, but she orchestrates the coming of night and day. Baba Yaga also doles out advice from her store of wisdom, counseling Vasilisa that not all questions have answers, and that it is not well for children to know too much.

A witch who dispenses useful advice cannot be all bad, especially since witches in fairy tales are not known for their helpful nature. The queen in *Snow White* does not tell the princess how to live her life, nor does she advise her on court etiquette. The witch in *Hansel and Gretel* does not instruct the children on table manners. She is too busy readying the oven and fattening up Hansel. Witches in fairy tales are not out to educate the children in the story. Baba Yaga is an exception. Though she is evil, she has redeeming virtues.

The nature of the world is such that sharp distinctions between good and evil usually are illusory. Good often is intertwined with the bad, something children come to appreciate as they grow older and are forced to confront life's inevitable moral dilemmas. By featuring a witch who is both good and bad, *Vasilisa the Beautiful* communicates to young readers that the moral issues of life are not as simple or straightforward as they seem.

This complicates matters, since killing Baba Yaga would be tantamount to destroying the good with the bad. Besides, Vasilisa doesn't seem to be in a position to do the old woman harm. Another solution must be found if the story is to have a happy ending. Before we find out what that solution is, we rejoin Baba Yaga, for she is not quite through with Vasilisa. She still has some advice to dole out.

"Why don't you ask me more?" said Baba Yaga.

"That will be enough," Vasilisa replied. "You said yourself that one who knows too much will grow old soon."

"It is well," said Baba Yaga, "that you ask only about what you have seen outside my house, not inside it; I do not like to have my dirty linen washed in public, and I eat the overcurious. Now I shall ask you something. How do you manage to do the work I set for you?"

Vasilisa answers innocently, "I am helped by the blessing of my mother."

"So that is what it is," shrieked Baba Yaga. "Get you gone, blessed daughter! I want no blessed ones in my house."

Baba Yaga provides Vasilisa with another tidbit of useful information, telling her it is best to keep one's business to oneself. It is not wise, the witch counsels her, to wash one's dirty linen in public. But she erupts in anger at the child's allusion to blessedness and orders her out of the house. Before she dismisses her, however, she provides Vasilisa with what she has come for—a light.

Baba Yaga dragged Vasilisa out of the house and pushed her outside the gate. Then she took a skull with burning eyes from the fence, stuck it on a stick, and gave it to the girl, saying, "Here is your light for your stepsisters. Take it; that is what they sent you for."

Vasilisa ran homeward by the light of the skull, and by nightfall of the following day she reached the house. As she approached the gate, she was about to throw the skull away, thinking that surely they no longer needed a light. But suddenly a dull voice came from the skull, saying: "Do not throw me away, take me to your stepmother." Vasilisa entered the house with the skull.

For the first time, Vasilisa was received kindly. Her stepmother and stepsisters told her that since she had left they had had no fire in the house; they were unable to strike a flame, and whatever light was brought by the neighbors went out the moment it was brought into the house. "Perhaps your fire will last," said the stepmother.

The skull was brought into the room, but its eyes kept staring at the stepmother and her daughters, and burned them. They tried to hide, but wherever they went the eyes followed. By morning they were all burned to ashes; only Vasilisa remained alive, her body untouched by the fire. The next morning Vasilisa buried the skull in the ground.

Why is it that the stepmother in *Vasilisa the Beautiful* perishes, whereas the stepmother in *Cinderella* does not? After all, she is a bona fide mother, as is her counterpart. Shouldn't that guarantee her survival? The difference is that the stepmother in *Cinderella* merely wished to elevate her own daughters to a higher status; she wasn't intent on destroying the heroine. The stepmother in *Vasilisa the Beautiful*, on the other hand, is a calculating murderess who deliberately tries to do the heroine in. She is evil, pure and simple, and must perish.

The good in *Vasilisa the Beautiful*, paradoxically, resides in Baba Yaga. Though she gets annoyed at Vasilisa and throws her out of the house, she provides the girl with a means of dealing with her dysfunctional family. Without Baba Yaga's help, Vasilisa would remain at their mercy and probably suffer repeated attempts on her life. The witch thus is the redemptive force in the story.

What about the doll? Does Vasilisa still have need of it now that the stepmother has been eliminated? At first glance, it would seem that she should be able to function on her own and not have to depend on magical devices to make her way in the world. But just as many of us hold on to cherished childhood objects, so the protagonists in fairy tales hold on to theirs. You can never tell when a teddy bear—or a doll—will come in handy. Besides, Vasilisa still has a way to go before her journey is over.

After she buries the skull, Vasilisa travels into town to wait for her father's return. There she meets a mysterious old woman who gives her shelter. Some time passes, and when her father fails to show up, Vasilisa asks the old woman to provide her with flax and a spinning wheel; she would rather do something useful than sit about idly doing nothing. The old woman fulfills her request.

Vasilisa spins a prodigious quantity of yarn and wants to weave it into cloth. But she has no loom. She takes the doll from her pocket and asks it to build one.

"Bring me an old comb, an old shuttle, and a horse's mane," the doll replies, "and I will make a loom for you."

In the morning, Vasilisa wakes to find the doll has built a wonderful loom during the night. The young girl uses it to weave the finest linen in the land. Once she is done, she asks the old woman to sell it, telling her she can keep the money for herself.

Her benefactor is so impressed by the quality of Vasilisa's work that she decides to show the linen to the tsar. He too is taken by the excellence of the cloth and orders twelve shirts made from it. But his servants cannot find anyone in the kingdom skilled enough to do the linen justice. The old woman informs the tsar that she knows someone who can do the job. She returns with the linen to Vasilisa and tells her of the tsar's wish.

"I knew all the time that I would have to do this work," said Vasilisa when she heard what the old woman had to say.

She locked herself in her room and set to work, sewing without rest until a dozen shirts were ready. The old woman took them to the tsar while Vasilisa washed herself, combed her hair, and dressed in her finest clothes.

Soon a servant of the tsar entered her courtyard. He came into her room and said: "The tsar wishes to see the needlewoman who made his shirts, and wishes to reward her with his own hands."

Vasilisa appeared before the tsar. When he saw Vasilisa the Beautiful he fell madly in love with her. As she was about to leave, he declared, "No, my beauty, I will not separate from you; you shall be my wife."

He took Vasilisa by the hand, seated her by his side, and the wedding was celebrated at once. When Vasilisa's father returned, he was overjoyed by his daughter's good fortune, and was invited by Vasilisa to live in the palace. Vasilisa took the old woman into the palace as well, and carried her doll in her pocket till the end of her life.

Vasilisa the Beautiful is unique in that it contains not one but three maternal presences: the doll, Baba Yaga, and the old woman in the village. Each fantasy figure represents an important aspect of the relationship between mothers and their offspring. The doll is the *rescuing* side of the mother, the part that comes to the child's aid when the child is forced to perform hopeless tasks. Baba Yaga is the part of the mother that imparts *wisdom*, the part of the good mother who draws on her store of experience to smooth the child's path in the world. The old woman, finally, inculcates *skills* and presents the child with an opportunity to put them into play; she provides the materials and tools that allow the child to succeed.

Vasilisa's comment, "I knew all the time that I would have to do this work," reflects her understanding that she would eventually have to prove herself a self-sufficient adult. She knew she would have to draw on her own resources—weave the linen and sew it into shirts—to prove she could stand on her own two feet. This she does, signifying she has fully internalized the good mother and taken her into herself. And though Vasilisa no longer needs a magic object to sustain her, she nevertheless keeps the doll, carrying the treasured object about in her pocket "till the end of her life." It never hurts to hedge one's bets.

Charles Horton, a psychiatrist who has written a book on transitional objects titled *Solace*, argues that the notion of a transitional object should be broadened to include intangible "objects" such as treasured places (a playroom, a back porch, a secret closet), fragments of poems, familiar jingles, and even works of art. In his book, Horton maintains that anything capable of triggering a "symbolic connection with an abiding, mainly maternal, presence" helps to promote what he labels "transitional relatedness." Whereas a teddy bear may work for some, for others a childhood nursery rhyme, a strain from a lullaby, or a mental image may do the job. In *David Copperfield*, the image of a book bequeathed to David by his mother fulfilled transitional needs, whereas for Marcel Proust it was the taste of a cookie.

Objects need not necessarily be inanimate to assume the status of a transitional object. Living creatures, especially pets, often fulfill transitional needs, particularly since animal fur evokes memories of soft downy blankets and mother's soft body. Pets, moreover, are dependable and forgiving. A child may have a disappointing day at school but return home to find the family pet waiting with anticipation.

In much the same way that animals in real life function as transitional objects, so do animals in fairy tales. The red calf and golden fish in *Rashin Coatie* and *Yeh-hsien* provide love and support when the mother is not physically able to dispense it. In *Cinderella*, the doves not only come to the heroine's aid when she is forced to perform impossible tasks but supply the clothes she needs to attend the ball. And in *The Goose Girl*, a magic horse looks after the princess after the handkerchief given to her by her mother is lost.

The transitional significance of animals was not lost on Walt Disney. Many of his fairy-tale films abound with magic birds and enchanted creatures. In *Snow White*, the enchanted animals of the forest keep the beleaguered princess company when she is lost in the woods. The flounder and crab in *The Little Mermaid* take the place of the mother, offering the child comfort and advice when she is alone and needs a helping hand.

One of the transitional objects in *The Wizard of Oz* is Dorothy's faithful companion, Toto. He is always by her side, and comes to her rescue on more than one occasion. It is Toto, for example, who reveals the Wizard's true identity by pulling down the screen that shields him from Dorothy, thus preventing her from being taken in by the Wizard's charade.

Blanketed by love

Transitional objects inhabit not only the world of childhood but also the world of adults. Winston Churchill and Queen Victoria are said to have held on to their teddy bears well into adulthood. A market survey some years back revealed that toy manufacturers no longer regard teddy bears solely as children's toys. "Teddy bears are not just for kids anymore," one toy analyst said. "They are infiltrating almost every market and industry."

It is not surprising that college students going off to school for the first time take along dolls, stuffed animals, and other transitional objects. Bruce, a college student in one of my seminars, admitted that he had extended the use of his childhood transitional object—a blanket—into grade school and even beyond. He revealed that he had been very attached to a particular blanket as a child and that it was his constant companion. Like Linus's blanket in "Peanuts," Bruce's blanket accompanied him wherever he went.

As Bruce got older, the blanket increasingly became a source of embarrassment. It was one thing to drag it to nursery school, but taking it along to kindergarten and first grade was another matter. Bruce nevertheless couldn't bring himself to part with his loyal friend. One day he came upon an ingenious solution: he took a pair of scissors, cut the blanket into four-inch squares, and stored the pieces in the bottom drawer of his bedroom chest. Each day before school he would take out one of the squares and stuff it into his pants pocket, secretly fingering it whenever he felt anxious and insecure. His cache of mini-blankets supplied him with a sense of security and well-being for most of his growing years.

The significance of transitional objects has made them a subject of more than a few fictional accounts. David Copperfield, as mentioned earlier, used the image of a book given to him by his mother as a source of comfort and solace. Dorian Gray in Oscar Wilde's *The Picture of Dorian Gray* kept the contents of his nursery in a locked room at the top of his mansion for his entire adult life. And then there is Rosebud.

In *Citizen Kane*, Orson Welles's thinly disguised account of the life of newspaper magnate William Randolph Hearst, the protagonist, Charles Foster Kane, dies with the name "Rosebud" on his lips. The film, told in flashback, chronicles Kane's life through the eyes of a newsman trying to uncover the meaning of Kane's final utterance. Was Rosebud one of Kane's secret female admirers? A racehorse? A password to a hidden hoard of riches?

The picture tracks Kane's meteoric rise to power and his fall from grace, but in the end the newsman is no closer to solving the riddle than in the beginning. In the film's last scene, workmen are tossing unwanted articles of furniture from Kane's estate into a furnace after the executors have separated out the more important items from his effects. The camera zooms in on a child's sled hidden among the remains. Just as the sled is about to be consumed by flames, the stenciled name "Rosebud" briefly appears on its surface, then quickly melts away. The sled recalls an earlier scene in the film in which the young Kane is separated from his parents and sent to boarding school. As he is led away from his mother and father, he drags behind him his cherished childhood possession—Rosebud.

A tongue-in-cheek parallel to Welles's depiction of a fictional transitional object is provided by Alfred Hitchcock in *Psycho*. Quirky Norman Bates, the protagonist in Hitchcock's film, manages the Bates Motel and is also an amateur taxidermist. We learn exactly how quirky when we find out that Norman has indulged his passion for taxidermy by literally preserving his dead mother, stashing her in the fruit cellar away from prying eyes. While Norman's creation is undoubtedly the most outrageous example of a transitional object, it comes as close as one can get to conveying the emotional importance of these objects. Still, Norman's devotion to his mother probably would have been better served by a teddy bear.

Fortunately, the use of transitional objects among adults is usually more benign and represents a healthy recognition that maternal caring remains an important element in people's lives. In his classic Wimbledon struggle with Arthur Ashe, Jimmy Connors kept a copy of an old letter from his mother tucked away in his sock. Between difficult points he pulled the letter out and glanced at it, relying on the contents for inspiration. Connors ultimately lost the match, but the sentiments in the letter would always be a part of him. It is doubtful that he would always need to keep the letter on his person, but sometimes a concrete memento of a soothing maternal presence comes in handy when the going gets tough.

Whether stuffed in a sock, stored away on a closet shelf, or found in a fairy tale, transitional objects possess the magical power to confer love. They bridge the psychological gap between the mother as an external object and the mother as an inner presence, acting as a hedge against loneliness and feelings of emptiness. Transitional objects are constant reminders that we are never alone. You may not currently have a teddy bear to cuddle with, or some other toy to comfort you, but it is not difficult to recall times when a special plaything made a difference. Fairy tales recall those times, reminding us that the magic objects in these stories are also the enchanted playthings of our youth.

7
Deceit
Spinning Tales, Weaving Lies

𝔒n *The Goose Girl*, a fairy tale by the Brothers Grimm, a servant woman usurps the position of a princess in order to marry a prince. Her prospective father-in-law, the king, suspects the woman is an impostor and asks her to propose a punishment for someone who would engage in such a deception. Believing her secret safe, the servant replies:

> "No better than this, that the woman be put naked into a cask studded inside with sharp nails, and be dragged along in it by two white horses from street to street, until she is dead."

Having tricked the impostor into prescribing an appropriate sentence, the king proclaims, "Thou hast spoken thy own doom; as thou hast said, so shall it be done."

What terrible sin has the servant woman committed to deserve such a fate? She has lied about who she is in order to perpetrate a fraud. Not only does she lie about her identity, but she betrays the princess's mother, who has charged her with looking after her daughter's welfare.

Lying, fraud, and other forms of deceit are frequent visitors in fairy tales. The evil queen in *Snow White* lies to her stepdaughter, telling her the stay-laces and comb will make her pretty whereas they are really meant to kill her. The cat in *Puss in Boots* tells a series of lies to deceive the king into believing his owner is the wealthy Marquis of Carabas. *The Goose Girl* is unique, however, in that the servant woman in the story lies to steal another person's birthright.

There once lived an old queen whose husband had been dead for many years. She had a beautiful daughter promised in marriage to a prince who lived at a great distance. When the time for the wedding approached, the queen packed up many costly things for her daughter's dowry: fine furniture, vessels of silver and gold, and adornments made of precious metals and jewels. She also provided the princess with a servant woman, a maid-in-waiting, who was pledged to deliver her safely into the bridegroom's hands. Each was given a horse for the journey, but the princess's horse, whose name was Falada, was magical for it possessed the faculty of speech.

If the servant woman's pledge is made in good faith, the princess has nothing to worry about. But the servant is duplicitous and schemes to take advantage of the young girl as soon as the opportunity arises. Her plan is to usurp the princess's position and marry the prince herself.

Just before the princess and the servant woman embark on their journey, the queen presents her daughter with an enchanted handkerchief.

When the time for parting came, the old queen went into her bed chamber, and cut her finger with a small knife so that it bled. She then held the finger over a white handkerchief and let three drops of blood fall onto it. Calling her daughter into the room, she pressed the handkerchief into the girl's hand, and said:

"Dear child, preserve this carefully, it will be of service to you on your way."

The princess put the napkin into her bosom, mounted her horse, and set out with the servant to meet the bridegroom.

The handkerchief is a transitional object. Impregnated with the mother's blood, it symbolizes the transcendental bond between mother and daughter. As long as she doesn't lose the handkerchief, the princess is protected from harm.

But lose it she does. After traveling for some time, the princess becomes very thirsty and halts by a stream at the side of the road to quench her thirst. She asks her maid to get down from her horse and fetch her some water, but the servant woman refuses. "Get down yourself," the servant woman replies, "If you are thirsty, get on your knees and stoop down to drink. I do not choose to serve you and will not be your slave." The princess is parched and has no other alternative but to dismount. As she stoops to drink, the three drops of blood declare, "If this your mother only knew, her heart would surely break in two."

This sequence of events is repeated a second time, with the princess forced again to dismount and get her own drink. The third time she loses the handkerchief as she bends over the stream.

Just as the princess was about to rise, the handkerchief with the three drops of blood fell out of her bosom and floated down the stream. In her distress she did not notice it, but it did not go unnoticed by the servant who rejoiced because she now had power over the princess. Without the handkerchief, the princess soon became weak and unable to defend herself.

Loss of the handkerchief bodes ill. Once the princess no longer has it in her possession, she is susceptible to the servant woman's influence. The story makes clear that loss of the handkerchief—the concrete embodiment of the mother's love and protection—is the result of the heroine's carelessness and has nothing to do with anything the servant woman has said or done. The princess's negligence signifies self-neglect; it suggests that she does not appreciate the contribution her mother makes to her psychological well-being.

Similar attitudes are harbored by children who deliberately disregard parental concern, interpreting it as a challenge to their emerging independence. This is most often seen in adolescence, but even young children will test the limits by courting danger, as when a young child tries to cross the street unattended. *The Goose Girl* conveys to young readers that a mother's concern is synonymous with concern for the self, and that it must be embraced in order for the self to be nourished and sustained. Without the handkerchief, the princess is sapped of vital life energy and is unable to stand up for herself.

When the princess, now weak and defenseless, tried to mount Falada, the servant woman grabbed the reins from her hands.

"Falada now belongs to me," she said, "and my nag will do for you." Then, with many hard words, the servant woman ordered the princess to exchange her royal apparel for her own shabby clothes. She forced her to swear she would say nothing about the incident when they reached the royal court, threatening to take her life if she refused.

Assuming the identity of another person is a common theme in fairy tales and a routine component of children's play. Many "make-believe" games of childhood—house, doctor, school—enlarge the experiential world of children by allowing them to try on different personas. When a little girl dons her mother's shoes and jewelry and poses in front of the mirror, she experiences what it feels like to be a mommy. Male children emulate their fathers by drawing charcoal mustaches on their faces and stomping around in their father's boots. By incorporating the mannerisms and behaviors of teachers, parents, and older siblings into ordinary play, children prepare themselves for the roles they are destined to play later in life.

But there is a difference between temporarily immersing oneself in a fantasy of otherness and actually becoming another person. Ferdinand Demara, whose exploits were chronicled in the book *The Great Impostor*—and in a movie of the same name—lived a good part of his life pretending he was someone else. At various times in his life, Demara posed as a physician, a college dean, a clergyman—and even the assistant warden of a Texas prison! Demara was skilled in practically every occupation he undertook and could have succeeded in most professions had he merely been himself. But he was unable to. Even after he was exposed, he continued his impersonations, betraying a deep dissatisfaction with who he truly was.

The princess and her maid-in-waiting travel on until they arrive at the prince's palace. Deprived of the handkerchief and the royal trappings that would identify her as the true bride-to-be, the princess watches helplessly as the prince greets the servant woman. The prince's father, the king, who is observing the welcoming ceremony, is curious about the beautiful but sad-looking maiden standing in the courtyard. Puzzled by the girl's sorrowful demeanor, he asks the impostor bride who the maiden is.

"Oh!" the servant woman exclaims, "I picked her up along the way and brought her along for company. Pray give her something to do, that she might not be forever standing idle."

The king summons Conrad, a local goose boy, and tells him to put the sad-looking maiden to work. "She can help you look after the geese," he tells him. Conrad takes the young girl's hand and leads her away.

The lie the servant woman tells the king about the princess's identity is the third in a series of lies. The first occurs when she promises the queen she will look after her daughter. The second occurs when she passes herself off as the princess. And now she lies about who the princess is. Most of the lies in *The Goose Girl* clearly are told by the servant woman. But in *Rumpelstiltskin*, practically everyone lies, including the heroine and the little man after whom the story is named. The most egregious lie, however, is told by the heroine's father.

A LIE BY ANY OTHER NAME

Rumpelstiltskin begins with a miller boasting to the king that his daughter can spin gold from straw. The miller's boast is, of course, a bald-faced lie. The daughter can no more turn straw into gold than water into wine. Her father's lie is especially loathsome since he tells it merely to elevate himself in the king's eyes, or as the story puts it, "to give himself consequence." He seems little concerned that his boast places his daughter's life in jeopardy.

The miller's lie is not only despicable but stupid. If his daughter can spin gold from straw, why tell the king? He could keep the girl at home, give her a spinning wheel, and keep the gold for himself. No one would be the wiser. If, on the other hand, he is lying about his daughter's supposed ability merely to inflate his status, he risks her life. You don't lie to a king, not when it comes to gold.

Psychoanalytic writers put a sexual twist on the miller's motives by suggesting that his behavior is driven by guilt originating in either an incestuous wish or actual incest. They claim the miller feels guilty about his illicit attraction to his daughter and unconsciously wishes her dead, either to remove her as a source of temptation or to eliminate evidence of previous illicit encounters. But if this were the case, the miller would merely be trading one type of guilt for another. Who's to say that guilt over planning the death of one's daughter is any less disturbing than guilt over incest? Regardless of the motive behind the miller's claim, he is intent on pursuing the deception.

> The king, on being told that the miller's daughter could spin gold out of straw, said to the miller,
>
> "That is an art that pleases me well; if thy daughter is as clever as you say, bring her to my castle tomorrow, that I may put her to the proof."
>
> When the girl was brought before the king, he led her to a room that was full of straw, and gave her a wheel and spindle, and said,
>
> "Now set to work, and if by the early morning thou hast not spun this straw to gold, thou shalt die." And he shut the door himself and left her there alone.

Like many fairy tales, *Rumpelstiltskin* contains more than one "sin." Avarice also figures into the plot. The king is a greedy monarch, so greedy he is ready to kill to satisfy his thirst for gold. But this is not the king's story. It belongs to the miller and his daughter—and to a wizened little man named Rumpelstiltskin.

The daughter, as everyone knows, is saved by the little man who offers to spin the straw in return for the necklace she wears. She readily accepts his offer, and he sets to work. When the king returns the next morning and sees the gold, he leads the girl to a larger room filled with straw, demanding that she spin that into gold as well. If she does not, her life will be forfeited.

Rumpelstiltskin appears once again, this time promising to spin the gold in return for the maiden's ring. She, of course, agrees to the bargain.

In the morning the king rejoiced beyond measure at the sight of all the gold. But he was greedy, and as he could never have enough of gold, he had the miller's daughter taken into yet a larger room full of straw, and said,

"This too must be spun in one night, and if you accomplish it you shall be my wife." For he thought, "Although she is a miller's daughter, I am not likely to find anyone richer in the whole world."

As soon as the girl was left alone, the little man appeared for the third time, and said,

"What will you give me if I spin the straw for you this time?"

"I have nothing to give," answered the child.

"Then you must promise me the first child you have after you are queen," said the little man.

Though the miller's daughter expresses misgivings, she relinquishes her claim to her firstborn. What choice has she? If she does not agree to Rumpelstiltskin's demand, she surely will die. She nevertheless does not intend to fulfill her end of the bargain. She agrees to his proposal only because she is sure it will never amount to anything. "But who knows whether that will happen?" she says to herself.

But the unthinkable does happen. A year later the miller's daughter, now the queen, gives birth to a child, and Rumpelstiltskin returns to claim his prize. The queen is stunned when she sees the little man and tries to renege on her bargain by offering him a vast treasure. But he refuses, insisting that he wants the child. He tells her, "I would rather have something living than all the treasures of the world."

So far in the story, both the miller and his daughter have engaged in deceit. Now it is Rumpelstiltskin's turn. He makes the queen a proposition, offering to relinquish his claim to the child if she guesses his name. But his seemingly gracious offer is steeped in duplicity.

For one, dwarfs and gnomes do not have names in fairy tales. The seven dwarfs in the Grimm brothers' *Snow White* are simply referred to as "the dwarfs." Sneezy, Grumpy, Bashful, and the rest were names invented by Walt Disney. The term "Rumpelstiltskin" is a combination of the Middle German *Rumpel*, meaning creased or wrinkled, and *steln*, to obtain by illegal means. Adding the suffix *kin*, signifying small, results in a description of a little man who is "a wrinkled dwarf that acquires things illicitly." It is not a name in the traditional sense of the word, like Fred or Hans, and the queen is left with little hope of guessing it.

Even if she could, there is no way Rumpelstiltskin is going to give up the child. Why should he? The little man has labored long and hard for the right to own the infant. Furthermore, he has announced that he cherishes the baby "more than all the treasures in the world." He makes his supposedly "humanitarian" gesture only because he is convinced the queen has absolutely no chance of divining his true identity. His offer is a cruel lie, a taunt, much like the lie Cinderella's stepmother tells when she promises Cinderella she can go to the ball.

The queen by sheer chance manages to foil Rumpelstiltskin's plan. The day before he comes to claim the child, one of her servants accidentally stumbles across a little man in the woods dancing about a fire, an activity characteristically associated with witches. The servant tells the queen that he paused to look at the strange spectacle and overheard the man sing a song in which he called out the name "Rumpelstiltskin." The queen is delighted to receive this news and waits for her nemesis to arrive.

When the little man finally appears, the queen teases him, addressing him first as Jack and then Harry, knowing full well that neither is his real name. She wants to pay him back for the torment he has put her through. Rumpelstiltskin laughs at her and prepares to exact his due. But just at the moment when he reaches out to seize the child, the queen cries out: "Rumpelstiltskin!"

"The devil told you that! The devil told you that!" cried the little man, and in his anger he stamped with his right foot so hard, that it went into the ground above his knee. Then he seized his left foot with both his hands in such a fury that he split in two, and that was the end of him.

The strange manner of Rumpelstiltskin's death—torn in two by his own hand—dramatically brings the splitting dynamic to the fore. People often speak about being pulled in two directions when forced to tell a lie, and Rumpelstiltskin's final act puts a concrete face on this conflict. Separation of the little man into two parts mirrors the psychological split in children who struggle with competing tendencies when it comes to telling the truth: the desire to be honest—to be good—versus the tendency to lie.

The servant woman in *The Goose Girl* has no such problem. Remember, she is the witch in the story and embodies all that is evil. Her main concern is to make sure things go according to plan. The one fly in the ointment—a rather large one—is Falada. The horse has the faculty of speech and can give her away by revealing what took place on the journey. To protect herself, she asks the prince to help her dispose of the animal.

"Dearest husband," the false bride said to the prince, "I pray thee do me a favor."

"With all my heart," he answered.

"Send for the knacker, that he may cut off the head of the horse which I came here upon, for the animal was very troublesome on the journey."

The prince promised it would be done.

The servant woman's statement to the prince that Falada has caused trouble on the journey is the fourth lie she tells. Her endless deceptions make clear that once you set out to deceive, there is no end of lies needed to cover up the lies that have come before. The tangled web one weaves just gets more and more complex and convoluted.

When the order to kill Falada reached the ears of the princess, she realized she was powerless to stay the animal's death. She nevertheless paid a secret visit to the knacker and promised him a gold coin if he would do her a service.

"There is a great dark gateway in the town through which I must pass every morning and evening," she said to him. "Please be so good as to nail Falada's head on it so that I might always see him when I pass by."

The man promised, and he nailed the animal's head over the gate.

Early the next morning, when the princess and Conrad drove their flock beneath the gateway, the princess looked up at her beloved steed and said, "Alas, Falada, hanging there."

The head answered,

> *Alas young Queen, how ill you fare!*
> *If this your mother only knew,*
> *Her heart would surely break in two.*

The words that issue from Falada's mouth echo the words that earlier emanated from the handkerchief, signifying that it too is a transitional object. The goose girl has not been abandoned; her mother's spirit is yet a part of her.

The exchange between the princess and Falada is repeated every morning and every evening. Just as the bones in *Rashin Coatie* and *Yeh-hsien* survive the animals of which they are a part, so the head of the horse—echoing, as it were, the mother's sentiments—survives Falada. Each time the goose girl passes through the gate, the horse's words exhort her to rise above her current circumstances and justify her mother's faith in her. Only in this way can she develop faith in herself.

The days pass by, and the princess toils in the meadow alongside the goose boy. Occasionally she pauses to comb her hair, allowing her golden tresses to fall free. The goose boy, thinking her hair must be made of gold, tries to pick some of the strands for himself. But every time he approaches the princess, a violent windstorm sends his hat flying, and he must run off to fetch it.

Frustrated by these strange occurrences, Conrad complains to the king about the goose girl. "I will not tend the geese with that girl any longer!" he says to the monarch.

When the king asks why not, the goose boy tells him of the incidents with the hat as well as the girl's mysterious conversations with the horsehead. Curious about what is going on, the king stations himself outside the village gate, where he overhears the interchanges between the horsehead and the young girl. He sends for her and insists that she tell him what is behind these strange events.

"That I dare not tell you," she answered, "nor can I tell any man of my woe, for when I was in danger of my life I swore an oath not to reveal it."

The king pressed her sore, and left her no peace, but he could not get anything out of her. At last he said, "If you will not tell it to me, tell it to the iron stove that stands in the corner," and he went away.

The princess crept into the iron oven and began to weep and lament. She at last opened her heart and said,

"Here I sit forsaken of all the world, and I am a king's daughter. A wicked waiting-woman forced me to give up my royal garments and my place at the bridegroom's side, and I am made a goose girl and have to do mean service. If my mother only knew, it would break her heart."

The old king was standing outside by the oven door and heard all the princess had said. He called to her and told her to come out of the oven. Then he caused royal clothing to be put upon her, and informed his son he had the wrong bride. The impostor bride was really only a waiting-woman, and the true bride was here at hand.

The stove episode exposes conflicting perspectives on lying and deceit. The princess, on the one hand, declines to tell the king what happened on the journey. Even though she was coerced into doing so, she vowed to the servant woman to keep her lips sealed. She refuses to go back on her word ("I swore an oath"), even though it means she cannot reclaim her rightful position. Although she pays a considerable price, keeping her word allows her to maintain an image of herself as a truthful person.

The king deceives the princess, but he does so in order to get at the truth. He tells the goose girl to "tell it to the oven," leading her to believe that she will be talking to herself when in fact he plans to eavesdrop on her "conversation." His behavior indicates that it is the intent behind the lie that counts rather than the lie itself. In other words, there may be instances in which telling lies is justified.

These contrasting approaches to deception reflect the ambivalence people harbor about telling the truth. On the one hand, we know that lying is wrong. At the same time, it is hard, as Diogenes discovered, to find an honest man. In a study by *U.S. News & World Report*, 94 percent of those interviewed said they believed that honesty in a friend was an important quality, more important perhaps than any other personal attribute. Yet in another poll reported in a book titled *The Year America Told the Truth*, over 90 percent of the respondents admitted to telling lies. The most common falsehoods had to do with sex, income, and age.

Adults intuitively recognize that treating the truth as inviolable may sometimes not be in one's best interest. Richard Nixon is reputed to have confided in a friend that "honesty is the best policy," adding, "but it isn't the only policy." Subsequent presidents seem to have adopted this advice, applying it not only to international affairs but to personal ones as well. President Clinton's lies about his sexual encounters set off a national debate about the extent to which deception can be forgiven or overlooked.

Most people acknowledge that it would be difficult to go through life without ever telling a lie. This idea is explored in a humorous way in the film *Liar, Liar*, in which the protagonist is rendered incapable of lying. Since he is a lawyer, his compulsion to tell the truth proves especially damning in the courtroom as well as outside of it. When a policeman pulls him over for speeding, he readily admits to exceeding the speed limit, then spontaneously opens his glove compartment to reveal a slew of unpaid parking tickets. When a woman to whom he has just made love asks, "How was it?" he answers, "I've had better."

In some fairy tales, lying is not merely treated with ambivalence but is actually rewarded. The cat in *Puss in Boots* lies to the king by claiming his owner is a marquis, tricking the monarch into believing the "marquis" is wealthy and owns vast tracts of land. Instead of being punished, the cat becomes "a personage of great importance," and his master—who colludes in the deception—marries the king's daughter.

Lying also is treated kindly in *The Frog Prince*. The princess tells the little frog that she will love and care for him—even share her bed—in exchange for a simple favor. All she asks is that the frog retrieve her ball from the well into which it has fallen.

"Do not weep," said the frog. "I can help you. But what will you give me if I fetch up your ball?"

"Whatever you like, dear frog," said she, "any of my clothes, my pearls and jewels, or even the golden crown I wear."

"Thy clothes, thy pearls and jewels, or thy golden crown are not for me," answered the frog. "But if thou wouldst love me and have me for thy companion, and let me sit by thy table and eat from thy plate, and drink from thy cup, and sleep in thy little bed—if thou wouldst promise all this, then I would dive beneath the water and fetch thee thy golden ball."

"Oh, yes," the princess answered, "I will promise it all, whatever you want, if you will only get me my ball."

But she thought to herself, "What nonsense he talks! As if he could do anything else but sit in the water and croak with the other frogs, or could possibly be anyone's companion."

The princess clearly does not plan to honor her vow. Once she gets the ball, she wants absolutely nothing to do with the frog. This becomes evident the moment he comes to the palace to claim his due. She refuses to let him eat from her plate, nor will she let him drink from her cup as promised. It is only when her father admonishes her about the need to keep one's word that she lets the frog sit by her side. But she does so reluctantly.

The princess draws the line when the frog follows her to her room and asks to climb into her bed. She refuses, but he persists, reminding her of the promise she made. The princess flies into a rage, picks up the frog, and smashes him against the wall. "Now will you be quiet, you horrid frog!" she cries out. To her astonishment, the frog is miraculously transformed into a handsome prince.

What is going on here? The princess is supposed to kiss the frog, not throw him against the wall. But there is no mention of a kiss in the story recorded by the Grimm brothers. There is a version of *The Frog Prince* in which the princess does indeed kiss the frog, but in that version she first sleeps with him for three weeks. The Grimm brothers never published this version—apparently it was too risqué—and very few people even know it exists.

So where did the notion of a kiss arise? Most likely it was added over the years by storytellers who felt obliged to portray the princess as more loving—and honest—than she actually is. After all, she shouldn't be rewarded with a handsome prince after she has lied so shamelessly, and certainly not after she hurled the frog against the wall. Altering the story so that the heroine rewards the frog with a kiss compensates for her earlier attempts to deceive him and brings her character more into line with the story's ending. But if we honor the original version of the story, the one published by the Grimms, the princess's true nature is clearly that of a liar.

The reason children's fairy tales sometimes reward rather than punish lying may have to do with the role lying plays in childhood development. We tell children there is nothing worse than a liar and that telling the truth is a virtue. We hold up the behavior of little George Washington, who confessed to his father that it was he who chopped down the cherry tree, announcing, "I cannot tell a lie."

Yet lying sometimes serves important developmental functions. Some researchers suggest that if a young child tells a lie to his or her mother, and the mother believes it, the child is able to conclude that the mother does not know what the child is thinking. And if she cannot know the child's thoughts, she cannot control them. Lying under circumstances such as these allows children to liberate themselves mentally from their parents, thereby fostering the development of personal identity.

Children obviously lie for different reasons. They lie to protect themselves when they have done something wrong and to aggrandize themselves in the eyes of parents and playmates. Children are also taught to lie in order to smooth over social situations. Parents will admonish children, for instance, not to tell their grandmother that she dresses funny or that they don't like the gift she gave him. Children are sometimes instructed to lie about their parents' whereabouts when they answer the telephone. And woe to the child who answers truthfully to a nosy neighbor who asks whether Mommy dyes her hair or Daddy drinks. Marie Vasek, a psychologist who studies lying in children, contends that the social fabric of society would unravel if children and adults didn't tell "little white lies."

Ultimately, though, children must learn the difference between so-called altruistic lies that are meant to spare the feelings of others and lies that do others harm. The latter constitutes sinfulness, and fairy tales like *The Goose Girl* make sure that the evil figure in the story who tells such lies, the putative witch, receives the punishment she deserves.

Once the king learns what happened on the trip, the servant woman's fate is sealed. But she first must be exposed. The king arranges a great feast to which he invites the impostor bride and the true princess as well as other members of the court.

At the head of the table sat the bridegroom with the princess on one side and the waiting-woman on the other; and the false bride did not know the true one, because she was dazzled with the princess's glittering braveries. When all the company had eaten and drunk and were merry, the old king posed a hypothetical story of a servant who betrayed her mistress, and asked the false bride what punishment should be meted out for such a crime.

"What doom," he asked the false bride, "does such a person deserve?"

"No better than this," the false bride answered, "that the woman be put naked into a cask, studded inside with sharp nails, and be dragged along in it by two white horses from street to street, until she is dead."

"Thou hast spoken thy own doom; as thou hast said, so shall it be done."

The precise method of the servant woman's death, while gruesome, is not simply the result of some medieval storyteller's overactive imagination. Gerhard Mueller, a distinguished professor of criminal justice and a student of legal lore, points out that many of the punishments described by the Grimm brothers reflect actual sentences carried out during the Middle Ages. Before legal doctrines became codified in imperial decrees and city codes, wrongdoings and the punishments attached to them were transmitted through parables, folklore, and other sources of folk wisdom. Fairy tales thus functioned as an unofficial form of legal jurisprudence.

Though there isn't a one-to-one correlation between fairy-tale justice and the actual penalties invoked for specific offenses, the two have much in common. Soliciting murder and actual attempted murder—crimes performed by the stepmother in *Snow White*—were offenses historically punished by a fiery death, symbolically depicted in *Snow White* by the witch being forced to dance to her death in red-hot shoes. Death by drowning, the fate suffered by the mother-in-law in Perrault's *The Sleeping Beauty*, was also commonly used to punish attempted murder as well as other heinous crimes. And stoning to death—a punishment recorded in Germany during the early Middle Ages—has its counterpart in *The Juniper Tree*, in which the stepmother is crushed to death for inciting murder and fostering cannibalism.

Impersonation of royalty—like murder, solicitation of homicide, and witchcraft—was also considered a capital offense in medieval times. We have seen the punishment accorded the duplicitous servant woman in *The Goose Girl*. In *Alyunuschka and Ivanuschka*, a Russian fairy tale, a sorceress is burned at the stake for taking the place of a newly crowned princess. And in *The Princess Who Couldn't Laugh*, a slave woman is buried alive for impersonating royalty. The message in fairy tales is clear: taking the place of another—trying to be who you are not—is a serious matter.

In addition to fairy tales that deal with taking another person's place, there are tales that describe the consequences of taking sexual advantage of others. One of these is *The Adroit Princess*. A French fairy tale written by Marie-Jeanne L'Héritier, a cousin of Charles Perrault, the story features a wicked prince who takes advantage of two sisters in order to destroy a third he has reason to hate.

BE SURE IT'S TRUE WHEN YOU SAY I LOVE YOU

The heroine of L'Héritier's story, Finette, is the youngest of the three. She is virtuous, thoughtful, and resourceful, whereas her two elder sisters, Nonchalante and Babillarde, are just the opposite. Nonchalante, appropriately named, is slovenly and lazy. Thoroughly lacking in ambition, she not only struts about all day with her buttons unbuttoned and her hair unkempt but refuses to take off her bedroom slippers, claiming she is too tired to get dressed. Her sister Babillarde (French for "chatterer") is not much of an improvement. She is an indefatigable gossip and babbles on about anything and everything. Unable to keep her mouth shut, she suffers from what L'Héritier refers to as "a frantic itch to talk."

One day the father of the three princesses decides to join the crusades. Concerned about his daughters' physical as well as moral well-being, he consults a wise fairy, who advises him to lock the three princesses in the castle. She tells him to give each a magical glass distaff, a traditional symbol of virginity, as a parting gift. The distaff of any daughter whose virtue fails will shatter, thus providing the king with evidence of her indiscretion.

The king was very wise to be concerned about his daughters for in a
nearby kingdom there lived another king who had a malevolent son
called Riche-en-Cautèle (Rich in Cunning). The prince bore a special
grudge toward Finette because she had foiled a treaty between their two
fathers. The treaty, unbeknownst to either of the two kings, contained a
hidden clause placed there by the prince that would have put Finette's
father at a sore disadvantage. Finette exposed the prince's underhanded
scheme at the last moment and had the treaty voided. Because of this,
Riche-en-Cautèle bore a great hatred toward Finette and vowed
vengeance on her and her entire family.

The moment the king sets off on the crusades, Riche-en-Cautèle disguises himself as a beggar woman in order to gain entry to the castle. He makes his way to the bed chambers of Nonchalance and Babillarde and swears his unending love for the them, seducing each in turn and thereby causing their magic distaffs to shatter. He marries each of the sisters in separate ceremonies and then goes looking for Finette.

> The prince searched all the rooms in the castle until he came across a locked door. He concluded Finette was on the other side, and proclaimed his love to her through the closed portal. Finette sat silently on the other side listening to the prince's overtures but was not moved. She was infinitely wiser than her sisters, and recognized Riche-en-Cautèle for the lying scoundrel he was.
>
> When Finette refused to open the door, Riche-en-Cautèle broke it down, only to find Finette defiantly standing before him with a hammer in her hand. She cried out, "Prince, if you come any nearer I will break your head with this hammer." The prince, realizing Finette was serious, retreated, resolving for the moment that discretion was the better part of valor.

It is obvious that Finette is not your run-of-the-mill princess. Unlike other heroines in fairy tales who tend to be docile and submissive, she is strong and self-assertive. She also has a keen mind and is interested in politics; it was she who was responsible for uncovering the prince's duplicitous scheme. About the only characteristic she shares with other fairy-tale princesses is an absent father.

Now she finds that she must deal with the vengeful prince. Realizing she can expect no help from her sisters, and that she has only herself to rely upon, Finette takes active steps to protect her interests. She senses that the prince may have already compromised her sisters, and she plays for time in order to come up with a plan to thwart him. In the meantime, she lets him know she will not be intimidated, threatening to crack his head in two if he persists in his advances.

But the prince is not easily dissuaded. He is bent on seducing Finette and shaming her in the same way he shamed her sisters. He returns a little later to convince Finette that he truly cares for her despite her threat.

> "Why, beautiful princess," the prince proclaimed in mock indignation,

"does my love for you provoke such cruel hatred?" He told her that he was captivated by her beauty and intrigued by her wonderful mind.

"Why then," Finette asked him, "did you find it necessary to enter the castle under false pretenses?"

"I only dressed as a beggar woman to gain entry to the castle so that I could offer my heart and hand to you," the prince answered. "I did not look for your sisters; I was only thinking of you."

Finette pretended to soften, and told the scheming prince, "I have to look for my sisters before I decide whether to marry you."

Riche-en-Cautèle answered, "I cannot allow you to consult them for they would deny me the privilege of marrying you. They are older and by custom must marry first."

Finette knows Riche-en-Cautèle is lying and begins to worry about her sisters when he refuses to let her see them. She is convinced that some mischief has befallen them and wants to find out if they are all right. To keep the wicked Riche-en-Cautèle at bay, she agrees to marry him but asks to postpone the marriage until the following day.

Riche-en-Cautèle agreed, and Finette asked him to leave her for a while so that she could think and pray, telling him she would take him to "a room with a bed" when he returned. As soon as the prince left, Finette rushed to a room high up in the castle and constructed a flimsy latticework of sticks over a hole in the floor leading to a drainage system below the castle. She then spread a clean sheet over the latticework and returned to her own chamber.

When the prince returned, Finette led him to the room and told him she had to leave for a few moments but would return shortly. Unable to restrain himself, Riche-en-Cautèle leapt onto the bed without even taking time to remove his clothes only to find himself crashing hundreds of feet into the castle sewer below.

Though the prince is bruised and battered, he manages to survive. You would think by now he would have learned that lies and deceit lead to disaster. Apparently not. Wallowing in filth, and covered with wounds suffered in the fall, he vows revenge and concocts a scheme to capture Finette, who in the meantime has located her sisters and discovered the shattered glass spindles. Her worst suspicions are realized when she learns that both are pregnant.

While Finette is admonishing her sisters for being such ninnies, Riche-en-Cautèle instructs his henchmen to place trees filled with fruit just beyond the palace gates, hoping to entice the princesses to venture outside. Finette correctly suspects the trees are a ploy, but her sisters, who are suffering from cravings brought about by their delicate condition, beg her to bring them some fruit. Though Finette has grave misgivings, she gives in to her sisters' pleas and opens the gate. The minute she ventures outside, the prince's henchmen overcome her and spirit her to an isolated mountain retreat where Riche-en-Cautèle is recuperating from the injuries suffered in the fall.

While Riche-en-Cautèle had been convalescing, he had prepared a barrel studded with knives, razors, and hooked nails. He planned to put Finette into the barrel once she was in his clutches and to roll her down the mountainside. The prince waited anxiously as his henchmen brought Finette before him.

"You are going to die," he told her, "as revenge for all the tricks you played on me."

The prince showed Finette the cask he had constructed and cried out triumphantly, "Now you will receive the punishment you deserve. I am going to put you in this barrel and roll you down the mountainside."

The evil prince paused to inspect his diabolical creation, gloating over the pain and torment Finette was about to suffer. He stooped to push Finette inside the barrel, but she nimbly stepped aside and kicked the prince into the barrel instead. Then she rolled him off the cliff, sending him hurtling down the mountain.

The story of *The Adroit Princess*, one of the "salon fairy tales" of the seventeenth century, speaks to the duplicity of men while at the same time showcasing a heroine who could well be a model for other fairy-tale heroines. L'Héritier's story illuminates the consequences of duplicitous dealings between the sexes and simultaneously offers a vision of femininity rather advanced for its time. And though the prince is not your traditional witch, he has many witchlike characteristics and is rewarded with a punishment usually reserved for them.

Fairy tales that feature deceit, whether they involve out-and-out lies, assumption of a fraudulent identity, or the use of sex to exact revenge, help to combat tendencies in the self that undermine meaningful relationships. Situations involving deceit crop up throughout life, and it sometimes is difficult to know the right course of action when the options are cloudy and the consequences murky. Is it permissible to lie and, if so, under what circumstances? What conditions must prevail to violate an agreement made in good faith? Fairy tales do not pretend to provide all the answers, but they teach readers there are important issues to be considered when the truth is at stake.

8

Lust

A Tail of the Sea

𝔍t was said that once upon a time, there lived a king of the Bushy Valley who had a daughter that never smiled. The afflicted father, having no other child, tried everything he could to lighten her melancholy. He summoned jugglers, magicians, and even a dancing dog. But 'twas all for naught.

The unfortunate father, not knowing what else to do, ordered a great fountain of oil to be constructed in front of the palace gate. The fountain was situated so that his subjects, all of whom passed by the palace each day, were forced to crowd like ants to avoid getting splashed by the oil. This caused some to scurry like hares, and yet others to push and knock one another about. The king hoped that such doings might cause his daughter to laugh. But to no avail.

One day as the princess is standing at her window, she sees an old woman approach the fountain with an earthen ewer. While she is filling the jar with oil, an unruly court page throws a stone at her. It misses her but strikes the ewer, breaking it and spilling its contents on the pavement. The old woman is enraged and calls the boy a scatterbrain, embellishing her remarks by labeling him "a knave, a pimp, and the son of a whore."

The lad, responding to this flow of abuse, repays her in kind by calling her "a farting old crone." The old woman is so inflamed by the boy's insolence, she flings herself at him but, in doing so, accidentally slips and falls on her back. Her skirt flies over her head, exposing what is referred to in the story as *la scena boschereccia*, the bushy landscape. The princess, viewing this spectacle, bursts into laughter.

Though one is hard-pressed to find explicit references to sex in fairy tales today, many older tales were filled with bawdy references and lurid encounters. Indeed, sex—or any incident with salacious content—was often a pivotal part of the plot. An early version of *Little Red Riding Hood* describes the wolf's efforts to entice Red Riding Hood into bed. The story begins with the wolf telling his innocent visitor, "Undress and get into bed with me." When she asks him where to put her apron, he replies, "Throw it on the fire for you won't need it anymore." The child receives the same answer for each piece of clothing—bodice, skirt, petticoat, and stocking—and so in essence performs a striptease for the wolf. In one version of *The Frog Prince*, the frog jumps into bed with the princess and sleeps with her for three weeks before revealing his true identity.

The princess in Basile's *The Princess Who Couldn't Laugh* doesn't have to wait this long to discover the identity of the old woman. Only a few moments pass before she finds out that the old woman is a witch. Humiliated by the princess, who not only glimpsed her private parts but laughed at her in the bargain, the witch sentences her to a life of celibacy. "Go!" she says to the princess, "and mayest thou never see the bed of a husband, unless thou take the hand of Prince Thaddeus."

"Who is Prince Thaddeus?" the princess asked the witch in bewilderment, "and where can he be found?"

The witch answered, "He is a wonderful creature who, having been cursed by a fairy, died and was laid outside the city walls of Campo Rotundo. Upon his tombstone is graven an inscription:

WHOSOEVER OF WOMANKIND IS ABLE IN THREE DAYS TO FILL WITH TEARS AN EARTHEN VESSEL WHICH HANGS UPON A HOOK WILL BRING THE PRINCE TO LIFE AND STRENGTH, AND TAKE HIM TO HUSBAND.

The witch went on to explain: "But it is impossible for two human eyes to weep so much as to fill an earthen flagon in three days' time. This curse I have given you in revenge for the injury done me."

And thus saying, the old woman went on her way.

The princess could, of course, remain in her father's palace and enjoy a life of leisure, but she recognizes that she would be denied the most fundamental of human needs: companionship and sexual fulfillment. Self theory recognizes the importance of intimacy and holds that relationships are the key to self-realization. Without meaningful relationships, life is as empty as the earthen vessel that hangs by the prince's tomb.

The princess wanders for years until she finally arrives at the town of Campo Rotundo, where she finds the marble sarcophagus described by the witch. Taking down the earthenware jug hanging on a nearby hook, she begins to fill it with her tears. She cries for days, shedding rivulets of tears until there are only two inches left to the top of the vessel. Then, troubled by her ordeal and weary from so much crying, she falls into a deep sleep.

While she was asleep, a passing slave woman who knew well the manner of the inscription passed by the tomb. Seeing the flagon almost full, she put it to her eyes and filled it to the brim. Hardly had the vessel been filled than the prince awoke and threw his arms about the slave, and leading her to his palace took the woman for his wife.

The princess awoke to find the grave open and the jug gone. In despair, she fared on and entered the city where she learned of the marriage between the prince and his new wife. Picturing what must have happened, she consoled herself by taking a house fronting the prince's palace from which she could at least gaze upon her beloved.

The remainder of the story describes how the princess smuggles a magic doll into the prince's palace that compels its owner to crave fairy tales. The slave woman, who by now has become pregnant, comes into possession of the doll and threatens to do away with her unborn child if her husband does not provide her with a constant supply of stories. Fearing she will carry out her threat, the prince summons ten women storytellers from the center of town, ordering each to tell five stories in Scheherazade-like fashion to appease his wife.

The last storyteller in the group is the princess herself in disguise. She spins a tale of a princess's fateful meeting with a witch who accidentally exposes herself, an ensuing curse, and the deception practiced by a slave woman at the tomb of a prince. The prince's wife tries to silence the princess, but the prince commands her to finish her tale. When the story is finished, the prince realizes what has happened and forces the slave woman to confess her evil deed. Upon hearing her confession, he orders her to be buried alive, thus putting an end to her treachery and bringing Basile's tale to a close.

The Princess Who Couldn't Laugh, like *The Goose Girl*, deals with the usurpation of an innocent princess by an impostor. But the intrigue in *The Princess Who Couldn't Laugh* is the direct result of a salacious incident: exposure of a witch's genitals. The ribald nature of the plot is telegraphed by Basile in the opening line of the story when he tells the reader that the father of the sullen princess is king of the Bushy Valley. With the story set in such a locale, it is not difficult to imagine the kinds of events that are bound to follow.

The Princess Who Couldn't Laugh is not a tale for young children to the extent that it depicts voyeurism as well as explicit references to abortion. Neither is *The Three Wishes*, a fairy tale that rarely finds its way into children's storybooks in the original version. In the children's version, a couple is given three wishes. The wife impulsively wishes for a large quantity of black pudding sausages. The husband, angry at the wife for squandering one of the requests, wishes that one of the sausages be permanently attached to the end of her nose. He immediately regrets what he has done and uses the third and final wish to request that the sausage be removed.

In the adult version, whose origins are traced to a Persian fairy tale, the couple also is granted three wishes. The wife, who clearly has ulterior motives, wishes her husband's sexual organ to grow larger in size, claiming he would be happier if he were more generously endowed. The husband's penis, however, grows so large it weighs him down, making it difficult for him to move about. He uses the second wish to shrink his penis, but it becomes so small it is practically undetectable. The third wish restores the shrunken organ back to its original size.

One wonders whether fairy tales would have been altered as much had they come into being in today's sexual climate. In a world where the sexual exploits of movie stars and political leaders are paraded before the public day after day on television, and children are explicitly instructed on proper and improper touching, material regarded as risqué hundreds of years ago probably would be considered tame. When fairy tales first became a part of children's literature, however, publishers were concerned about tales that might conceivably damage the sensibilities of the very young.

As fairy tales increasingly became a part of children's literature, "obscene" tales were consequently toned down or completely deleted from children's storybooks. *The Pig Prince*, a story about a mother's attempt to find a bride for her son, born a pig, was deleted from children's books because of its lustful overtones. Publishers apparently were convinced that parents would be repulsed by a story in which a pig repeatedly drives his hoofs into the breasts of young maidens because they find him sexually repulsive. Not that sex isn't a central component of some children's tales. But these stories are not so much about sexuality per se as about premature sexuality—sex before its time. A prime example is *Rapunzel*.

There once lived a man and his wife who had long wished for a child, but in vain. Now there was at the back of their house a little window which overlooked a beautiful garden full of the finest vegetables and flowers. There was a high wall all round the garden, and no one ventured into it for it belonged to a witch of great might, of whom all the world was afraid.

One day the wife was standing at the window, and saw a bed of the finest rampion in the garden; it looked so fresh that she began to develop a great longing for it. Her desire for the rampion grew with each passing day so that she pined away and became pale and miserable.

The wife's longing for rampion, a European salad green, suggests that she is pregnant, and that her craving is the product of her delicate state. In the Italian version of the tale, *Petrosinella*, the sought-after green is *petrosine* (the Neapolitan word for parsley), whereas in France, where parsley is *persil*, the story goes by the name of *Persinette*.

Parsley or rampion, the wife's longing for the green is so compelling, she tells her husband, that she must have some or she will die. The husband, convinced that she will indeed perish, climbs over the wall and steals some. He gives the rampion to his wife, who eats it and instantly demands more. When he scales the wall a second time, he is challenged by the garden's owner, the witch.

"How dare you climb over into my garden like a thief, and steal my rampion?" the witch cried, looking at him with angry eyes. "It shall be the worse for you!"

"Oh," answered he, "be merciful rather than just. I have done it only out of necessity, for my wife saw your rampion out of the window, and became possessed of a great longing. She would have died if she could not have some to eat."

The witch replied, "If it is all as you say, you may have as much rampion as you like, on one condition—the child that will come into the world must be given to me. It shall go well with the child, and I will care for it like a mother."

The witch's demand—reminiscent of Rumpelstiltskin's request—serves to remind us that witches, despite their wicked nature, have maternal longings. They are, after all, the other side of the good mother. As such, they harbor the same maternal feelings. This can be seen in the witch's promise to cherish and protect the child. "I will care for it like a mother," she tells the husband.

The husband agrees to the bargain. Whether his decision is prompted by fear for his life or a concern that his wife will wither away for lack of the rampion, he promises the child to the witch. When the baby finally is born, the witch comes to claim the child and names her Rapunzel—the German word for rampion.

When Rapunzel is twelve years old and on the verge of puberty, the witch shuts her up in a tower to safeguard her virtue. The tower has neither steps nor a door, but only a small window at the very top so that whenever the witch wants to be let in, she stands below and calls out, "Rapunzel, Rapunzel! Let down your hair."

Upon hearing the voice of her "mother," the young maiden unbinds the plaits of her hair and lowers it down the tower so that the witch can climb up. The ritual is repeated year after year, during which time the witch is the only person with whom Rapunzel has contact.

After they lived thus a few years, it happened that a king's son was riding through the wood, and passed the tower. As he drew near, he heard a voice singing so sweetly that he stood still and listened. It was Rapunzel in her loneliness trying to pass the time with sweet song. He wished to go into the tower, and sought to find a door, but there was none. So he rode home, but every day he went into the wood and listened to the song.

Once, as he was standing beneath a tree, he saw the witch come up. He listened while she called out,

"Rapunzel, Rapunzel, let down your hair."

Then he saw how Rapunzel let down her long tresses, and how the witch climbed up by it, and he said to himself,

"Since that is the ladder, I will climb it and seek my fortune."

And the next day, as soon as it began to grow dusk, he went to the tower and cried,

"O Rapunzel, Rapunzel, let down your hair."
And she let down her hair, and the king's son climbed up by it.

The element of sexual curiosity enters the story, for this is the first time in her life Rapunzel has seen a man. Although she is terrified at first, other emotions soon come to the fore. She and the prince fall in love and conspire to meet when the witch is away. The prince asks Rapunzel to run away with him, and she instructs him to bring a skein of silk every time he visits so she can weave a ladder from it. "When it is ready, I will descend, and you will take me away on your horse."

Little is revealed about what transpires during the prince's visits. All we are told is that the two decide to meet at night since the witch makes her rounds during the day. Although the story does not spell it out in so many words, it is obvious the two engage in lovemaking during their rendezvous. Proof of this is supplied at a later point in the story when Rapunzel gives birth to two children, a boy and a girl.

The witch ultimately learns of the couple's clandestine meetings even before Rapunzel gives birth. In the children's version of the story, Rapunzel asks her surrogate mother, "How is it you are so much heavier to draw up than the prince?" Her foolish slip of the tongue informs the witch that Rapunzel has secretly been meeting with someone, and that she is doing more than just innocently passing the time away. In earlier adult versions of *Rapunzel*, the witch learns of the prince's visits when she notices that Rapunzel's stomach is getting larger. Whether through a slip of the tongue or some physical indication of the girl's pregnant state, the witch's discovery of Rapunzel's illicit behavior throws her into a rage.

"O wicked child," cried the witch, "what is this I hear? I thought I had hidden thee from all the world, and thou hast betrayed me."
In her anger, she seized Rapunzel by her beautiful hair, struck her several times with her left hand, and then grasping a pair of shears in her right—snip, snap—the beautiful locks lay on the ground. And she was so hard-hearted, she took Rapunzel and put her in a waste and desert place where she had to live in great woe and misery.

The price Rapunzel pays for her nightly indiscretions is disfigurement and banishment. Not only does she lose her beautiful tresses for consorting with the prince, but she is cast from her home. As punishment for her sexual recklessness, she is exiled to a desert wasteland to live out the rest of her life.

The prince also is punished for contributing to Rapunzel's fall from grace. When he arrives to take Rapunzel away, he finds the witch in her place. She mocks him and issues a curse:

> "Aha," cried she, "you came for your darling, but the sweet bird sits no longer in the nest, and sings no more. The cat has got her, and will scratch out your eyes as well. Rapunzel is lost to you, and you will see her no more."

The curse is fulfilled when the prince leaps from the tower in despair and is blinded by thorns.

The harsh punishment of both the prince and Rapunzel highlights the seriousness with which premature sex is treated in fairy tales. Not only is Rapunzel forced to live out the rest of her years in isolation, but the prince is deprived of his sight. *Rapunzel* is nevertheless a fairy tale, and fairy tales by definition demand a happy ending. The story consequently ends with the prince and Rapunzel reunited. After years of wandering about sightless, he stumbles across his lost love in the wasteland where she has been raising his twin children, a boy and a girl.

> He heard a voice he thought he knew, and it seemed so familiar to him he went toward it. When he approached, Rapunzel knew him and fell on his neck and wept. And when her tears touched his eyes they grew clear again, and he could see with them as before. Then he took her to his kingdom, where he was received with great joy, and there they lived for a long time afterward, happy and contented.

What could have been a tragic ending turns into a joyous occasion. The prince is reunited with Rapunzel and the children, and his sight is miraculously restored.

But what about the witch? Though she punishes both Rapunzel and the prince for their illicit behavior, forcing them to live apart without knowing the other is alive, she also survives. Why? Because, like Baba Yaga, she is not evil through and through. Her decision to keep Rapunzel in the tower flowed not from malice but from maternal concern. Unlike the evil queen in *Snow White*, who is out to destroy the heroine, the witch in *Rapunzel* wants to protect Rapunzel. If she were destroyed, it would be tantamount to destroying parts of the self charged with safeguarding one's sexual well-being, a theme explored in Robert Louis Stevenson's *The Strange Tale of Dr. Jekyll and Mr. Hyde*.

DESPERATELY SEEKING SEX

In Stevenson's dark and brooding tale, a dedicated and respected London physician, Dr. Henry Jekyll, grapples with the problem of indulging a part of himself that society finds distasteful and morally reprehensible. Stevenson never makes it explicit, but it is clear in light of the Victorian preoccupation with sex that lustful feelings constitute Jekyll's "sinful" side. The doctor's conflicting feelings about his sexual nature reflect the conflicts woven into late-nineteenth-century English society. Forced to adhere to prevailing social codes and the need to appear "proper," many Victorians led double lives, maintaining high moral standards for public consumption while indulging private desires by means of fantasy or clandestine behavior.

Jekyll refers to the split between his virtuous and sinful sides as a "primitive duality" and believes the sinful side deserves as much consideration as its virtuous counterpart. He sets out to develop a potion that will separate the two sides from one another so that they can peacefully coexist.

If each . . . could be housed in separate identities, life would be relieved of all that was unbearable; the unjust might go his way, delivered from the aspirations and remorse of the more upright twin; and the just could walk steadfastly and securely on his upward path, doing the good thing in which he found his pleasure, and no longer exposed to disgrace and penitence by the hands of this extraneous evil.

The desire to split off the "wicked" part of himself and place it in a separate entity is closely aligned to efforts on the part of children to place objectionable parts of themselves in the witch. The difference is that Jekyll, like Dorian Gray, embraces the bad part of himself, whereas children try to dissociate themselves from their sinful side: it is the witch who is bad, not the child.

The creature that Jekyll gives birth to, Edward Hyde, is a shrunken miscreant, a deformed and foul-looking creature described by Stevenson as "less robust and less developed" than Jekyll. Lifted from the pages of a child's fairy tale, Hyde's physical appearance is not unlike that of a witch. He is ugly and hunched over, the child's bad self transformed into an adult representation of sin.

Jekyll nevertheless feels an affinity for this creature. He protects Hyde and lovingly accepts him as an intrinsic part of his being—which, of course, he is. The acceptance of his dark side is telegraphed by his reaction the first time he catches a glimpse of Hyde in the mirror: "And yet when I looked upon that ugly idol in the glass, I was conscious of no repugnance, rather of a leap of welcome. This, too, was myself."

Jekyll's response to his wicked self contrasts sharply with the child's response to the witch in a fairy tale. It is a rare child who responds to a witch with "a leap of welcome." The more typical reaction is fear and loathing; the witch is not someone with whom you would want to spend much time. Jekyll, on the other hand, is delighted with his other self.

But as time goes by, Jekyll's grand design starts to unravel. In the beginning he is able to regulate the coming and going of his other self by means of the potion, but eventually he wakes one day to find that he has spontaneously turned into Hyde. When this happens a second time, Jekyll begins to fear that Hyde will take over and inadvertently give him away, thus jeopardizing both their existences. Dorian Gray, it will be recalled, shared a similar fear about his portrait.

Jekyll sends his servant scurrying to chemists all over London to find chemicals for a more powerful potion, but none of the combinations work. He is left with but one alternative: Hyde must be destroyed. In a final act of desperation, Jekyll takes poison and destroys the evil Hyde and, in the process, destroys himself as well.

Both *Dr. Jekyll and Mr. Hyde* and *The Portrait of Dorian Gray* take their cue from the splitting dynamic that is at the core of children's fairy tales. But there is a difference. In a child's fairy tale, destruction of the witch leads to everyone living happily ever after. The death of the witch signals the death of unwanted tendencies, the banishment of all that is undesirable in the self. Once she is gone, the story progresses to its inevitable happy ending. Not so in adult splitting tales. Except in rare instances, no one lives happily ever after. Killing off the sinful part of the self ends in the destruction of the entire self.

This is why the witch in *Rapunzel* is allowed to survive. She is a complex character who incorporates both good and bad qualities. To destroy the bad would destroy the good. As we grow older, we come to appreciate that viewing the world in black-and-white terms is counterproductive. Whereas there is a need to protect children from prematurely engaging in sex, it is foolhardy to mount an all-out attack on sex—or on any other "sin" for that matter. This is the message conveyed by adult splitting tales, as well as by stories like *Rapunzel* that depart from the traditional fairy tale formula. Although precocious sex—childhood lust—is to be frowned upon, we cannot lock children in their rooms to protect them from sexual perils.

In fairy tales where the hero or heroine is older and presumably more mature, sexual involvement tends to be viewed more charitably. Once one is grown, there is no need to pair sex with punishment. This is why there is no witch in *The Twelve Dancing Princesses*, and why the princesses are able to embark on their nocturnal adventures without dire consequences. Their journey across a subterranean lake where they "dance" the night away with twelve handsome princes is eminently understandable. They are ready for love.

But what about the Little Mermaid? Is she ready? Is she mature enough to enter into a sexual relationship with a man? The story suggests otherwise. In Hans Christian Andersen's *The Little Mermaid*, the grandmother in the story tells the child that her life is below the sea with her own kind. She warns her granddaughter that she is not ready to enter into a relationship with a male, especially a mortal. The Little Mermaid, however, has other ideas.

DESIRE BENEATH THE WAVES

The struggle of Andersen's heroine to rise above her aquatic origins, to transcend her animal nature and enter into a mature relationship with a man, forms the basis for one of the most beloved stories in children's literature. Andersen's story, however, is not, technically speaking, a fairy tale. For one, it lacks a happy ending; in stark contrast to other fairy tales, the heroine perishes at the end. Furthermore, the Sea Witch, who ranks among the most malevolent witches in fairy-tale literature, escapes unscathed.

The story, however, achieves fairy-tale status in the Disney movie. Not only does the Disney version provide a happy ending, but it makes sure that the witch receives her just reward. More important, it offers a sharply etched portrait of the witch. In doing so, it clearly delineates the struggle between sexual restraint and sexual fulfillment that lies at the heart of the story.

Far below the sea on the ocean floor where no mortals have even been, there lived a sea king who ruled over a great underwater kingdom. He was a widower so his aged mother kept house for him and looked after his six daughters. Of the six, one was the prettiest. Her skin was clear and delicate as a rose, and her eyes as blue as the sea. But like the others, she had no feet, only a fish's tail.

There was a garden in front of the king's palace where the daughters frolicked. And in the garden were strange things that had been obtained from the wrecks of various ships that had either sunk or run aground. While her sisters were exhilarated by all manner of objects that lay in the garden, the Little Mermaid was most taken by a statue of a handsome youth hewn out of pure white marble.

"Tell me about the world where such people live," she implored her grandmother. "I want to know about ships, towns, and people. Will I ever be able to see the upper world for myself?"

Like most fairy tales, *The Little Mermaid* starts off with the mother missing. But rather than being replaced by a stepmother, her place is taken by the heroine's grandmother, a maternal substitute who cares for the heroine and her five sisters. A wise and protective force, she functions as a counterweight to the witch who appears later in the story.

The Little Mermaid, like all young girls, is eager to increase her knowledge of worldly things. She wants to know about the handsome youth in whose image the statue was patterned; she wants to learn about matters of which she is only dimly aware; she wants to know where she fits into the grand scheme of things. Though she is only ten years old when she comes across the statue, she nevertheless is intent on journeying into the "upper world" so that she can taste adventure and untold pleasures.

Her grandmother tells her that she is not ready to venture into unfamiliar territory. The older woman maintains that there is a time and place for everything, and that the time is not ripe for romantic involvement. Perhaps later the Little Mermaid can "rise up out of the sea, and sit on the rocks in the moonlight, and look at ships sailing past." The implicit message for the Little Mermaid and young readers is to be patient, and the wider world will reveal itself in time.

Years pass, and one day the princess swims to the top of the sea where she spies a large ship in the distance. She swims close and peers through a cabin window, where she sees a lively celebration taking place. It is the sixteenth birthday party of a young prince. As she watches the event, a fearful storm blows in that breaks the mast of the ship and capsizes the vessel, spilling its occupants overboard. The princess sees the young prince sinking into the water and swims toward him. Keeping his head above water, she waits for the waves to carry her and the unconscious prince to shore.

While the two float on the waves, the Little Mermaid's sexual feelings for the prince similarly float to the surface. Stroking his wet hair, she kisses his forehead: "She fancied he was like the marble statue in her garden, and she kissed him again." She leaves him on the shore and swims out to sea, watching from afar as a young maiden and her entourage find him lying on the sand. The prince wakes and mistakenly thinks the maiden has rescued him. The Little Mermaid sadly watches all the proceedings, then dives into the water with a heavy heart.

From this point on, the princess becomes more and more obsessed with the prince: "She remembered how his head had rested on her bosom, and how heartily she kissed him." The more she thinks about him, the more her passions are aroused—and the more she wants to be human. These are impossible dreams, warns her grandmother. Her tail would be considered a deformity on earth, and humans would consider her ugly. Besides, "it is necessary to have two stout props, which they call legs, to be beautiful," she tells her.

Is it merely that human legs are more attractive than a fish tail? Or is there something else? There is, and it has to do with sexuality. Aside from allowing those who possess them to walk about, legs part to reveal the female genitalia. As long as she has a tail, the Little Mermaid's chances of attracting the prince, or any other human being for that matter, are virtually nonexistent. A tail is an impediment when it comes to making love.

If the Little Mermaid hopes to achieve sexual satisfaction and romantic fulfillment, something must be done about her tail. Enter the witch. A reprehensible and ruthless creature, the Sea Witch is one of Hans Christian Andersen's most formidable creations. Residing in an underwater swamp and protected by polyplike sea serpents, she is surrounded by corpulent sea snakes and toads who feed off the debris that spills from the sides of her mouth. Her home is as awesome as any witch's home, constructed, as it were, out of the bones of shipwrecked sailors. Andersen's Sea Witch is nothing less than a marine version of Baba Yaga with none of Baba Yaga's redeeming virtues. This is the vile creature to whom the Little Mermaid turns for help.

"I know what you want," the witch said to her visitor. "You want to be rid of your fish's tail, and have legs so the young prince may fall in love with you." She gave a repulsive laugh and added, "I will prepare a potion for you that will make your tail disappear, and shrivel up into what

THE WITCH MUST DIE

human beings call legs. But every step you take will be like treading upon sharp knives. If you put up with sufferings like these, I have the power to help you."

The reason the witch knows what the Little Mermaid wants—even before the child has a chance to speak—is that she *is* the child. She is the part of the heroine that lusts for forbidden fruit, the external manifestation of the child's sexual desire. Unlike the good mother (the grandmother), who cautions the child to wait until she is psychologically prepared to handle sexual demands, the Sea Witch encourages the child to pursue her lustful cravings. She tells her she will give her legs, but at a terrible risk. If she fails to win the prince's heart, she will dissolve into sea foam—in other words, die. But if the prince chooses her for his bride, she will become fully human and gain an immortal soul.

"I am resolved," said the Little Mermaid, who had turned as pale as death.

"But you must pay me my dues," said the witch. "You have the loveliest voice of all the inhabitants of the deep, and you think to enchant him with it; but you must give over that voice to me. I must have the best of all you possess in exchange for my powerful potion."

"But if you take away my voice," said the Little Mermaid, "what shall I have left?"

"Your lovely form," replied the witch. "Come put out your little tongue and let me cut it off for payment; then you shall be given the valuable potion."

"So be it," said the Little Mermaid, and the witch put the cauldron on the fire to prepare the potion. After scouring the kettle with a bundle of snakes she had tied into a knot, she pricked her breast, and let her blood drip down into the vessel. When the potion was ready, she gave it to the Little Mermaid.

The maternal tie that links the witch and the Little Mermaid is symbolized by the potion, which includes, among its other ingredients, the witch's blood. In much the same way that blood in *Snow*

White and *The Goose Girl* solemnizes the bond between mother and child, the blood of the Sea Witch—soon to flow in the body of the Little Mermaid—re-creates the commingling of the mother and child's blood in the womb. The bad mother, though a pernicious force, is an integral part of the Little Mermaid's—and the reader's— psychological makeup.

Moments after delivering the potion, the Sea Witch exacts her part of the bargain: "Then she cut off the child's tongue so that she could neither sing nor speak." The significance of the mutilation points up the intimate connection between the witch's character and the mermaid's sexual longings. In folklore, a woman's voice is traditionally associated with seductiveness and thus symbolizes lustful feelings. Odysseus, in *The Odyssey*, orders his men to stuff their ears with wax so that they will not be bewitched by the sirens' call. In orthodox Judaism, men are prohibited from listening to female singers to guard against the seductive nature of their voices. By taking away the Little Mermaid's voice, the Sea Witch appropriates part of the child's sexuality, adding it to her own store of sexuality.

But at the same time, the witch makes sure not to entirely do away with all of the child's potential for sexual conquest. She leaves the Little Mermaid with enough residual sensuality to do the job. When the princess asks, "If you take away my voice, what shall I have left?" the witch replies, "Your lovely form." Even though she is deprived of her voice, the princess can rely on her physical charms to entice the prince. Possessed of a pair of legs to prop up her "lovely form," she crosses over into the upper world.

When the sun rose, she found the handsome prince kneeling over her. Her fish tail had disappeared and in its place was a pair of the nicest white legs a maiden could desire. The prince asked who she was and how she got there, but she could only stare at him with her sorrowful blue eyes, for she could not speak. The prince took her by the hand and led her into the palace.

Each day the Little Mermaid grew to love the prince more fondly, and he loved her just as one loves a dear good child. But as to choosing her for his queen, such an idea never entered his mind.

"Don't you love me the best of all?" the Little Mermaid's eyes would seem to ask when he embraced her and kissed her lovely brow.

"Yes," said the prince, "I love you best for you have the dearest heart of all. You are the most devoted to me, and you remind me of a young maiden I once saw, but shall probably never meet again. She found me when I almost drowned and is the only one I could love in this world. But your features are like hers, and you almost take the place of her image in my soul."

Almost, but not quite. The prince's emotional response to the Little Mermaid is more like that of a brother for a sister than that of a lover. Though he calls her "his foundling" and professes to care for her, it is not the kind of affection the Little Mermaid has in mind. His love is more platonic than sexual. Even though the Little Mermaid does indeed possess legs, she lacks the maturity and social wherewithal that might attract a man. Lacking a tongue, she cannot even engage in conversation.

The distinction between mature love between a grown man and a grown woman and lustful impulses hints at the nature of sex as it gets played out in fairy tales. It is not sex per se that is sinful, but rather premature sexual desire. The Little Mermaid's craving for human legs is as disastrous as Snow White's craving for stay-laces. Desires that would be considered appropriate at a later time in life are inappropriate in fairy tales where the heroine is not yet psychologically prepared to handle them.

The message in these stories is that mere desire is not the same as sexual readiness. Like the children who read the story, the Little Mermaid is still a child. Her rejection by the prince in favor of someone who is sexually *and* emotionally mature hammers the point home. As the Little Mermaid helplessly stands by, the prince turns to his betrothed, the woman who earlier found him on the beach.

"It is you," he cried. "You were the one who saved me when I lay like a lifeless corpse upon the shore." And he folded the blushing princess in his arms.

Then he turned to the Little Mermaid. "Oh, I am too happy. My fondest dream has come to pass. You will rejoice at my happiness, for you wish me well, more than any of them."

The Little Mermaid kissed his hand but felt as if her heart was about to break. She would never have the prince's hand nor would she gain an immortal soul. His wedding morning would bring the death that had been prophesied for her by the Sea Witch.

We now can see what a foolish bargain the heroine entered into. Throwing caution to the wind, she ignored positive messages emanating from within (the grandmother's sage advice) and surrendered herself to sexual impulses (the promises of the Sea Witch). She relinquished her lithe, fluid form and melodic charm—her tail and voice—in exchange for a vision of adulthood that was illusory, premature, and ultimately self-destructive.

The story nears its conclusion with the disillusioned heroine sadly pondering her fate. Suddenly her sisters rise out of the water, their beautiful tresses noticeably shortened. They tell their sister they made a bargain with the Sea Witch—their hair for a knife—in order to save her life. If she plunges the knife into the prince's heart, her feet will close up into a fish's tail and she will be able to live out the rest of her days as a mermaid. Otherwise she will die and turn into sea foam.

The Little Mermaid took the knife and lifted the scarlet curtain of the tent. She saw the prince and his beautiful bride, her head lying peacefully on the prince's chest. She bent down and kissed the prince's forehead. Then she gazed on the sharp knife, and again turned her eyes toward the prince, who was calling his bride by her name in his sleep. Her fingers clutched the knife instinctively—but in the next moment she hurled the blade into the waves. It gleamed redly where it fell, as though drops of blood were gurgling up from the water. The Little Mermaid gave the prince one last dying look, and then jumped overboard, and felt her body dissolve into foam.

The Little Mermaid spares the prince but, in doing so, gives up her life.

What's wrong with this picture?

Andersen's story deviates markedly from the usual fairy tale formula. The heroine not only endures the loss of her tongue and a painful lower body metamorphosis but loses the prince. Her hope of sexual union with the man of her dreams dissolves, as does she, into "foam on the waves."

There is, however, partial recompense. Soon after she floats off, she is "rescued" by ethereal spirits—"daughters of the air"—who lift her out of the water and tell her that an immortal soul may still be hers because of her suffering and self-sacrifice: "You, poor little mermaid, have suffered and endured, and have raised yourself into an aerial spirit, and now your own good works may obtain you an immortal soul and entrance into Heaven."

While this high-minded ending compensates somewhat for the story's overall depressing tone, it is a radical departure from the usual fairy tale ending where the witch dies, the girl gets the prince, and everyone lives happily ever after. In a bona fide fairy tale, the witch, as the embodiment of the heroine's forbidding longings, is destroyed. This is exactly what happens in the Disney version of the story, in which the sexual nature of the Sea Witch clearly is a major component.

In Disney's *The Little Mermaid*, the Sea Witch, dubbed Ursula, oozes sexuality from every pore: gigantic breasts threaten to spill over the edge of the screen, lascivious eyes peer out from beneath arched eyebrows, sensual lips promise pleasure. An oversexed incubus out to conquer the world, Ursula practically tells Ariel, the Little Mermaid, to take off her clothes and use her feminine wiles to seduce the prince. Marina Warner, author of *From the Beast to the Blond*, masterfully captures the essence of Ursula in the following passage:

The Sea Witch . . . expresses the shadow side of desiring, rampant lust; an undulating, obese octopus, with a raddled bar-queen face out of Toulouse-Lautrec and torso and tentacles sheathed in black velvet, she is a cartoon Queen of the Night, avid and unrestrained, what the English poet Ted Hughes might call "a uterus on the loose."

If Ariel's lustful impulses are to be overcome, this rampaging uterus and all she represents must be destroyed.

This is a formidable task, since the witch is determined to destroy the heroine. She first tries to drown Ariel and the prince in a maelstrom. When that fails, she rains down bolts of lightning on the prince's ship, forcing it to veer out of control. But the prince seizes the wheel and drives the ship straight at the Sea Witch, impaling her on the end of the vessel's narwhal-like bowsprit. The wicked creature sinks to the bottom of the sea, her demise signaling the destruction of unbridled sexuality. The Little Mermaid not only regains her voice at the end of the film but gets her man.

A purist might argue that changing Andersen's tale corrupts the story by diluting the spiritual message of self-sacrifice the author intended to convey. But fairy tales are products of their time and constantly take new form. We earlier saw how Perrault changed Basile's *Sleeping Beauty* and how the Grimms changed Perrault's. It may be that the Disney studio's transformation of *The Little Mermaid* is the next evolutionary step in fairy tales. Although Walt Disney's early undertakings altered age-old stories to make them conform to his vision of what a fairy tale should be, current norms regarding sex and violence may bring fairy tales closer to what they were originally meant to be.

9
Greed
The Beanstalk's Bounty

There once lived a farmer who had the good fortune to own a goose who laid golden eggs. With every passing day, the man and his wife grew more and more prosperous. But they felt they were not getting rich fast enough. In order to increase their wealth at a more rapid pace, they decided to kill the bird so as to collect all the eggs at once. But when they cut open the bird, they discovered no eggs at all. Thus they not only lost the goose, but the source of all their riches.

Of the over two hundred fables in Aesop's collection, *The Goose That Laid the Golden Eggs* is one of the most well known and widely quoted. It describes not only the impossibility of ever satisfying a lust for wealth but also the consequences of coveting more than one really needs.

Greed in its myriad forms is the stuff of novels, plays, and myths. When Dionysus tells King Midas of Phyrigia to name anything he would like in exchange for a favor the king performed, Midas asks for the ability to change all he touches into gold. The gift turns out to be a curse instead of a blessing, for not only does the king's touch turn his food and drink to gold, but also his beloved daughter.

Greed is also a major theme in a number of fairy tales, including *Jack and the Beanstalk*. The story of an encounter with a cannibalistic giant, the English fairy tale recounts a young boy's journey to a land "beyond the sky," and the temptations he faces along the way. Like most fairy tales, the story begins with a dilemma: Jack and his widowed mother are running out of food. To compound matters, the family's only cow, Milky-White, has stopped giving milk.

> "What shall we do, what shall we do?" said the widow, wringing her hands.
>
> "Cheer up, Mother, I'll go and get work somewhere," said Jack.
>
> "We've tried that before, and nobody would take you," said the mother. "We must sell Milky-White and with the money start a shop, or something."
>
> "All right, Mother," said Jack. "It's market day today, and I'll soon sell Milky-White, and then we'll see what we can do."

The family's dependence on a single cow for its subsistence underscores the precarious conditions experienced by peasants when hunger was a frequent visitor. But there is a major difference between *Jack and the Beanstalk* and other "food tales" like *Hansel and Gretel*. The family at least has a cow to trade. Jack's mother sends Jack to the market to see if he can sell Milky-White, thus setting the stage for his adventure. On the way, he meets a funny-looking man who bids him good morning.

"Well, Jack, and where are you off to?" asked the man.

"I'm going to market to sell our cow," Jack replied, wondering how the man knew his name.

"Oh, you look the proper kind of chap to sell cows," said the man. "I wonder if you know how many beans make five."

"Two in each hand and one in your mouth," said Jack.

"Right you are," said the man, "and here they are, the very beans themselves," he went on, pulling a number of strange-looking beans out of his pocket. "As you are so sharp," said he, "I don't mind doing a swap with you—your cow for these beans."

"Go along," said Jack. "Wouldn't you like that."

"Ah, but you don't know what these beans are," said the man. "If you plant them overnight, by morning they will grow right up to the sky."

"Really," said Jack. "You don't say so."

"Yes, that is so, and if it doesn't turn out to be true, you can have your cow back."

"Right," said Jack. He pocketed the beans and handed over Milky-White's halter.

Jack, like the hero or heroine in most fairy tales, gives in to temptation and finds himself at the short end of a foolish bargain. Like Red Riding Hood, who ignores her mother's instructions to go straight to her grandmother's house, he ignores his mother's instruction to sell the cow for cash. Jack's foolhardy behavior makes it easy for young readers to identify with him, for what child has not ignored parental advice so as to indulge a childish whim?

Jack is so ecstatic about the trade—and the prospect of growing a stairway to the sky—that he believes his mother will be as delighted as he. But he is in for a rude awakening.

"What!" said Jack's mother. "Are you such a fool, such a dolt, such an idiot, as to have given away my Milky-White, the best milker in the parish, and prime beef to boot, for a set of paltry beans? Take that! Take that!" she said, beating him over the head. "And as for your precious beans, there they go out the window." She threw the beans out the window, and sent Jack to bed, saying, "Not a sip shall you drink, and not a bit shall you swallow this very night."

Jack wakes the next morning to find that the beans his mother threw out the window have sprung up into an enormous beanstalk that reaches high into the sky. Curious to see where the beanstalk leads, Jack decides to climb to the top.

> The beanstalk grew up quite close past Jack's window, so all he had to do was open and give a jump onto the beanstalk which ran up just like a big ladder. Jack climbed and he climbed and he climbed until at last he reached the sky. And when he got there, he found a long broad road going as straight as a dart.

Like the yellow brick road in *The Wizard of Oz*, the road at the top of the beanstalk introduces Jack to a very different world—the alternative world of the fairy tale. The "crossover" holds the promise of a great adventure, and Jack eagerly heads down the "long broad road" to see where it leads.

At the end of the road is a house. Jack knocks at the door, and a large woman comes out to greet him. The wife of an ogre, she takes an immediate liking to Jack and invites him in. At the same time, she warns him that her husband is a cannibal who eats little children for breakfast, broiled on toast no less.

Since the ogre is presently out, the wife sets a table for Jack. But before he has a chance to put a piece of bread in his mouth, he hears the ogre's footsteps. There is no time to escape, so the wife tells Jack to hide in the oven. And not a moment too soon, for the door swings open to reveal the giant.

The giant strides into the room and deposits several dead animals on the table, his bounty from the day's hunting expedition. He raises his nose in the air and utters the words that have sent shudders down the spines of countless young listeners:

> *Fe fi fo fum!*
> *I smell the blood of an Englishman;*

Be he alive, or be he dead,
I'll grind his bones to make my bread.

Jack, who is hiding only steps from where the giant is standing, real-izes that he is in danger of becoming the ogre's next meal. Fortu-nately, the wife draws her husband's attention away from his hiding place.

"Nonsense, dear," said his wife, "you're dreaming. Or perhaps you smell the scraps of that little boy you had for yesterday's dinner. Here, you go wash and tidy up. By the time you come back, your breakfast will be ready for you."

So off the ogre went, and Jack was just going to jump out of the oven and run away when the woman told him not to. "Wait till he's asleep," she said to Jack. "He always has a doze after breakfast."

The wife's concern for Jack's well-being suggests that she is more than just the ogre's wife. Not only does she feed Jack when he comes to the door, but she makes sure her husband doesn't find him. Her special connection to Jack is demonstrated by the fact that she shows little concern for her husband's other victims but goes out of her way to protect Jack. She even risks the ogre's wrath to shelter the boy. A pro-tective maternal force, she is Jack's mother away from home.

Following the wife's direction, Jack gets back into the oven and waits for the ogre to finish his breakfast. But instead of dozing off, the ogre strolls over to a large chest and removes two sacks of gold. Jack watches wide-eyed as the ogre sits down and proceeds to count his money.

PENNIES FROM HEAVEN

At this point, the narrative veers off in a different direction. What began as a story about the scarcity of food turns into a tale about a boy's lust for riches. Whereas Jack earlier was willing to forgo what-ever money he could get for Milky-White in exchange for a handful of beans, he now becomes obsessed with the ogre's gold. The more Jack watches the ogre count his money, the more he covets it. He waits until the ogre dozes off, then grabs one of the bags of gold and heads out the door.

One of the problems with an excessive appetite for money is that it often leads to tragic consequences. We already have seen what happened to King Midas. It was not until he lost his daughter that he came to appreciate how costly greed can be. The grief wrought by greed is a familiar theme and also finds its way into modern drama. In Arthur Miller's *All My Sons*, a World War II manufacturer of sensitive aircraft components skimps on the quality of the parts he produces in order to increase his profits. When his son, a combat pilot, learns that his comrades have gone to their deaths in a plane containing parts from his father's factory, he commits suicide.

But profiteering is not merely the stuff of myths and stage plays. It is a part of everyday life and often is expressed in questionable business practices. Pesticides outlawed in this country are shipped abroad, and manufacturers of flammable baby clothes that have been improperly treated send their goods to Third World countries where product liability is virtually unknown. Examples of cutting corners to increase profits are not difficult to find.

Because they constitute a form of social commentary, fairy tales reflect attitudes about wealth that were prevalent at the time folktales circulated among the peasantry. The source of the king's gold in *Donkeyskin* leaves no doubt as to what early storytellers thought about unearned riches, particularly in regard to royalty. The king's dirty intentions toward his daughter are matched only by the dirty money stored in his treasury. Although "modern" versions of *Donkeyskin* have gold coins issuing from the donkey's ears, the orifice from which the gold flows in the original story leaves little doubt as to how the lower classes felt about excessive wealth.

Money, we tell children, is the root of all evil. But money itself obviously is not evil; rather, it is the lengths to which people are willing to go to get it. It is the craving to amass more than one really needs, the willingness to do anything to ensure that you have more than the next person, that makes for greed.

But what about Jack? Is it fair to consider him a greedy person merely for stealing a bag of gold? He is, after all, only a poor country boy trying to get money for food; some gold would also help compensate for the foolish bargain he made earlier. To his credit, Jack pilfers only one sack of gold; he conceivably could have taken two, or even more. It may be premature to label Jack greedy—at least at this point in the story.

Jack's mother is relieved to see her son. She takes the gold and uses it to stock the larder with food. But the money soon runs out, and Jack is forced to go back for more. He climbs the beanstalk and once again sets out down the long broad road. Before long, he arrives at the ogre's house, where the wife again invites him in. But before he can make himself comfortable, the ogre returns unexpectedly. The wife hides Jack a second time, and from his hiding place he waits for the ogre to bring out his gold. This time the ogre orders his wife to fetch a magic hen.

"Bring me the hen that lays the golden eggs," he roars.

The wife returns with the hen, and the ogre commands it to produce an egg. "Lay," he calls out, and a golden egg falls from the hen's body. He calls out again, and more eggs appear.

The giant's obsession with gold betrays his greedy nature. His daily ritual of reviewing his wealth—counting bags of gold and watching the hen lay golden eggs—demonstrates how much of his life is taken up with money. For the ogre, money is a source of comfort and contributes to his sense of well-being, a sentiment rooted in childhood that is shared by many.

The author and financial guru Andrew Tobias traces his involvement with money and finances to the time his father, an advertising executive, gave him five dollars for his fifth birthday. He liked the feel of dollar bills in his pocket, he confessed to a reporter, and came to see money as a way of coming out ahead. Child psychologists report that acquisitiveness in children is natural, and that children as young as two accumulate toys and possessions for the security they provide. Try taking any child through a toy store and see whether you can leave without making a purchase. It doesn't matter that the child's room is already full of toys.

Jack too is not satisfied with what he has. He waits until the ogre nods off, and then goes after the hen.

Jack crept out of the oven on tiptoe and caught hold of the golden hen, and was off before you could say, "Jack Robinson." But the hen gave a cackle which woke the ogre, and as Jack ran out of the house he heard the ogre cry out, "Wife, wife, what have you done with my golden hen?"
And the wife said: "Why, my dear?"
But that was all Jack heard, for he rushed off to the beanstalk and climbed down like a house on fire. And when he got home he showed his mother the wonderful hen. Jack said, "Lay," and the hen laid a golden egg every time.

You would think that a child who owns a hen capable of producing an endless supply of golden eggs would be satisfied with what he has. But not Jack. His craving for wealth knows no bounds: "Jack was not content, and it wasn't very long before he determined to have another try at his luck." Though he already has all the wealth a boy could reasonably hope for, he craves more.

It can be useful in reading the story to children to pause at this juncture and ask why Jack decides to go back after he already has the hen. Children often ignore this aspect of the story because they are so caught up in the adventure or dazzled by Jack's derring-do. Exposing Jack's motives adds to the story's complexity and gives children something to think about. Though most of a fairy tale's work takes place unconsciously, a little direction ensures that children do not miss the story's underlying meaning.

The next morning Jack rises early and climbs the beanstalk for the third time. He returns to the house at the end of the road and hides inside a large copper pot, waiting to see what treasure the ogre will bring out next. Only a few moments pass before the giant orders his wife to bring him his golden harp.

"Sing!" commanded the giant and the harp sang most beautifully. And it went on singing until the giant fell asleep, and commenced to snore like thunder.

Then Jack lifted up the copper-lid very quietly, and crept on his hands and knees till he came to the table. He crawled to the top, caught hold of the golden harp, and dashed toward the door.

But the harp called out quite loud, "Master! Master!" and the ogre woke up just in time to see Jack running off with his harp.

Bruno Bettelheim ennobles Jack's theft of the harp by contending that it stems from Jack's desire to attain "the higher things in life." In *The Uses of Enchantment*, he claims that the harp symbolizes beauty and art, and that Jack's desire to possess it represents sublimation of the boy's sexual impulses into more noble pursuits. Absconding with the instrument is less a sign of greed than a growth experience, an indication that Jack's interest in material goods has been transcended.

Once again, the psychoanalytic interpretation ignores the context of the story and all that has occurred beforehand. To transform Jack into a cultural aesthete at this point ignores the motives behind his earlier behavior. It is telling that the harp is made of gold, not wood from which most string instruments are made. Besides, how many farmboys in medieval Britain were so obsessed with taking up a musical instrument that they were willing to risk their lives for it? Jack's interest in the harp is more rightly interpreted as an expression of the greed he displays in climbing the beanstalk a third time.

The scene that ensues is one of the great chase scenes in fairy-tale literature. How many children have listened in breathless suspense as the ogre pursues Jack down the beanstalk? How many eyes open wide as the giant gets closer and closer? Just as the giant is about to catch him, Jack calls out to his mother to bring him an axe.

And his mother came rushing out with the axe in her hand, but when she came to the beanstalk she stood stock still with fright, for there she saw the ogre with his legs just through the clouds.

But Jack jumped down and got hold of the axe and gave a chop at the beanstalk. The ogre felt the beanstalk shake and quiver, so he stopped to see what was the matter. Then Jack gave another chop with the axe, and the beanstalk was cut in two and began to topple over. The ogre fell down and broke his crown, and the beanstalk came crashing down after him.

As in other fairy tales, the evil presence in the story pays the price for sinful tendencies shared with the hero. As the embodiment of Jack's sins, the giant must perish. His death expunges all vestiges of greed in the reader, thus helping to overcome the tension generated by greedy impulses. Though greed gets more complex as children grow older, the death of the giant represents a primitive way of addressing selfish inclinations early in life.

Once the ogre is vanquished, a happy ending is all but ensured. Both Jack and his mother reap the benefits of Jack's adventure: "What with showing the harp and selling the golden eggs, Jack and his mother became very rich." To add icing to the cake, Jack marries a great princess and lives out his days a happy man. It perhaps is more than he deserves, but he is, after all, a figure in a fairy tale.

Who gets the farm?

The lengths to which some people will go to satisfy their greed is seen in fairy tales where there is an inheritance at stake. In *The Juniper Tree*, a stepmother commits a heinous murder to ensure that she and her daughter inherit the family fortune, and then follows it up with an even more loathsome act. One of the lesser stories in the Grimm brothers' collection, *The Juniper Tree* tends to be omitted from children's books because of its gruesome sequences. It nevertheless is a poetic example of the consequences born of unbridled greed.

Once upon a time, there lived a rich man and his beautiful wife, and they loved each other dearly. However, they had no children even though the woman prayed day and night for a child. In front of their house was a courtyard that contained a juniper tree. One day in winter the woman was sitting beneath the tree paring an apple when the knife slipped and cut her finger. As she watched the blood from her finger fall upon the snow, she sighed, "Ah, if I had but a child with lips as red as blood and skin as white as snow." And while she thus spoke, she became quite happy in her mind, and felt just as if that were going to happen.

The longing to create new life commonly begins many fairy tales and often sets the tone of the story. In *Snow White*, the unborn princess's mother also longs for a child with lips as red as blood and skin as white as snow. In *The Pig Prince*, the barren queen wishes for a son who will be "the most handsome child in the world." To her great consternation, she gives birth to a son with the body and limbs of a pig.

The desire to bring life into the world constitutes a deep and powerful wish on the part of parents. At the same time, it reassures young readers they are loved and wanted. The child's belief that he or she will be loved, no matter what, is reinforced by fairy tales. Despite her initial disappointment, the queen in *The Pig Prince* caresses her son by "stroking his bristly back with her hand and embracing him as though he were human." Even the father, who initially considers killing his son to spare his wife shame, accepts him and vows to bring him up with love and respect.

The wife in *The Juniper Tree* also is granted her wish and soon finds herself pregnant. Sitting in the garden beneath the juniper tree, she waits for her baby to arrive. But in the eighth month of pregnancy, she falls gravely ill. She calls her husband to her side and says, "If I die, bury me beneath the juniper tree." Before she succumbs, she gives birth to the child she wished for: a baby boy with skin as white as snow and lips red as blood.

Her grief-stricken husband fulfills his wife's last request and buries her beneath the juniper tree. After a time of mourning, he takes a new wife.

The husband had a daughter by the second wife. When the woman looked at her daughter, she loved her very much, but when she looked at her stepson, it cut her to her heart for she knew he would inherit her husband's fortune.

One day, the woman went upstairs to her room, followed by her daughter who wanted an apple.

"Mother, may I have an apple?" she asked.

"Yes, my child," replied the mother, reaching into a great chest that had a heavy lid.

The young girl took the apple, and said to her mother, "Is Brother not to have one too?"

This made the woman angry, and she snatched the apple back from her daughter and threw it back into the chest, shouting, "Yes, but you shall not have one before your brother."

The daughter left to fetch the brother. When the little boy entered the room, his stepmother asked whether he would like an apple.

"Yes," replied the boy.

"Take out an apple for yourself," the stepmother said. While the little boy was stooping down, she shut the lid down so hard that his head flew off and fell amongst the red apples.

The stepmother was overwhelmed by terror, and thought: "If I could but make them think it was not done by me." So she took a white handkerchief from the top drawer of her chest, set the head on the neck again, and folded the handkerchief about the boy's neck so that nothing could be seen. Then she set him on a chair in front of the door and put the apple in his hand.

The murder of a child—whether a natural child or a stepchild—is a phenomenon that defies comprehension. Yet we all too often are exposed to situations in which a parent or parents kill their offspring. The South Carolina housewife Susan Smith drowned her two boys in a lake and tried to make it look like a case of car-jacking. In her case, money wasn't a motive. But is it possible it could be in others? Would a parent kill a child solely to satisfy greed? An incident in New England indicates that this can, in fact, happen.

In 1994 Sandra Dostie was convicted by a Massachusetts court of murdering her five-year-old stepson. The trial revealed that the boy suffered from hemophilia, and that his father had incurred significant medical costs as part of the support agreement with the child's mother. Dostie—who already had one child by the boy's father and wanted more—became convinced that she and her husband would never have a second child as long as they had to spend money caring for her sick stepson.

On the day of the child's death, the father, who shared custodial rights with the boy's biological mother, brought the boy home for the weekend. While the father was out of the house, Dostie crept into the child's room and smothered him with a pillow. Then she went into the basement, bound herself with tape, and waited for her husband to return home. She told him that two mysterious intruders had broken into the house, forcefully overcome her, and murdered the child. The jury saw through the fabrication and sentenced Dostie to life imprisonment for murder.

The stepmother in *The Juniper Tree* is even more diabolical. She not only kills her stepson but contrives to make her daughter believe that the girl is responsible for the crime. When the daughter, named Marlinchen (little Marlene), asks her brother to share his apple, he, of course, does not respond. Marlinchen is annoyed and complains to her mother. "Brother is sitting by the door looking quite white and will not say anything to me," she tells her.

"Go back to him," the mother orders, "and give him a box on the ear if he refuses to answer."

So Marlinchen went to him and said, "Brother, give me the apple." But he was silent. Following her mother's instructions, she gave her brother a box on the ear whereupon his head fell off. Marlinchen was terrified, and began to cry and scream. She ran to her mother, and said, "Alas, Mother, I have knocked my brother's head off!" and she wept and wept and could not be comforted.

To kill a child is reprehensible enough, but to shift the blame onto an innocent child, the murdered boy's sibling no less, qualifies the perpetrator as a witch. And the stepmother is not yet finished. Like the wife in *Talia, Sun, and Moon*, she intends to make a stew of the stepson's remains and feed it to her husband to cover up the crime. She tells Marlinchen to keep her mouth shut so that no one will suspect what happened.

When the father came home and sat down to dinner, he asked, "Where is my son?" The mother answered, "He has gone across the country to visit his mother's great-uncle," and proceeded to dish out the stew to her husband. The father ate the food, commenting on how delicious it tasted, and asked for more. When he was finished, he threw all the bones under the table.

Marlinchen ran to her chest of drawers, took her best silk handkerchief from the bottom drawer, and collected all the bones from beneath the table. She tied them up in the handkerchief and carried them outside, all the time weeping. Then she lay under the juniper tree, and after a while her tears stopped.

Suddenly the juniper tree began to stir, and the branches parted asunder. A mist seemed to rise from the tree from which a beautiful bird flew. It rose out of the mist and singing magnificently, flew high into the sky. When the bird was gone, the handkerchief with the bones was no longer there.

This phoenix-like scene of reunion and rebirth recalls a similar scene in *Aschenputtel*. But in *The Juniper Tree*, it is the child who is resurrected. The commingling of the son's bones with those of the dead mother symbolically reiterates the primal connection between mother and child. In much the same way that the mother's wish for a child culminated in the boy's birth many years earlier, she again gives him life.

The spiritual resurrection that comes of Marlinchen's efforts to preserve her brother is not the end of the story. Rather, it marks the beginning of a journey in which the son, now an enchanted bird, sets out to seek retribution. The journey begins with the bird lighting on the house of a goldsmith.

The goldsmith was sitting in his workshop making a golden chain when he heard the bird singing on his roof:

> *My mother slew her little son;*
> *My father thought me lost and gone;*
> *But pretty Marlinchen pitied me,*
> *and laid me under the juniper tree.*

Overcome by the haunting refrain, the goldsmith asked the bird to sing the piece for him once again.

The bird tells the goldsmith he will only do so in exchange for a golden chain. The goldsmith hands the chain to the bird, and the bird sings the song again.

After he is finished, he flies to the home of a shoemaker, where he repeats the refrain. The shoemaker is also enchanted by the song and, like the goldsmith, asks to hear it again. The bird agrees to do so only if the man also gives him something in return. The shoemaker tells his wife to fetch a pair of red shoes sitting on a shelf in his workshop. The bird sings his song a second time, takes the shoes in his left claw, and flies away.

The third stop on the bird's odyssey is a mill, where a group of workmen are hewing a gigantic millstone. The scene is reenacted a final time, with the men agreeing to give the bird the millstone for repeating the song.

> Then the workers all set to work with a beam and raised the stone. The bird stuck his neck through the hole, wearing it as if it were a collar, and flew onto a tree where he sang his song again. When the bird had done singing, he spread his wings and flew far away to his father's house. In his right claw he had the chain, in his left the shoes, and round his neck the millstone.

The bird's journey is a journey of empowerment. Earlier in the story, the stepson was powerless to deal with the stepmother and so was prematurely deprived of life. The song heralds his rebirth and provides him with the objects he needs to combat the stepmother.

With the objects in his possession, he flies home, where the father, mother, and Marlinchen are eating dinner. The father hears the bird singing outside on the juniper tree, and a feeling of joy comes over him: "I feel just as if I were about to see an old friend," he remarks.

The mother responds quite differently. "I feel so anxious," she confesses. "My teeth are chattering, and the blood in my veins is on fire." She senses that the moment of reckoning is at hand.

The father goes outside to hear the bird better, and when he does, the bird lets the golden chain fall onto his neck. The father is overwhelmed and returns to the house to show the others the gift he has received.

Marlinchen decides to go out to see if the bird has something for her. She steps out the door, and the bird throws down the red shoes; they fit the sister's feet perfectly. She, too, goes back in the house, proclaiming her joy. "I was so sad when I went out," she cries out, "and now I am so happy and lighthearted."

The stepmother hopes the magic bird has brought something for her as well. Deep down she knows the bird bodes ill, but greed overcomes her.

"I too will go out and see if my heart feels lighter," said the woman.

She went out the door and as she did, the bird dropped the millstone. Crash! It landed on her head, and crushed her to death. The father and Marlinchen heard what had happened and rushed out of the house. Smoke, flames, and fire were rising from the spot where the millstone had fallen, and there stood the little brother. He took his father and Marlinchen by the hand, and the three went inside the house and had dinner.

The story of *The Juniper Tree* ends with the son transformed and the greedy stepmother dispatched. The theme of avarice, first spelled out in the stepmother's murder of her stepson, is repeated in the woman's desire for the bird's bounty. But the gift she receives is not what she expected. It nevertheless is the one she deserves.

WHEN ENOUGH IS NOT ENOUGH

An unquenchable thirst for wealth, whether it takes the form of lusting after gold or coveting an undeserved inheritance, are but two of the ways avarice is depicted in fairy tales. Another is the pursuit of exalted status, the tendency to be dissatisfied with one's station in life. This is the underlying theme of *The Fisherman and His Wife*.

There once was a fisherman and his wife who lived in a hovel by the sea.

One day, the fisherman was sitting with his rod looking into the water, and when he drew his line up he found a great flounder on the hook.

"Fisherman," the flounder said to the man, "let me go; I am not a real fish but an enchanted prince. What good shall I be to you if you land me? I shall not taste well; so put me back into the water, and let me swim away."

The fisherman lets the fish go and tells his wife of his adventure. She is annoyed that he granted the fish's request without getting anything in return. "Did you not wish for anything first?" she scolds him.

The fisherman confesses that he did not, since he wouldn't know what to wish for.

His wife points out that they live in an evil-smelling hovel and could make use of better living quarters. "It is hard to live in this disgusting pig sty," she says to her husband. "Go back and tell him we want a little cottage."

The husband reluctantly obeys and returns to the spot where he caught the flounder.

When he got there, the sea was green and yellow, and no longer so clear. So he stood by the water's side, and cried out,

> *Oh, flounder, flounder in the sea,*
> *Come, I pray thee, here to me;*
> *Such a tiresome wife I've got,*
> *She wants for me what I do not.*

The flounder came swimming up, and said, "Now then, what does she want?"

"She does not want to live in a hovel anymore, and would rather have a cottage," replied the man. "She said I should have wished for something when I let you go."

"Go home with you," said the flounder, "she has it already."

The fisherman returns home but finds his wife is not so easily satisfied. After only two weeks in the cottage, she decides she wants a large stone castle, and she sends her husband back to the fish to demand one.

The fish grants the wife's wish, but her needs are insatiable. She next decides she wants to be king. Once she is king, she will be the most powerful person in the world—at least, that is what she thinks. She sends her husband back with her latest wish.

The fish grants her wish, but the wife soon becomes dissatisfied with her new designation. She is not content merely to be king; she wants to be emperor. But even this does not satisfy her. The story moves to its inexorable conclusion as the wife makes her final request: she demands to be God! "If I cannot have the power to make the sun and moon rise," she tells her husband, "I shall never have a quiet hour." She sends him back to the fish to submit her demand.

The flounder saw the man approach, and rose from the sea a final time. "Well, what does she want now?" he asked.

"Alas," said the fisherman, "she wants to be like unto God."

"Go home with you," said the flounder, "you will find her in the old hovel."

And there you can find them living to this very day.

The *Fisherman and His Wife*, though a part of the Grimm brothers' collection, is not really a bona fide fairy tale. There is no witch, and no climactic struggle between the forces of good and evil. More an Aesop-like parable featuring a fish with the powers of speech, the story nevertheless points up the consequences of greed. The wife is a self-centered harridan who is dissatisfied not only with her living conditions but with her station in life. And though she doesn't die in the end, she is punished for her sinful ways.

Collectors and collecting

The final shape that greed takes in fairy tales is a compulsion to collect things. The impulse to hoard, to amass not only money but everything from art to antiques, is a problematic disposition in people, especially when the objects collected are human beings.

> There was once a man who had fine houses, both in town and country, a great deal of silver and gold plate, embroidered furniture, and coaches gilded all over with gold. But this man was so unlucky as to have a blue beard, which made him so frightfully ugly that all the women and girls ran away from him.

This singular detail, that of a strangely colored beard, introduces one of the most sinister and disturbing fairy tales of all times, one that in some ways is more gruesome than *The Juniper Tree*. The story of a serial killer, *Bluebeard* tells of a man who marries women and then disposes of them after taking them for his bride. And though the story is ostensibly about killing, its underlying meaning centers on what it means to treat human beings as objects, as things to be collected much as one collects art, jewelry, and other valuables.

The story, a Charles Perrault fairy tale, starts off with Bluebeard coveting the affection of his neighbor's daughters, both of whom are described as "perfect beauties." The daughters are not particularly attracted to their neighbor; in fact, they are repulsed by him. It is not only his beard but the fact that he has been married before and all his wives have disappeared without leaving a trace.

Scorned by both daughters, *Bluebeard* nevertheless persuades one of them to marry him. After the wedding, the two return to the bridegroom's castle, at which point Bluebeard announces he must go off on a journey to attend to business. Before he leaves, he presents his new wife with the keys to two large cabinets, one filled with silver plate and the other with jewels. He also gives her a small key that opens the lock to a room located at the end of a great gallery.

"Open them all," he tells her, "except for that little room, which I forbid. If you happen to open it, you can expect my just anger and resentment."

The wife, of course, cannot resist and goes to the great gallery soon after her husband leaves. Ignoring his warning, she reaches into her pocket and pulls out the key.

She took the little key and opened the door, trembling for it was dark inside and she could not see. The windows were shut and did not let in light. After some moments she began to perceive the floor was all covered with clotted blood. To her horror, she noticed the bodies of several dead women lying against the wall. They were the wives Bluebeard had married and murdered, one after another. She thought she should have died of fear, and the key, which she pulled out of the lock, fell out of her hand. She stooped to pick it up and noticed it was stained with blood. And though she tried to wipe the blood off, it would not come off for the key was magical.

Upon returning home, Bluebeard asks for the keys back. The wife returns all but the small one. He demands that she return it as well, and when she does, he sees the blood.

"How came this blood upon the key?" he asks her. The wife pleads ignorance, but Bluebeard forces her to admit that she had indeed entered the small room and viewed its contents.

"You were resolved to go into the room, were you not?" Bluebeard says to her. "Very well, madam; you shall take your place among the ladies you saw there."

WHEN ONE IS NOT ENOUGH

What are we to make of this story? Some writers have suggested that *Bluebeard* represents a caution against curiosity, a warning to readers, especially young women, that too much knowledge can be dangerous. Marina Warner, author of *From the Beast to the Blonde*, notes that in some editions of Perrault's works, the story is subtitled, "The Effects of Female Curiosity." She claims that the story contains the message that curiosity has disastrous implications for women who fail to be obedient. A similar message is contained in *Cupid and Psyche*, where the heroine almost loses her life by opening the forbidden "jar of beauty."

But though stories such as these may indeed say something about curiosity, *Bluebeard* says more about acquisitiveness than inquisitiveness. Bluebeard's sin is the compulsion to amass innocent women. His vast collection of silver plate, embroidered furniture, and jewels is matched only by his collection of wives. Though he kills them, he stores their bodies in a little room, treating them as possessions much as one would treat jewels or furs.

Stories involving the tendency to acquire human beings are not as rare as one might think. It also forms the basis for *Princess Olympia*, a fairy tale by Marie-Jeanne L'Héritier, the author of *The Adroit Princess*. In L'Héritier's story, a princess is abandoned on an island occupied by a sadistic fiend who allegedly murders his female victims. The monster, it turns out, is not a monster in the fairy-tale sense of the word, but rather an ordinary man who collects women. Instead of killing his victims, he keeps them captive underground, where he maintains dominion over them.

Real-life variations on this acquisitorial theme are seen in cultures where potentates and the wealthy keep harems and concubines. On the fictional side, the tendency is described by James Patterson in *Kiss the Girls*. In Patterson's book, the story's central character assembles a collection of attractive young women and keeps them hidden away in an underground bunker where he forces sex upon them. Like Bluebeard and the protagonist in *Princess Olympia*, the protagonist is driven by a need not so much to kill women as to collect them.

The ultimate sin in stories of this sort is the way the protagonist regards his victims. His "possessions" are not human beings, but rather assets designed to satisfy his avaricious needs. This is the hidden perversion in greed, whether it involves a desire to collect gold or people. The pilots and navigators who perish in Miller's *All My Sons* are not human beings insofar as the father in the story is concerned; they are unknown faces in an unknown sky. The children scarred by improperly treated pajamas are little more than ciphers in far-off lands, not laughing children sitting on their parents' knees. And industrial polluters who dump toxic waste into streams do not envision the potential cost in health and life to their victims. What counts is the bottom line. As greed grows, human sensibilities decline until people become little more than objects.

The wives in *Bluebeard* can be amassed like silver plates and pieces of jewelry precisely because they are regarded as objects by their owner. The heroine realizes that she is about to become a part of her husband's macabre collection and tries to save herself.

> When the wife heard her husband's pronouncement, she threw herself at his feet and begged forgiveness, promising she would never again be disobedient. But Bluebeard's heart was harder than a rock:
>
> "You must die, Madam," said he, "and that presently."
>
> "Since I must die," answered she, looking upon him with eyes bathed in tears, "give me some little time to say prayers."
>
> "I give you a quarter of an hour," replied Bluebeard, "but not one moment more."

A quarter of an hour is all the heroine needs. She beholds a great cloud of dust in the distance and sees two horsemen rapidly approaching the castle. "God be praised," she cries out. "They are my brothers come to rescue me."

Bluebeard takes hold of his wife's hair with one hand and lifts his cutlass with the other, preparing to strike off her head.

> At that very instant, there was such a loud knocking at the gate that caused Bluebeard to start. The gate was opened, and presently entered two horsemen, who, drawing their swords, ran directly at Bluebeard. He knew them to be his wife's brothers, one a dragoon, the other a musketeer, so he ran away immediately to save himself. But the two brothers pursued so close that they overtook him before he could escape, and ran him through with their swords.

There is a folk saying that greed is still young when other sins are old. Perhaps this is why avarice is so ubiquitous a theme in fairy tales. The battle to conquer greedy inclinations is ongoing, and stories like *Jack and the Beanstalk*, *The Juniper Tree*, and *Bluebeard* represent attempts to combat and overcome impulses that threaten to corrupt the self. They may not always succeed, but they at least constitute a beginning.

10

Sloth

Geppetto's Dream

An old king lay upon his deathbed, and as he had no son to reign after him he sent for his three nephews, and said to them:

"My dear nephews, I feel that my days are drawing to an end, and one of you will have to be king when I am dead. But though I have watched you all closely, I know not which is most fit to wear the crown, so my wish is that you should each try it in turn. The eldest shall be king first, and if he reigns happily, all well and good; if he fails, let the next take his place; and if he fails, let him give it to the one who is left. In this way you will know which is the best fitted to govern."

On this, the three young men all thanked their uncle, each declaring he would do his best. Soon after, the old king died and was buried with great state and ceremony.

When the eldest was crowned, there was great rejoicing everywhere. "'Tis a fine thing to be king," cried he in much glee. "Now I can amuse myself and do just as I please, and there will be no one to stop me. I can lie in bed as late as I like in the morning, for who dares blame one, if one is king?"

Next morning, the prime minister and the chancellor came to the palace to see the new king and settle affairs of state, but they were told that his majesty was in bed and had given orders that no one should disturb him.

"That is a bad beginning," sighed the prime minister.

"Very bad," echoed the chancellor.

THE MAN WHO WOULD NOT BE KING

Both the prime minister and chancellor rightly sense that the kingdom has inherited a shiftless king. Now that he has ascended the throne, all the new king can think of is staying in bed. The king's agents realize that they are saddled with a lazy monarch, and that the kingdom may be in trouble.

The situation in the palace goes from bad to worse as affairs of state are neglected in favor of leisurely pursuits. The king is not oblivious to the consequences of his behavior; he realizes that the kingdom will be ruined if he continues to rule. Acknowledging that he was not cut out to be king, he relinquishes the throne and travels into the countryside, where he secures work as a goose boy.

"This is capital," he cries, "and much better than being king. Here there are no prime ministers or chancellors to come worrying." And he lies on the grass very contentedly tending to the geese all day.

The other two brothers try their turn at being king but fare no better, though for different reasons. One cannot manage money, and the other is an insensitive boor. The middle brother comes perilously close to bankrupting the royal treasury, and the youngest brother tells his subjects what kinds of clothes they must wear and the kinds of homes they should live in; he even orders them to stop making pea soup because he cannot stand the smell of peas. Like the eldest brother, both siblings eventually quit the palace to pursue less demanding careers, leaving the chancellor and prime minister combing the kingdom for a man who would be king.

The Three Clever Kings, published by Mary De Morgan in 1888, is a humorous commentary on incompetence and sloth. Neither of the youngest brothers are punished for their ineptitude, nor does the eldest suffer for his slothful ways. This does not mean that early storytellers considered sloth anything less than a serious failing. Carlos Collodi considered it one of the most pernicious childhood vices. For the author of *Pinocchio*, laziness was the major obstacle that prevented children from succeeding in life.

THE TOY WHO WOULD BE A BOY

The story of a marionette who must overcome his lazy ways to fulfill his dream of becoming "a real boy," *Pinocchio* was published by Collodi as a series of magazine articles in 1881. Two years later, it was published in book form and quickly became one of the best-selling children's stories of all time. Though many consider *Pinocchio* a children's story rather than a fairy tale, perhaps because of its length—two hundred pages as opposed to the usual fairy-tale length of five to ten pages—the story contains most of the ingredients typically found in fairy tales. There is a journey through a world filled with magical figures, a series of encounters with menacing forces, and the requisite happy ending. The story even features a fairy godmother. But the theme that binds these elements together and fuels the plot is sloth.

Pinocchio starts off in the workshop of an old cabinetmaker named Antonio who is surprised when a piece of wood he is carving yells out, "Oh! You have hurt me." The cabinetmaker, thinking he has imagined the voice, takes a plane to the wood only to hear the voice cry out, "Stop, you are taking the skin off my body." Convinced he is dealing with a ghost, Antonio sells the wood to an elderly puppet-maker named Geppetto, who wants to build a dancing puppet so that he can tour the world and make a living. "With this marionette," he tells his friend Antonio, "I will travel through the world and earn for myself a little bread."

Geppetto's character sets the tone of the story by establishing industriousness as a major theme. Although he is along in years, the old man continues to toil at his craft, working long hours without complaining. But he is literally unable to carve out a decent living and is on the lookout for other work that will earn him "a little bread." A dancing puppet presents an opportunity to make a living as a traveling entertainer.

The puppet that Geppetto constructs turns out to be as unmanageable as the piece of wood from which it was carved. Christened Pinocchio by his maker, the puppet is unruly in public and soon gets Geppetto thrown into jail for disturbing the peace. While Geppetto languishes in a cell, Pinocchio runs away from home hoping to find food. His initial foray into the world is a disaster, and he returns home cold, tired, and hungry.

As Pinocchio sits alone in the house waiting for Geppetto to be released from jail, he hears a small voice call his name. The voice belongs to a talking cricket, who proceeds to lecture Pinocchio on the virtues of obedience, hard work and the value of an education. Pinocchio scoffs at the cricket, dubbed Jiminy Cricket by Walt Disney, and tells him that he doesn't want to study; he would rather run after butterflies and climb trees. The cricket warns him that should he persist in this attitude, he will grow up to be a donkey and everyone will make fun of him. This plainly is not the advice Pinocchio wants to hear.

"Be quiet!" shouted Pinocchio, but the cricket went on patiently. "If you don't want to go to school, at least learn a trade so that you can make an honest living."

"There is only one trade that I fancy," replied Pinocchio, "and that is to eat, drink, sleep, and enjoy myself, lazing about from morning to night."

"People in that trade usually end up in hospital or in prison!" said the cricket calmly. "Poor Pinocchio! I really pity you! After all, you are only a puppet and, worst of all, you have a wooden head."

Pinocchio, like the eldest brother in Mary de Morgan's tale, is lazy. He has little use for work or school and is content to while away the day in bed. He also exhibits other character flaws, such as a tendency to lie, but it is his lazy nature that continually lands him in trouble and prevents him from making something of himself.

Collodi makes it abundantly clear that sloth is more than just a minor failing that can be dealt with through lectures or an occasional scolding. It is a serious psychological defect that breeds moral turpitude and mental illness. The cricket plainly states that children who are lazy not only grow up to be donkeys but risk becoming criminals or mental patients.

Sloth in children is more than just an individual concern; it strikes at the very heart of society. Before the Industrial Revolution, parents depended on children to help with farm and household chores. As labor moved from farm to factory, children were sent to work outside the home in order to supplement the meager wages of parents. Working long hours, the young contributed significantly to a nation's economic well-being even though they often were exploited. Even today many countries look to children as a cheap labor source.

If children work all day in a factory, however, they have neither the time nor the energy to get educated. With the passage of child labor laws, Western industrial nations recognized that education must be a priority in children's lives, and that the principal work of the young is study. Children today are urged to apply themselves in school and to travel as far up the educational ladder as they can.

Whether sloth interferes with the production of goods or prevents one from getting an education, it is a liability. It thus is understandable that themes involving hard work were prominently featured in children's literature, and that fairy tales trumpeting the rewards of hard work became a significant part of a storyteller's repertoire. In times when fairy tales circulated among the populace, industriousness—or even the appearance of industriousness—could elevate a peasant to royal status. It could even get you married to a prince. This fantasy forms the basis of the Grimm brothers' *The Three Spinsters*.

There was once a girl who was lazy and would not spin, and her mother could not persuade her, do what she would. At last the mother grew angry and out of patience, and gave the girl a good beating which caused her to cry out.

At that very moment, the queen was going by and heard the girl's cries. She stopped and went into the house where she found the mother pummeling the girl. The queen asked her mother why she was beating her daughter so.

The mother was ashamed to tell of her daughter's laziness, so she said, "I cannot stop her from spinning. She is forever at it, and I am poor and cannot furnish her with enough flax."

The queen answered, "I like nothing better than the sound of a spinning wheel, and always feel happy when I hear it humming. Let me take your daughter with me to the castle; I have plenty of flax, and she can spin to her heart's delight."

The mother was only too glad to take the queen up on her offer, and the queen left with the girl. When they reached the castle, the queen showed her three rooms filled with the finest flax.

"Now spin me this flax," said she, "and when you can show it to me all done, you shall have my eldest son for a bridegroom. You may be poor, but I make nothing of that—your industry is dowry enough."

The queen is not only delighted to take the girl home with her, she is willing to give away her eldest son as a reward for the girl's industriousness. So much does she value hard work that she is willing to accept it in lieu of a dowry.

The notion that a lowly maiden could ascend to royalty because of her ability to spin reflects the wish fulfillment that is at the core of every fairy tale. Only in a fairy tale can a spinning wheel provide a ticket out of poverty. Only in a fairy tale can the heroine become a princess or a queen because she has the ability to spin and the willingness to apply herself. The maiden in *The Three Spinsters* has neither. Apparently she never learned how to operate a wheel, nor does she have the inclination.

She nevertheless is saved by the maternal equivalent of the cavalry. One day while she is standing by her window wondering how she is going to spin the flax, three strange-looking women pass below in the street. One has a broad flat foot, another a big lower lip, and the third a broad thumb. The girl calls out to them, explaining her predicament, and the three offer to spin the flax. All they ask in return is an invitation to the girl's wedding. "Will you invite us to your wedding, and not be ashamed of us?" they ask. The girl replies, "With all my heart."

The three spinsters are maternal icons. But they are icons of a specific sort: they represent the industrious side of the heroine, a part of her that is yet to be realized. A tripartite manifestation of the good mother, they appear in the heroine's time of need, ensuring her place in the royal hierarchy by offering to spin the flax. Like all mothers, the three demand very little in return, only an invitation to her wedding. What greater joy for a mother—even a composite one—than to see her daughter married to a bona fide prince?

The three spinsters proceed to spin the yarn for the maiden. The first operates the treadle that turns the wheel, the second moistens the thread, while the third twists it. When they are finished, the girl calls the queen into the room and shows her the result, making sure the spinsters are hidden from view. The queen is delighted and arranges for the wedding to take place. Before the invitations are sent out, the girl asks her future mother-in-law and the prince for a favor.

"I have three cousins," said the girl, "and as they have shown me a great deal of kindness, I would not wish to forget them in my good fortune; may I be allowed to invite them to the wedding?"

"There is no reason against it," said the queen and the bridegroom.

So when the feast began, the three spinsters appeared in strange guise, and the bride said, "Dear cousins, you are welcome."

"Oh," said the bridegroom, "how come you to have such dreadfully ugly relations?"

And then he went up to the first spinster and said, "How is it that you have such a broad flat foot?"

"From treading," answered she, "from treading."

Then he went up to the second and said, "How is it that you have such a great hanging lip?"

"From licking," answered she, "from licking."

Then he asked the third, "How is it that you have such a broad thumb?"

"From twisting thread," answered she, "from twisting thread."

Then the bridegroom said that from that time forward his beautiful bride should never touch a spinning wheel.

And so she escaped that tiresome flax spinning.

Spinning is indeed tiresome. The princess is spared from having to do any spinning in the future because she is royalty. But it is eminently clear that her good fortune is due to the intervention of the three spinsters. As elements of the heroine's self, these three convey to young readers that they too harbor a latent potential for hard work, and that cultivating this potential can be rewarding.

Because spinning contributed to the economic viability of the community, it is a common metaphor for industriousness in fairy tales. The fairy tale historian Jack Zipes points out that before the Industrial Revolution, spinning was an essential occupation for women and considered a measure of a woman's worth. Not only could a woman earn a living as a spinner, but she could more easily attract a husband by dint of her ability to spin. The term "spinster," used today in a pejorative way, in early times had positive connotations: it described a woman who earned her livelihood because of her spinning skills.

Since fairy tales often were spun, so to speak, by women working side by side in communal spinning rooms, it is not surprising that spinning became a way of describing how young girls might improve their lot in life. Though the miller's daughter in *Rumpelstiltskin* gets into trouble because of her father's ill-conceived boast, she nevertheless can become queen if she is able to spin—in her case, straw into gold. The maiden in *The Three Spinsters*, similarly, can elevate herself to the status of princess if she can produce yarn. Both girls obviously can use as much help as they can get, but this is where maternal forces come into play. *The Three Spinsters*, representing industrious aspects of the self, as it were, promotes the notion that work is self-enhancing.

Though spinning wheels were increasingly replaced by machines during the nineteenth and twentieth centuries, they remained symbols of industriousness and self-determination. In the 1920s, Mahatma Gandhi believed that a nationwide program of spinning could help free India from British colonial rule. By working to make India self-sufficient in cloth manufacture, Gandhi hoped to drive a wedge between India and Great Britain, at the same time lending dignity to the Indian worker. Spinning as a craft was regarded so highly that a spinning wheel was used to decorate the flag of the Indian independence party.

Pinocchio is not concerned with political matters, nor does he have a spinning wheel to help him. Even if he did, it is unlikely that he would expend the effort learning how to use it. Shunning anything that smacks of work, the lazy puppet ignores the cricket's advice and leaves home a second time in search of food. He again comes up empty-handed and returns to find Geppetto waiting for him, having recently been released from jail. Relieved to find the little puppet unharmed, the old man feeds Pinocchio and puts him to bed. The next day Geppetto sells his overcoat to buy an alphabet book for Pinocchio and sends him off to school, determined that he get a proper education.

But Pinocchio never gets there. He is waylaid by a conniving fox and a supposedly blind cat, who seduce him with promises of wealth and fame. The two charlatans sell him to a puppet master—christened Stromboli in the film—who adds Pinocchio to his troupe of performing marionettes. This marks the beginning of a journey that takes the little wooden figure through a series of harrowing adventures.

In one of these adventures, Pinocchio travels to an island Collodi calls "the Land of the Busy Bees." There Pinocchio observes people busily carting wagons of coal and carrying pails of water. Everyone has been assigned a specific task, and everyone is busy doing his part. But the little puppet is not impressed. Surveying the scene before him, he declares, "This country is not for me. I was not born to work."

The story once again reiterates the puppet's major failing—his unwillingness to work. When a miner offers Pinocchio money to help him pull a wagon filled with coal, the puppet declines. "I was not made a mule; I have never pulled a wagon in all my life," he tells the man. Presented with numerous opportunities to abandon his slothful ways, Pinocchio rejects them all.

ENTER THE GOOD MOTHER

Left to his own devices, Pinocchio repeatedly gets into trouble because of his slothful disposition. But he is repeatedly saved by the Blue Fairy, a magical figure who materializes at critical moments to save Pinocchio from himself. As the symbolic representation of the good mother, she urges him to reject sloth as a way of life and to follow the path of industry. In the Land of the Busy Bees, she appears in the guise of a peasant woman and gets Pinocchio to help her carry several buckets of water. Once they arrive at her home, she reveals her true identity and pardons him for his past transgressions, declaring her faith in his essential goodness.

> "And that is why I have forgiven you," the Blue Fairy said to him. "I saw that you have a good heart and there is hope for you in spite of all your bad habits. That is why I came back to be your mother. But from now on you must do everything I say."
>
> "Oh, I will, I will," cried Pinocchio.
>
> "Good. Tomorrow you must find some work that you would like to do. Now why are you muttering to yourself?"
>
> "I was just thinking," said Pinocchio seriously, "that it's too late for me to start school now, and I don't really want to find work."
>
> "And why not?" asked the fairy angrily.
>
> "Because work tires me out," replied Pinocchio weakly.
>
> "People who talk like that," said the fairy, "usually end up in prison or in hospital. You must learn, my boy, that everyone has to work in this world. Sloth is a dreadful illness and must be cured at once, in childhood. If not, when we are old it can never be cured."

The words of the Blue Fairy echo the words uttered by the cricket earlier in the story: slothful tendencies are a sure path to prison or a mental hospital. Pinocchio and young readers once again are reminded of the dire consequences of sloth. Laziness, if indulged, is a scourge that can grow into a serious defect of the self if steps aren't taken to eradicate it. Once it progresses beyond childhood, it is impossible to reverse. Though the message is scary, it contains hope since it suggests that change is possible if one is willing to make the effort.

Despite the Blue Fairy's willingness to stand by the little puppet, and in spite of his good intentions, Pinocchio falters. He leaves the Land of the Busy Bees and is persuaded by a friend named Lampwick to join him and some other boys on a journey to a land where children are never obliged to study or go to school. Dubbed "the Land of Fools" by Collodi and rechristened "Pleasure Island" by Walt Disney, their destination is a utopia where pleasure reigns and work is virtually unknown. Lampwick tells Pinocchio, "On Saturdays you do not go to school, and every day is a Saturday except one, which is Sunday." The little puppet cannot resist. It is every child's dream come true.

The temptation to succumb to a life of leisure, to be entirely free of responsibility, is enticing, but the reality often is not as rewarding as it seems. Many children become bored during long summer vacations and look forward to returning to school and to the structure that school provides. In addition, mastering new skills and acquiring knowledge is gratifying. Adults also need to be involved in productive pursuits to maintain a positive sense of self.

Pinocchio's dream turns into a nightmare. He discovers that children in this fool's paradise are transformed into donkeys shortly after they arrive. To his dismay, he wakes one morning to find that he has grown a set of donkey ears. Soon afterward his hands and feet turn into hooves and his face takes on a muzzle shape. His horror is complete when he looks behind him and sees that he has grown a tail.

The little puppet, now a donkey, cries out in despair. A squirrel who tends to the lost boys tells him, "There is nothing you can do about it. All children who are lazy, who hate school, and spend all their time amusing themselves eventually turn into little donkeys." Once again, the cricket's words come back to haunt Pinocchio. If one's goal is to caution young readers about the consequences of sloth, it would be hard to find a more horrible fate than the one that befalls Pinocchio.

Punishment for slothful tendencies forms the focus in other fairy tales that feature laziness, one of which is *Mother Hulda*, a lesser-known story in the Grimm brothers' collection. Like *The Three Spin-*

sters and *Rumpelstiltskin*, the tale utilizes spinning as a metaphor for industriousness. But whereas *The Three Spinsters* and *Rumpelstiltskin* describe the adventures of just one maiden, *Mother Hulda* describes the exploits of two. Each is the opposite of the other, especially when it comes to hard work.

> A widow had two daughters; one was pretty and industrious, while the other was ugly and lazy. And as the ugly one was her own daughter, she loved her much the best while the other was forced to do all the work, and be the drudge of the house. Were this not enough to cause the stepdaughter misery, the poor girl had to sit by a well on the high road every day and spin until her fingers bled.
>
> Now it happened one day that as the spindle was bloody, she dipped it into the well to wash it. While doing so, the spindle slipped out of her hand and fell in the water. She began to cry, and ran to her stepmother, reporting her misfortune. But her stepmother showed no pity and scolded her without mercy:
>
> "As you have let the spindle fall in, you must go and fetch it out again," she told the girl.
>
> So the girl went back to the well, but knew not what to do. In the despair of her heart, she jumped down into the well the same way the spindle had gone. After that she knew nothing; and when she came to herself she was in a beautiful meadow, and the sun was shining on the flowers that grew round her.

The heroine's leap into the well signals a descent into the unconscious, a fairy-tale crossover that delivers her into an enchanted world very different from the world she left behind. The bright sunshine and flowers stand in stark contrast to the oppressive existence in which she was forced to sit by the side of the road and spin until her hands bled. But though she is temporarily freed from her previous surroundings, she is frightened and does not know where to turn. She decides to cross the meadow and see where it leads.

> The girl walked on through the meadow until she came to a baker's oven full of bread.

The bread called out to her, "Oh, take me out, take me out, or I shall burn; I am baked enough already."

She drew near and with the baker's peel took out all the loaves, one after another. Then she continued on her way until she came to a tree weighed down with apples.

"Oh, shake us, shake us," the apples called out. "We are all ripe."

So she shook the tree until the apples fell like rain and there were no more to fall. Then she gathered them in a heap and went on farther. At last, she came to a little house with an old woman in it. The woman had such great teeth that the girl was terrified. She was about to run away but the old woman called her back.

"What are you afraid of, my dear child? Come and live with me, and if you do the house-work well and orderly, things shall go well with you. You must take great pains to make my bed well. Shake it up thoroughly so that the feathers fly about, because then it snows in the world, for I am Mother Hulda."

Who is Mother Hulda, and why does she instill such fear in the child? Her looks provide the answer. Mother Hulda's "great teeth," an allusion to her destructive potential, identify her as a witch. Her witchlike nature is complemented by her ability to effect changes in the weather, something only mighty sorceresses like Baba Yaga are able to do. Like her Russian counterpart, Mother Hulda is a great earth mother capable of controlling the heavens. According to the Grimms, peasants in their home province of Hesse often were heard to remark, "Mother Hulda is making her bed," whenever it snowed. The old woman also is capable of wreaking destruction on innocent children. No wonder our heroine is frightened of her.

The threat that Mother Hulda poses to the heroine leaves the girl little choice but to go along with the old woman's proposal. She cooks, cleans, and shakes the witch's bed with such determination that feathers fly about "like snowflakes." Eventually, though, she becomes homesick and asks Mother Hulda whether she can return home. To her surprise, the old woman greets her request with understanding rather than rancor. The young girl has performed the duties she assigned her without complaint and deserves to be rewarded.

Mother Hulda answered, "It pleases me well that you should wish to go home, and as you have served me faithfully, I will undertake to send you there."

She took her by the hand and led her to a large open door. As the girl passed through it, there fell upon her a heavy shower of gold. And the gold hung all about her, so that she was covered with it.

"All this is yours, because you have been so industrious," the old woman said to the girl. On saying that, Mother Hulda returned the spindle to her, the same one the girl had dropped in the well. Then the door was shut again, and the girl found herself back again in the world, not far from her mother's house.

The return of the spindle confers on the heroine the mantle of industriousness that literally fell from her grasp when the spindle fell into the well. By faithfully performing the tasks set forth by the witch, the heroine proves her mettle, regaining her status as a hard worker. She is prepared to return to the "real world," wiser for her experience and proud of her accomplishment. And though the gold is a reward of the highest order, it is not as significant as the positive regard earned from Mother Hulda.

Mother Hulda teaches that the regard of significant others is more precious than gold. Young children don't understand the value of money; how many children know the difference between a five-dollar bill and a ten-dollar bill, or the purchasing power of each? What they do know is that they feel good when a parent or teacher praises them for their efforts. The positive responses of adults are incorporated into the child's inner world as feelings about the self and result in heightened self-esteem and positive self-regard. This is what the girl derives from her encounter with Mother Hulda. This is the deeper meaning of her experience.

Having regained the spindle, our heroine crosses back into the real world and tells her stepmother about her adventure. The stepmother insists that her own daughter also deserves to be showered with gold. She commands her to sit by the well and to reenact the original circumstances that led to her stepsister's good fortune. To make sure everything is precisely the same, the stepmother bloodies her daughter's hands by thrusting them into a thornbush and smears the spindle with the girl's blood. Then she casts the bloody spindle into the well and tells her to jump in after it.

The lazy daughter found herself, like her sister, in the beautiful meadow, and followed the same path. When she came to the baker's oven, the bread cried out,

"Oh, take me out, take me out, or I shall burn; I am quite done already."

But the lazy-bones answered, "I have no desire to blacken my hands," and she went on farther.

Soon she came to the apple tree who called out, "Oh, shake me, shake me, my apples are all ripe."

But she answered, "That is all very fine, but suppose one of you should fall on my head?" And she continued on.

When she came to Mother Hulda's house, she did not feel afraid, as she knew beforehand of her great teeth, and entered into her service at once.

The first day she put her hand well to the work, and was industrious. She did everything Mother Hulda bade her, because of the gold she expected. But the second day she began to be idle, and the third day even more so. She would not even get out of bed in the morning.

Mother Hulda soon grew tired of her, and gave her warning that she would have to leave, at which the lazy thing was well pleased since she thought the shower of gold was coming. Mother Hulda led her to the door, and as the girl stood in the doorway, a great kettle of pitch was emptied over her head.

"That is the reward for your service," said Mother Hulda, and shut the door.

So the lazy girl came home all covered with pitch. And the pitch remained sticking to her fast, and never, as long as she lived, could it be got off.

In rewarding the industrious sister with gold and punishing the lazy one with pitch, *Mother Hulda* graphically depicts the consequences of sloth. Being covered with pitch for the remainder of your days is as devastating as having to spend the rest of your life as a donkey. Just as

Pinocchio is punished for his lazy ways, so the indolent sister is punished for hers. But the sister at least has her mother to look after her. Pinocchio is alone and still far from home.

THE ROAD TO SALVATION

Having been transformed into a donkey, Pinocchio's stay in the Land of Fools soon comes to an end. The coachman who rules the diabolic animal farm sells him to a circus, where Pinocchio is placed in a stable and subjected to brutal whippings. Every night he is taken out of his stall and forced to perform difficult tricks in front of an audience. On one of these occasions, he notices the Blue Fairy in the stands. Her presence, a testimony to the unflagging nature of maternal devotion, communicates to young readers that as bad as one is, or has been, there is always hope.

One night during one of his performances, Pinocchio stumbles and injures himself jumping through a hoop.

"A lame donkey is no good to me," the circus owner grumbles. "There is little use in a circus for an animal who cannot perform."

The next day the circus owner takes him to the marketplace and sells him to a sinister-looking man. Pinocchio is alarmed to learn that his new owner intends to drown him and to use his skin to make a drum. The man ties a large stone around Pinocchio's neck and throws the donkey into the sea. Pinocchio, fortunately, manages to survive. He miraculously changes back into a wooden puppet when he is underwater and rises to the surface.

While floating on the waves, Pinocchio spies the Blue Fairy on a distant cliff disguised as a blue-haired goat. He gathers up all his strength and swims toward her. But before he can reach shore, he is faced with yet another challenge. A monstrous sea creature, termed "the Attila of all fishes" by Collodi, threatens to devour him. Pinocchio tries to escape the creature but is swallowed whole and swept into the monster's stomach. Inside the great fish—christened Monstro the Whale by Disney—he discovers a weak and emaciated Geppetto hovering on the brink of death.

The lone survivor of a ship that had been swallowed by the sea monster, Geppetto has been living in the animal's stomach since he and Pinocchio were separated. The old man is both amazed and overjoyed to find his long-lost "son" alive. The two embrace, after which they manage to escape from the fish's belly and return home. Safely back in familiar territory, Pinocchio gets a job on a farm and nurses Geppetto back to health.

> For the next five months, Pinocchio got up at five o'clock every morning to pump water from the well in return for food. That was not all; he also learned to make baskets which he sold at the local market. With this money he was able to look after his father and, since Geppetto was still too weak to walk very far, he made him a wheelchair so that he could take him out on fine days for a breath of fresh air.

The essence of Collodi's tale is revealed in the previous passage. Pinocchio's salvation comes about through hard work. He pumps water, makes baskets, and builds a wheelchair for his adopted father so that he can take him for walks. He even gets up at five o'clock in the morning to make sure everything is done.

The good part of Pinocchio's split self has finally gained ascendance and now guides his behavior. His positive side, symbolically represented by the Blue Fairy and her insect ambassador, the cricket, has won out over the negative tendencies that previously dominated his life. The puppet relinquishes his shiftless ways once and for all and becomes the good son, an industrious child willing to work hard to support those he cares for and who care for him.

But the story is not over. Though Pinocchio has renounced his old ways, he still is a puppet. His dream of becoming a real boy has yet to be realized. One night he falls onto his bed exhausted and dreams of the Blue Fairy. In the dream, the fairy kisses him and says, "Well done, Pinocchio! As you have been so good, I will forgive you for all the bad things you have done in the past. Try to behave like this in the future and you will always be happy."

When Pinocchio wakes, he is astonished to find that he has turned into a real boy. He dresses and runs excitedly to Geppetto, who has also undergone a magical transformation: "Pinocchio found Geppetto as well and as young as when he first began his profession of carving." The story ends on an exultant note as the two join hands and rejoice. Everyone's fondest dream has come true: Pinocchio has become a human being, the Blue Fairy sees her ne'er-do-well protégé abandon his former ways, and Geppetto inherits a live son.

THE BAD, THE GOOD, AND THE WOOD

But where is the witch in the story? Is it the coachman who rules the Land of Fools and trades Pinocchio to the circus master for a handful of gold? Is it the circus master who whips Pinocchio and sells him when he can no longer perform tricks? Or is it the sinister drum-maker who tries to drown Pinocchio? Each certainly is wicked in his own right. On the other hand, none of these characters are really witches in the true sense of the word. None of them were out to destroy Pinocchio, except perhaps for the drum-maker—and he thought he was slaughtering a donkey. So where is the witch?

"He's over there," said Geppetto, pointing to a puppet leaning against a chair with its head on one side, its arms dangling, and its legs crooked and bent. The discarded "other Pinocchio," embodying, as it were, the bad part of the self, lies lifeless in a corner of Geppetto's workshop, having been reduced to an inanimate piece of wood. On the other side of the room stands a "bright and intelligent boy with chestnut hair and large bright eyes."

The jettisoned Pinocchio, while not a witch in the conventional sense of the word, nevertheless personifies all that is bad in the story. He is lazy, unreliable, and incorrigible. Collodi decides the puppet's fate by robbing it of life and then destroying it in much the same way as the witch is destroyed in traditional fairy tales. By doing away with the "old Pinocchio," Collodi eradicates sloth, leaving in its place a Pinocchio with all the qualities one expects in virtuous children: concern for their parents, obedience, and, most important, an affinity for hard work.

Carlos Collodi was passionately committed to school reform. In addition to being a talented writer and creative storyteller, he published professional articles on childhood education and fought for changes in the schools. In Collodi's view, laziness was a dangerous trait that had to be thoroughly eradicated because of its deleterious effect on education. Unless steps were taken to eliminate sloth early on, it would prevent children from making use of school and leading useful lives. One could not expect sloth to disappear on its own. Active steps needed to be taken to ensure its elimination.

Collodi, accordingly, eliminates the puppet entirely and replaces it with a new creation: "a young man with chestnut hair and large bright eyes." There is absolutely no physical resemblance between the old Pinocchio and the new Pinocchio. The Disney version, on the other hand, transforms Pinocchio into a recycled version of his former self. The "new" Pinocchio is still a puppet, differing from his predecessor only in that he lacks hinged knees and hinged elbows.

But the most important difference between Collodi's *Pinocchio* and the Disney version is not the fate of the puppet but the fact that the film virtually ignores sloth as a psychological consideration. In the film, Pinocchio ends up on Pleasure Island, not because he is lazy, but because he is disobedient and self-indulgent. Once on the island, he and his friends smoke, play pool, and fight with one another to pass the time of day. There is even an arcade in which he and his companions are allowed to indulge their destructive impulses.

In Disney's eyes, the puppet's major failing is his inclination to tell lies, a character fault graphically depicted by the growth of his nose. This is the scene most people recall from the film even though it occupies only a couple of paragraphs in a book of over two hundred pages. Sloth, on the other hand, is mentioned or alluded to on practically every page.

It is unclear why Disney altered Collodi's story so as to eliminate sloth as a psychological dynamic. Perhaps he felt that laziness no longer was a pressing concern by the time the film came out in 1940. Child labor laws had been in place in the United States for a number of years, and children weren't expected to work. Disney may have felt that lying, smoking, and the destruction of property were more reprehensible sins and thus deserved more attention. Whatever the reason, sloth virtually disappeared from the story once it made the transition from the printed page to the screen.

Laziness nevertheless continues to be a concern for children and parents alike. We expect children to do household chores, and we become annoyed when they shirk their responsibilities. As parents and teachers, we recognize that sloth can pose a serious problem when it comes to schoolwork. Such concerns are reflected in the familiar Mother Goose nursery rhyme about a child who has trouble getting up in the morning.

> *A diller, a dollar, a ten o'clock scholar!*
> *What makes you come so soon?*
> *You used to come at ten o'clock,*
> *But now you come at noon.*

But nursery rhymes are merely playful reminders that lazy inclinations can be problematic; they do not attack sloth in the same way fairy tales do. Stories about a child covered with pitch for exhibiting laziness and a boy turned into a donkey for the same reason make powerful statements about sloth that cannot be conveyed through lectures, reprimands, or nursery rhymes. Parents searching for ways of introducing children to matters having to do with sloth could do worse than read their offspring stories like *The Three Spinsters, Mother Hulda,* or the original version of *Pinocchio.*

This doesn't mean that the movie version of *Pinocchio* and the storybooks it spawned have no redeeming social value. There is much to be said for using powerful graphic images to take a stand against smoking, destruction of property, and telling lies. For years, after seeing *Pinocchio* on the screen, I imagined my nose growing whenever I was tempted to tell a lie. One nevertheless needs to understand that the Disney version of *Pinocchio* has very little to do with sloth and thus is not of much psychological value when it comes to conflicts concerning laziness.

Despite their differences, both the Disney film and the Collodi original share one very important characteristic. Both are stories of transformation. Both champion the view that it is possible to change no matter how many times you have sinned in the past, or how great your shortcomings are. This is a reassuring message for young and old alike, one that is predicated on the successful completion of a fairy-tale journey. For some, the road leads though the Land of Fools, for others through the Land of Oz.

11

Inside Oz

Off to See the Wizard

"Give me back my shoe!"

"I will not," retorted the Witch, "for it is now my shoe, and not yours."

"You are a wicked creature!" cried Dorothy. "You have no right to take my shoe from me."

"I shall keep it, just the same," said the Witch, laughing at her, "and some day I will get the other one from you too."

> This made Dorothy so very angry that she picked up the bucket of water that stood near and dashed it over the Witch, wetting her from head to foot.
>
> Instantly the wicked woman gave a loud cry of fear, and then, as Dorothy looked at her in wonder, the Witch began to shrink and fall away.

Dorothy watches with a mixture of horror and amazement as the Wicked Witch of the West melts into a shapeless mass that spreads across the floor. She then announces to her companions that the Witch is dead, and together they set off to the Emerald City to receive the rewards promised them by the Wizard: a brain for the Scarecrow, a heart for the Tin Woodman, and courage for the Cowardly Lion.

There is hardly a child who is not intimately acquainted with Dorothy and her adventures in the Land of Oz. Media gurus estimate that more than one billion people have either seen the screen version of *The Wizard of Oz* or read L. Frank Baum's famous book, and the number continues to grow every day. It is a rare child who cannot recite the words to "Ding dong, the Witch is dead," or who doesn't know what a Munchkin is. Each year countless children and their parents gather in front of their TV sets to watch Dorothy set out on her journey down the yellow brick road.

Though most people tend to view *The Wizard of Oz* as a children's adventure, it is very much a fairy tale. But unlike stories like *Snow White*, *Cinderella*, and other traditional fairy tales, *The Wizard of Oz* focuses on perceived shortcomings in the self as opposed to excesses. Characters in classical fairy tales are typically plagued by sins of *indulgence*—vanity, gluttony, greed, and the like—but Dorothy's three companions suffer from sins of *deficiency*. The Scarecrow, the Tin Woodman, and the Cowardly Lion are convinced that they are not as intelligent, feeling, or courageous as others. Their hope is that Dorothy will help them remedy these shortcomings, and our heroine is more than happy to oblige. And though she has no way of knowing it at the beginning of the story, helping her companions fulfill their destinies helps her fulfill her own.

A FAIRY TALE FOR OUR TIME

Frank Baum's book begins with Dorothy seeking refuge from a deadly cyclone headed toward the farm where she lives with her Aunt Em and Uncle Henry. She is about to follow them into a storm cellar when Toto, her pet dog, jumps from her arms and hides under a bed. Before Dorothy has a chance to retrieve Toto, the cyclone lifts the farmhouse from its foundation, sending it sailing high into the sky. In the book, the gentle swaying of the house lulls Dorothy to sleep, and when she awakes she finds that the house has landed in the Land of Oz.

Dorothy's arrival in a magical kingdom filled with enchanted figures is heralded in the film by the screen suddenly bursting into color. This dramatic crossover signals that she no longer is bound by the drab confines of Kansas—reality—but has entered the realm of the unconscious. She opens the door leading into this magical universe and is immediately approached by a little white-haired lady who informs her that her house has fallen on a witch, killing her on the spot. To Dorothy's surprise, the old woman doesn't appear particularly upset. On the contrary, she seems relieved.

> "Welcome, most noble Sorceress, to the land of the Munchkins," the old woman said. "We are most grateful to you for having killed the Wicked Witch of the East, and for setting our people free from bondage."
>
> Dorothy listened to this speech with wonder. What could the little woman possibly mean by calling her a sorceress, and saying she had killed the Wicked Witch of the East? Dorothy was an innocent, harmless little girl, who had been carried by a cyclone many miles from home; and she had never killed anyone in all her life.
>
> But the little woman evidently expected her to answer, so Dorothy said with hesitation,
>
> "You are very kind; but there must be some mistake. I have not killed anything."
>
> "Your house did, anyway," replied the little old woman with a laugh. "And that is the same thing." She continued, pointing to the corner of the house. "See, there are her two toes, still sticking out from under a block of wood."

Dorothy looked, and gave a little cry of fright. There, indeed, just under the corner of the great beam the house rested on, two feet were sticking out.

"Oh, dear! Oh, dear!" cried Dorothy, clasping her hands together in dismay; "the house must have fallen on her. What ever shall we do?"

"There is nothing to be done," said the little woman, calmly.

"But who was she?" asked Dorothy.

"She was the Wicked Witch of the East, as I said," answered the little woman. "She has held all the Munchkins in bondage for many years, making them slave for her night and day. Now they are all set free, and are grateful to you for the favor."

Were the Wicked Witch of the East the only witch in the story, the narrative could end there and then. Dorothy could spend some time visiting with the Munchkins, take a couple of turns around Munchkinland, and wait for Glinda to whisk her back to Kansas. But things aren't that simple. The witch has a sister who undoubtedly will seek revenge once she learns of Dorothy's involvement in her sister's death.

The presence of two witches in the story, even though one dies before the story even gets off the ground, cautions readers that evil is not easily disposed of. Negative influences abound in the universe, and one needs to be constantly on guard. Kill one witch and another takes her place; eliminate one unwholesome thought and another pops up in its stead.

Dorothy has other problems besides the Witch. She desperately wants to get back to Kansas, for she is certain that Uncle Henry and Aunt Em are worried sick over her whereabouts. The Munchkins inform her that the only person who can possibly help her get home is the great and powerful Wizard of Oz. If she hopes to return to Kansas, she must travel to the Emerald City where the Wizard holds court and request his help. Dorothy puts on the magic shoes that only recently adorned the feet of the Wicked Witch of the East and heads down the yellow brick road. She has delivered the Munchkins from bondage and set them free. Now she must free herself.

The yellow brick road is marked by many twists and turns. A metaphor for personal growth, the road suggests that the path to self-realization is not only tortuous but filled with dangerous obstacles. Like the road at the top of the beanstalk that leads Jack to a confrontation with a murderous ogre, so the yellow brick road leads Dorothy to a confrontation with a deadly witch. But before this takes place, she must overcome a series of challenges and travel to the Emerald City to meet the all-powerful Wizard of Oz.

If i only had a brain

Soon after Dorothy starts out on her voyage, she spies a scarecrow languishing in a field. To Dorothy's astonishment, he calls out for help. She stops to speak to him and learns that he suffers from a unique failing: he lacks a brain. When he finds out that Dorothy is headed to a great wizard whom she believes can help her get back to Kansas, the Scarecrow wonders whether the Wizard might be able to help him as well.

> "Do you think" he asked, "if I go to the Emerald City with you, that the great Oz would give me some brains?"
>
> "I cannot tell," she returned; "but you may come with me, if you like. If Oz will not give you any brains, you will be no worse off than you are now."
>
> "That is true," said the Scarecrow. "You see," he continued confidentially, "I don't mind my legs and arms and body being stuffed, because I cannot get hurt. If anyone treads on my toes or sticks a pin into me, it doesn't matter, for I can't feel it. But I do not want people to call me a fool, and if my head stays stuffed with straw instead of with brains, as yours is, how am I to know anything?"

The Scarecrow's discomfort underscores how truly miserable it is to feel stupid. How many children—how many adults, for that matter—suffer intense embarrassment when they do not know the answer to a question or how to behave in a difficult situation? How often do we feel like hiding under a bush when our ignorance becomes obvious, or we are unable to perform a simple task? To feel like a dummy—to have others call you a fool—is a painful experience.

Children all too often are made to feel this way. Their teachers pose questions they cannot answer; they find themselves at a loss for words when their parents ask why they've done something they shouldn't have; their friends make fun of them because they cannot come up with the solution to a simple riddle. The opportunities for ridicule are endless, especially since young children do not have the wherewithal to think quickly on their feet. Few children would turn down a chance to join a quest that might make them more intelligent; fewer still would give up an opportunity to vanquish feelings of intellectual inferiority forever.

The issue of intelligence—more accurately, the lack of it—is a common theme in fairy tales. *Ricky with the Tuft*, one of the stories in Charles Perrault's collection, features a beautiful princess who suffers a shortage of brains. In Perrault's tale, Ricky, a prince, promises the princess the gift of intelligence in exchange for her hand in marriage. The prince knows what it means to suffer from a personal shortcoming, for he is extremely ugly. The relative merits of beauty and intelligence are debated before the two even meet, at the moment of their births.

There once was a queen who bore a son so ugly that it was doubtful his mother could ever come to love him. But a fairy who was present at his birth promised he should have plenty of brains and by virtue of this gift, would be able to bestow the same degree of intelligence to the person whom he should love. This consoled the queen, who came to love the child for when he grew older and learned to speak, his sayings proved very shrewd and he was so clever he charmed everyone. Because the child was born with a little tuft of hair upon his head, he was called Ricky with the Tuft.

Not long thereafter, the queen of a neighboring kingdom gave birth to twin daughters. The first was more beautiful than the dawn but exceedingly stupid while the second, born a few minutes later, was extremely ugly. The queen was deeply mortified, and expressed her distress. The same fairy who had attended Ricky's birth and was now assisting the queen, examined the second daughter and said,

"Do not be distressed, Madam, your daughter shall be recompensed in another way. She shall have such good sense that her lack of beauty will scarcely be noticed."

"May heaven grant it," said the queen, "but is there no means by which the elder, who is so beautiful, can be endowed with some intelligence?"

"I can do nothing for her in this regard," said the fairy, "but I will bestow upon her the power to confer beauty on whomever she falls in love with."

As the two princesses grow to adults, their perfections and imperfections become magnified: the elder becomes prettier and less intelligent, while the younger becomes uglier, but more clever. The difference between the two affects the way they are received at court.

At first, everyone gathered around the beauty to see and admire her, but very soon they were all attracted by the graceful and easy conversation of the clever one. In a very short time the elder sister was left entirely alone, while everyone clustered round her sister.

The notion that intelligence can compensate for, even outweigh, physical attributes is a comforting thought for many children, particularly those not fortunate enough to be endowed with good looks. Children with attractive features usually are more popular and are spared the taunts and jokes experienced by children who may be overweight or are saddled with unattractive features. The ability of the younger sister to compensate for a homely or offensive appearance by her intellectual prowess assures children that looks aren't everything, that there are other ways to gain acceptance and recognition.

The older sister is not so stupid as to be unaware of her "disability." She retires to a nearby wood to bemoan her fate, thinking she would willingly surrender all her good looks to be half as clever as her sister. Suddenly an ugly little man dressed in magnificent clothes appears be-

fore her. It is none other than Ricky with the Tuft. The young prince
has seen a portrait of the lovely princess and has traveled a great distance to admire her in person.

The prince is taken aback to see the object of his admiration so unhappy. He tries to console her, and she reveals the reason for her misery. The two discuss the relative merits of beauty and intelligence,
after which the princess declares to Ricky, "I would rather be as plain
as you are and have some sense, than be as beautiful as I am and at the
same time stupid."

Ricky, possessed of the gift awarded him at birth by the fairy, offers
to confer intelligence on the princess if she will marry him. The
princess consents but nevertheless expresses some misgivings, for
Ricky is truly unattractive. Ricky acknowledges her concern and tells
her that he will give her some time to get used to the idea. He will return in a year's time, and the two can get married then.

At the end of a year's time, Ricky returns to claim his bride. But the
princess tries to renege on the deal. She insists that it is unfair for
Ricky to press his claim since she didn't have enough sense to know
what she was getting into when she promised to marry him. She tries
to renounce her vow, but Ricky insists that she honor it, reminding
her she is a princess.

"A princess must keep her word," Ricky with the Tuft declared. "You
must marry me because you promised to."

The princess replied, "But I am speaking to a man of great taste, and I
am sure you will listen to reason." She continued, "As you are aware, I
could not make up my mind to marry you even when I was entirely
without sense; how can you expect that today I should take a decision
which I could not take then, now that I possess the intelligence you
bestowed on me. If you wished so much to marry me, you were very
wrong to relieve me of my stupidity, and to let me see more clearly than
I did."

Fairy tales teach that words can deceive as much as looks. Just as
one can smile and smile, and be a villain, so one can use words to mask
intentions. But Ricky refuses to be put off. He resolves the conun-

drum by asking the princess whether she would marry him were it not for his frightful looks. When she answers yes, he tells her it is within her power to make him handsome. He explains the earlier prophecies, indicating that all she has to do is love him. The princess proclaims her love, upon which Ricky is instantly transformed into "the most handsome and attractive prince in the world." The two embrace and are happily wed the following day.

Though the ultimate union between Ricky and his bride is predicated on Ricky turning into a handsome prince, the story nevertheless champions the importance of intelligence. The younger sister, though unattractive, is admired for her intellect while the pretty sister is ignored because she lacks brains. The advantage of having "brains" is not lost on the Scarecrow. He too knows his lot in life will be vastly improved if he can make sense of the world. And while intelligence does not necessarily guarantee happiness, it definitely has its advantages.

To feel, perchance to love

The next character Dorothy meets along the yellow brick road is the Tin Woodman. Immobilized by rust, he tells Dorothy that he too lacks an important part of his anatomy: a heart. Baum's original tale describes the peculiar circumstances under which the crucial organ was lost, something the movie fails to explain. In the book, the Tin Woodman informs Dorothy that his heart was lost in the course of wooing a Munchkin girl, and that he has been unable to experience emotion since then.

The Munchkin girl, the Woodman explains, worked as a servant in the home of an old woman. He and the girl planned to marry, but the old woman became alarmed at the prospect of having to do her own housework. She went to the Wicked Witch of the East and promised her two sheep and a cow if she would stop the couple from going through with the wedding. The Witch accepted the offer and enchanted the woodcutter's axe, forcing it to slip from his hand and severing his leg from his body.

The Woodman fortunately was able to find a tinsmith who fashioned a new leg for him out of metal. But the Witch, intent on preventing the wedding, made the axe slip once more, causing the other leg to fly off. The Woodman returned to the tinsmith, who fitted him with yet another leg. This scenario was repeated three more times, with the woodcutter losing both his arms and finally his head. Against all odds, the tinsmith was able to replace the missing parts, and the woodcutter felt confident the wedding could proceed as planned.

"I thought I had beaten the Wicked Witch then, and I worked harder than ever; but I little knew how cruel my enemy could be. She thought of a new way to kill my love for the beautiful Munchkin maiden, and made my axe slip again, so that it cut through my body, splitting me in two halves."

This time the damage was nearly irreparable. Although the tinsmith was able to put the woodcutter together again, the Woodman's heart was gone for good. The result was that his affection for the Munchkin girl was irretrievably lost. But it wasn't just his love for the Munchkin girl that he lost; the tragedy deprived him of all feeling. For without a heart, he was unable to experience emotion. He sadly tells Dorothy, "No one can love who has not a heart."

The ability to feel is perhaps the most human of human qualities and constitutes the building block of empathy. To be able to empathize, to understand and share another person's joy and sorrow, is the glue that binds people together. Without empathy, without the ability to feel what other people feel, human beings are forced to communicate exclusively through intellectual channels, making relationships barren and colorless.

The noted psychologist and self theorist Heinz Kohut believed that empathy grows out of two important childhood needs. On the one hand, children need to show off and be admired for their unfolding capabilities; on the other, children need to feel close to a loving caretaker, usually the mother. The growing intimacy between a mother and child in relation to these needs leads to shared emotional experiences that act as the foundation for empathy. When a mother smiles or hugs her child to indicate positive feelings, or frowns to show her displeasure, the child learns to decipher and share these reactions, a development that forms the basis for understanding and sharing the feelings of others.

Although the capacity for empathy develops early in life, children can be notoriously cruel and insensitive. Youngsters often taunt their playmates and pick on weaker children until the latter are reduced to tears—or worse. In England a teenager committed suicide after being ruthlessly taunted by her schoolmates for being overweight. Her teenage tormentors tossed salt into her school lunch, dumped her clothes into the garbage, and pelted her home with butter, eggs, and other cake ingredients. The night she took a fatal overdose of pain killers, she told her parents that she could no longer tolerate the abuse heaped upon her by her classmates.

This is not an isolated incident. The director of the Anti-Bullying Campaign in Great Britain reports that harassment of children by children is common, and that ten children die every year as a result of bullying. The organization fields sixteen thousand calls annually from callers, mostly children, who desperately need to speak to someone about the psychological brutality of their peers.

Why children behave "heartlessly" is not altogether known. Some children ally themselves with bullies to gain a sense of power or importance, and others because they see qualities in their victims they want to deny in themselves, thus compensating for their own feelings of vulnerability. Whatever the reason, behaving cruelly toward playmates takes its toll. Victimizing others forces children to doubt their own powers of compassion and raises questions about a child's ability to transcend cruel tendencies.

The Woodman wants a heart not merely because he wants to love, but because he intuitively recognizes that he may become as cruel as the witch if he lacks one. Confessing his worry to Dorothy, he asserts that he would like "never to be cruel or unkind to anything." Dorothy listens sympathetically and welcomes him aboard when he asks whether he can join the entourage on their voyage to the Emerald City.

COWARDS DIE A THOUSAND DEATHS

The final figure Dorothy encounters on her magical journey is the Cowardly Lion, who intercepts the little band as they are walking through the woods. After a failed attempt to intimidate the others, he breaks down and confesses his weakness. Beneath his false bravado, he is a coward.

> "What makes you a coward?" asked Dorothy, looking at the great beast in wonder, for he was as big as a small horse.
>
> "It's a mystery," replied the Lion. "I suppose I was born that way. . . . "
>
> "But that isn't right. The King of the Beasts shouldn't be a coward," said the Scarecrow.
>
> "I know it," returned the Lion, wiping a tear from his eye with the tip of his tail; "it is my great sorrow, and makes my life very unhappy. But whenever there is danger my heart begins to beat fast."

Like the Scarecrow and the Tin Woodman, the Lion voices a concern shared by all children. Most children would like to be brave, to feel unafraid, to know they can fall back on a reserve of inner fortitude if and when the need arises. No child wants to be thought of as a coward.

The Cowardly Lion's desire to be stout-hearted in the face of adversity is shared by the main character in *The Gallant Tailor*. The Grimm brothers' fairy tale tells of a meek and unassuming tailor who stitches the words "Seven at one blow!" on a belt after killing seven flies that have landed on some jelly. The belt impresses a neighboring king as well as a number of giants the tailor encounters on his journeys throughout the land, all of whom are convinced that he has killed seven men. The "gallant" tailor eventually comes to believe that he is in fact courageous, so much so that he defeats all his enemies and marries the king's daughter.

Courage is a major component of George Lucas's *Star Wars* trilogy. Tracking Luke Skywalker's journey from the ranks of inexperienced adolescence to Jedi warrior, Lucas draws on mythic themes to come up with a complex coming-of-age fairy tale that centers on timeless issues of loyalty, honor, and bravery. Each episode in the trilogy describes how Luke and his fellow space voyagers are forced to travel deep into themselves to find the courage needed to overcome the forces of evil (the dark side of "the Force").

To become a full-fledged Jedi warrior, Luke must conjure up the fortitude to confront forces that are more powerful than he. Han Solo must overcome selfish considerations and allow his latent courageous instincts to take precedence. Even Princess Leia joins the emotional fray. In standing side by side with her comrades in battle, she discards the stereotype of passive damsel in distress and adopts the role of woman warrior.

The Force drives this intergalactic drama. The cosmic equivalent of the self, it fuels the behavior of the various characters in the story, much as the self does in fairy tales. But instead of fairy godmothers and witches, Lucas offers up Obi-Wan Kenobi and Darth Vader, each personifying the good and bad sides of the self.

The struggle between good and evil culminates in a duel in which Luke—the spiritual heir of Obi-Wan Kenobi—is pitted against the evil Darth Vader. The final confrontation leads to the revelation that Darth Vader is actually Luke's father, a good Jedi knight gone bad. In much the same way as the witch figure in traditional fairy tales represents the externalized bad mother, so the evil Darth Vader in Lucas's fairy tale represents the externalized bad father. Each gives concrete expression to offensive parts of the self that must be overcome if good parts of the self are to prevail.

The psychological struggle between courage and cowardice, between good and bad, reaches its zenith when Luke delivers a near-lethal blow to his adversary. Spurred on by the evil emperor to kill Darth Vader, Luke refuses to administer the coup de grâce, intuitively recognizing that yielding to vengeful impulses is itself a form of cowardice. By refusing to surrender to destructive forces in the self, Luke and the viewer acknowledge a different kind of courage. Although Luke is not the instrument of his father's death, Darth Vader nevertheless perishes, thus suffering the same fate as other witch figures in fairy tales.

The Cowardly Lion, thankfully, does not have to confront the intergalactic forces faced by Luke and his comrades. But his problem looms just as large. Practically everything the blustery beast comes into contact with scares him to death. It is only natural that he seeks to join the others when they explain the purpose of their journey.

> "I am going to the great Oz to ask him to give me some brains," remarked the Scarecrow, "for my head is stuffed with straw."
> "And I am going to ask him to give me a heart," said the Woodman.
> "And I am going to ask him to send Toto and me back to Kansas," added Dorothy.
> "Do you think Oz could give me courage?" asked the Cowardly Lion.
> "Just as easily as he could give me brains," said the Scarecrow.
> "Or give me a heart," said the Tin Woodman.
> "Or send me back to Kansas," said Dorothy.
> "Then, if you don't mind, I'll go with you," said the Lion, "for my life is simply unbearable without a bit of courage."

The three figures Dorothy encounters on her excursion to the Emerald City are not fantasy figures who materialize from out of the blue; they represent emotional aspects of her own inner world. No child, Dorothy included, wants to think of herself as stupid, heartless, or cowardly. Children want to believe they are intelligent, compassionate, and brave. They want to believe they will follow their hearts and live up to the courage of their convictions. But childhood is a time of doubt, of reservations, of uncertainties. In joining Dorothy on her trek to find the Wizard, children seek to resolve questions about themselves so that they too may arrive at a more satisfactory vision of who they are.

LIONS AND TIGERS AND BEARS — OH, MY!

The voyage to the Emerald City, like most fairy-tale journeys, is fraught with dangers and pitfalls. In the book, Dorothy and her companions must ford a steep divide, cross a deadly poppy field, and battle Kalidahs, great hairy beasts with the bodies of bears and heads like tigers. Yet the obstacles serve only to strengthen their resolve, illuminating their inherent capabilities.

The Lion, for example, gets in touch with the courageous part of his self by attempting to leap a gorge lined with treacherous rocks. Measuring the distance to the other side in his mind, he tells the others to get on his back. He will vault the divide and carry them over. When the Scarecrow reminds him that they might all fall to their deaths, the Lion confesses he is not without misgivings.

"I am terribly afraid of falling, myself," he tells the Scarecrow.

He nevertheless screws up his courage and leaps to the other side. Everyone breathes a sigh of relief as the Lion lands safely on all fours, delivering his passengers to safety.

The Lion's display of courage is an inspiration to the others and encourages them to call on their own latent strengths. When the foursome fight a brief but intense battle with the Kalidahs, they emerge victorious owing largely to the quick thinking of the Scarecrow. He figures out a way to cut off one end of a large tree the Kalidahs are using as a bridge to cross a ravine and sends them hurtling to their deaths. When Dorothy collapses from fatigue in the deadly poppy field, the Scarecrow devises a way to rescue her and Toto from the lethal fumes.

"Let us make a chair with our hands and carry her," he tells the Tin Woodman, once again calling upon his native intelligence. Dorothy and Toto are saved from certain death as a result of the Scarecrow's quick thinking.

The journey to the Emerald City provides the members of Dorothy's entourage with numerous opportunities to overcome their fears and shortcomings. The Scarecrow demonstrates that he indeed has a brain, and the Lion displays more courage than he ever believed possible. Only the Woodman has not achieved his goal. But the journey is not yet over.

The indomitable foursome finally arrives at the Emerald City only to find that the Wizard is occupied with matters of state and much too busy to see them. But Dorothy and her friends refuse to take no for an answer and insist on an audience. They finally are admitted into a large chamber where they are confronted by an enormous head seated upon a throne of green marble. A voice from the head calls out, "I am Oz, the Great and Terrible. Who are you and what do you want?"

Dorothy introduces herself and tells the Wizard her story. She is worried that her Aunt Em and Uncle Henry are concerned about her whereabouts, and she asks for his help in getting back to Kansas. The Wizard grudgingly agrees to help her but tells her that she must return the favor.

> "You have no right to expect me to send you back to Kansas unless you do something for me in return. In this country everyone must pay for everything he gets. If you wish me to use my magic power to send you home again you must do something for me first. Help me and I will help you."
>
> "What must I do?" asked the girl.
>
> "Kill the Wicked Witch of the West," answered Oz.

The Wizard's command—the witch must die—is the driving force in *The Wizard of Oz* and propels the story to its inevitable conclusion. Dorothy must destroy the Witch if she hopes to return to Kansas. Her three companions, moreover, must assist her in doing what needs to be done. Each is a part of Dorothy, and so they must join her in the Witch's destruction. Their participation is made explicit by the "bargains" the Wizard makes with each of them.

He tells the Scarecrow, "If you will kill for me the Wicked Witch of the West, I will bestow on you a great many brains." He next tells the Woodman, "When the Witch is dead, come to me, and I will then give you the biggest, and kindest and most loving heart in all the Land of Oz." He concludes by promising the Lion courage when he returns with proof of the Witch's death.

THE FINAL FRONTIER: CONFRONTING EVIL

The encounter with the Witch constitutes the decisive turning point in Dorothy's journey, as it does in all fairy tales. The Witch, representing all that is "bad" in Oz—and in Dorothy—must be destroyed. But the Wicked Witch of the West, like all witches, is a powerful figure with many resources at her disposal. She will stop at nothing to make sure Dorothy is defeated.

In the Baum original, the evil woman dispatches a pack of ferocious wolves to attack the interlopers. To assist the wolves, she sends a flock of crows to peck out their eyes. The Woodman makes short shrift of the wolves by chopping their heads off with his axe, and the Scarecrow kills the crows by wringing their necks.

The Witch responds by sending a swarm of bees to sting Dorothy and her friends to death. The Scarecrow, who is growing more resourceful by the moment, comes up with a scheme to destroy the bees. He takes the straw from his body and scatters it over Dorothy and the Lion to protect them from the bee's deadly stings. Only the Woodman is left exposed. The bees attack the Woodman and perish when their stingers break off against his metal exterior.

But the Witch is not to be denied. Her servants, a troupe of winged monkeys, overcome Dorothy and her friends. They dump the Woodman and Scarecrow in a field and deliver Dorothy and the Lion to the Witch's castle. The Wicked Witch of the West imprisons Dorothy and her companion, threatening to kill the girl unless she hands over the magic shoes. Dorothy refuses, knowing they are her only defense against the Witch's onslaughts.

Like the doll in *Vasilisa the Beautiful*, and the blood-stained handkerchief in *The Goose Girl*, the magic shoes are transitional objects. They have protected Dorothy up to now and will continue to protect her as long as she has them in her possession. Dorothy intuitively recognizes their value and knows she must hold on to them at all costs.

The Witch flies into a rage and retaliates by treating Dorothy cruelly, forcing her to perform unpleasant tasks not unlike those demanded of heroines in other fairy tales. She makes her clean the pots, sweep the floor, and keep the fire fed, threatening to beat her with an old umbrella if she doesn't obey. Dorothy has no alternative but to carry out the Witch's commands.

While Dorothy is laboring away, the evil woman turns her attention to the Lion, who is tied up in the castle courtyard; her plan is to harness him and ride him like a horse. She approaches the Lion's cage, fully expecting him to be docile, but he surprises her by rearing up on his hind legs and throwing himself at her: "As she opened the gate, the Lion gave a loud roar and bounded at her so fiercely that the Witch was afraid, and ran out and shut the gate again."

The Lion once again draws on resources he thought he lacked and responds in a courageous fashion. Earlier in the story, he proved his mettle by fearlessly bounding over the ravine. Now he directly challenges the Witch's authority, refusing to be cowed even though he is her prisoner and in chains.

Finally it is Dorothy's turn. Taunted and harassed by the Witch, she rises up against her tormentor. When the evil woman tries to steal one of her shoes, Dorothy reaches for a nearby bucket of water and dashes it over the Witch's head.

> Instantly the wicked woman gave a loud cry of fear, and then, as Dorothy looked at her in wonder, the Witch began to shrink and fall away.
>
> "See what you have done!" she screamed. "In a minute, I shall melt away."

And so she does. The description of the Witch's death in the film, while paralleling that in the book, is different in one important respect. In the film, Dorothy *accidentally* splashes the Witch in her effort to save the Scarecrow from going up in flames. In the book, she *deliberately* douses the witch for not only stealing her shoe but threatening the lives of her companions: "Dorothy [was] so very angry that she picked up the bucket of water that stood near and dashed it over the Witch." The vision of a courageous young woman boldly asserting herself is much more in line with modern notions of female capabilities than the image portrayed in the film. Actively destroying the witch underscores Dorothy's newfound self-assurance and the progress she has made in overcoming her insecurities.

The death of the Witch sets the stage for a triumphant return to the Emerald City. But before Dorothy heads back to the Wizard, she rushes to the field where the Scarecrow and the Woodman have been languishing. The two are relieved to see her, especially the Woodman, who is overcome by emotion. Feelings he thought he was incapable of experiencing well up in him as he sheds tears of joy over Dorothy's safe return. Like her other companions, he comes to realize that the personal attribute he has been searching for has always been a part of him. Dorothy wipes the tears from his eyes, and the foursome sets out to find the Wizard.

Though Dorothy still needs to make her way home, she is already home psychologically: she is at home with herself. In defeating the Witch and transforming her friends, she has transformed her sense of who she is. Her final meeting with the Wizard only confirms what she always intuitively knew, that the positive qualities her companions were searching for were qualities she was searching for in herself. By joining her three friends in confronting the Witch, she actualized her latent strengths and was able to overcome her own self-doubts.

The inherent struggle between conflicting forces in the self, coupled with the need to regard oneself as essentially good, affects not only Dorothy but the Wizard. His response to Dorothy once he is exposed by Toto confirms this. When Dorothy realizes that the Wizard is just an ordinary man, she accuses him of being deceitful.

"I think you are a very bad man," she tells the Wizard after his elaborate charade is exposed.

"Oh, no, my dear," he replies, "I'm really a very good man; but I'm a very bad Wizard."

The Wizard, like all of us, needs to believe he is a good human being. His only sin, he intimates, is that he tried to exaggerate his powers. Fearful of revealing his true self, that of an ordinary man with ordinary failings, he resorted to a complex deception to hide himself from the world. The result was that he relinquished all chances of authentically interacting with other human beings. The screen he used to mask his true identity—the false front that separated him from others—prevented him from being who he truly was.

Accepting who you are is the emotional chord that reverberates throughout *The Wizard of Oz*. The various psychological malaises from which people suffer—anxiety attacks, phobias, psychosomatic disturbances, and the like—often are the result of fears they harbor about what might happen if they interacted with others in an open and honest way. Personal concerns about being shown up—of revealing imperfections—cause many individuals to erect barriers that frustrate meaningful relationships. Ralph Waldo Emerson wrote, "Make the most of yourself, for that is all there is of you." *The Wizard of Oz* also teaches that we must accept ourselves if we hope to fulfill our destinies.

AND THEY LIVED HAPPILY EVER AFTER

The final chapter of Baum's tale describes Dorothy's return to Kansas. True to every fairy tale's maternal underpinnings, the heroine's return involves a reunion with her surrogate mother, Aunt Em. It is not purely an accident that the first letter in "mother" is "em."

> Aunt Em had just come out of the house to water the cabbages when she looked up and saw Dorothy running toward her.
>
> "My darling child," she cried, folding the little girl in her arms and covering her face with kisses. "Where in the world did you come from?"
>
> "From the Land of Oz," said Dorothy, gravely. "And here is Toto too. And oh, Aunt Em! I'm so glad to be at home again!"

Though the story concludes on a happy note, there is something missing. Where are Hunk, Zeke, and Hickory? The three farmhands who so closely resemble Dorothy's fellow travelers in the film are nowhere in sight. They seem to have disappeared. That's because they never were in the story to begin with. The characters of Hunk, Zeke, and Hickory were added to the film version of *The Wizard of Oz* when Baum's story made the transition from the printed page to the screen.

While adding Dorothy's farmhand friends introduces a fanciful twist to the film, their inclusion suggests that Dorothy's adventure was only a dream, that "it really didn't happen." This does a disservice to young moviegoers and undermines the story's cathartic value. Children need to feel that fairy tales are authentic, and that what takes place in the story really can happen. They need to believe that the magic in fairy tales is genuine, not the product of chicanery or sleight of hand. To make fairy tales less than real, to transform make-believe into non-belief, trivializes them and detracts from their ability to inspire and empower.

Children need to feel that Dorothy's odyssey is more than just a hallucination brought about by a cyclone-induced bump on the head or that Snow White's adventure is more than just a dream. Imagine if Snow White woke to find that the seven dwarfs were really her playmates from school, and that the evil queen was her mean Aunt Tilly. Changing the Scarecrow, Tin Woodman, and Cowardly Lion into Kansas farmhands undermines the phantasmagorical nature of the story and detracts from its psychological impact.

Nevertheless, it is difficult to regard *The Wizard of Oz* as anything other than a cinematic masterpiece, a marvel of twentieth-century storytelling. Dorothy's journey to the Land of Oz is the premier fairy tale of our time, offering children both an enchanted adventure and an opportunity to confront their own self-doubts as they travel down the yellow brick road of life. For these reasons, *The Wizard of Oz* must be considered a fairy tale not only for our time but for all time.

12

Once Upon a Future

One afternoon a big wolf waited in a dark forest for a little girl to come along carrying a basket of food to her grandmother. Finally, a little girl did come along and she was carrying a basket of food. "Are you carrying that basket to your grandmother?" asked the wolf. The little girl said yes, she was. So the wolf asked her where her grandmother lived and the little girl told him and he disappeared into the wood.

When the little girl opened the door of her grandmother's house she saw that there was somebody in bed with a nightcap and nightgown on. She had approached no nearer than twenty-five feet from the bed when she saw that it was not her grandmother but the wolf, for even in a nightcap a wolf does not look any more like your grandmother than the Metro-Goldwyn lion looks like Calvin Coolidge. So the little girl took an automatic out of her basket and shot the wolf dead.

Moral: It is not so easy to fool little girls nowadays as it used to be.

James Thurber's *The Little Girl and the Wolf* presents us with a much different vision of Little Red Riding Hood than we are accustomed to. The image of the little girl in the red cape defending herself—with a forty-five automatic, no less—is a far cry from the traditional picture of Red Riding Hood found in children's storybooks.

As we enter the twenty-first century, our notions of fairy tales and the meaning they have for children are likely to undergo change. But that is to be expected. Fairy tales have always been products of the culture and era of which they are a part. It thus is not surprising that an entire genre of feminist tales has appeared in recent years that seeks to challenge many of the underlying fairy-tale assumptions about male-female relationships. Rather than giving us heroines who are passive, submissive, and self-sacrificing, tales with a feminist bent feature a heroine who is bold, resourceful, and sassy. She is more likely to rescue the prince than the other way around. Indeed, in some contemporary fairy tales, there isn't even a prince.

Jane Yolen's Cinderella-like tale *The Moon Ribbon* is a case in point. In it, the widowed father of a girl named Sylva decides to remarry after many years without a wife. Much to Sylva's consternation, the woman he marries is selfish and mean-spirited, as are her two daughters from a previous marriage. Soon after arriving, the new wife dismisses the servants and saddles Sylva with all the household chores, forcing her to clean, cook, and toil in the fields.

One day, when Sylva is cleaning out an old desk, she comes across a silver-tinted ribbon that had belonged to her mother. The ribbon is the color of her mother's hair, and Sylva cherishes it as a reminder of her mother and their time together. Her stepsisters are attracted to the pretty ribbon and try to take it from Sylva, but she manages to safeguard it. It is the only concrete reminder she has of happier days.

One night while Sylva is lamenting her circumstances, the ribbon magically turns into a river and transports her to a distant kingdom. There she meets a silver-haired woman living in a great house at the edge of a forest. The woman identifies herself as Sylva's mother and, in an emotional exchange, exhorts Sylva to reach deep within herself for strength and inspiration. The young girl returns home with a memento of her visit, a precious crystal.

When Sylva tells her stepmother about her adventure, she scoffs at the girl's story. Though she cannot explain how Sylva has come into possession of the gemstone, she confiscates it, sells it, and keeps the proceeds for herself. Through the magic of the ribbon, Sylva returns a second time to the mysterious house by the forest, where she again encounters her spiritual benefactor. This time her mother presents her with two fiery-red jewels. Sylva returns home, where she is again confronted by her stepmother and ordered to turn over the stones. Sylva refuses.

"I *cannot*," she tells her stepmother.

"Girl, give it here," the stepmother insists, a menacing look in her eyes.

This time Sylva responds, "I *will* not."

The change from "I *can* not" to "I *will* not" signifies Sylva's transformation from a passive, subservient child to an active, self-assertive young woman. Her transformation, significantly, takes place without the help of a prince but rather from her experiences with a nurturant adult female. In Yolen's tale, there is no fancy ball, no magic slipper, and no male presence to save Sylva from a malevolent stepmother. Left to her own devices, the heroine asserts her independence and carves out a new identity for herself.

As in most stories that owe allegiance to *Cinderella*, the stepmother and her daughters in *The Moon Ribbon* are punished for their evil ways. The stepmother, believing that the ribbon will point the way to great riches, takes the ribbon from Sylva in lieu of the jewels and heads across a meadow, triumphantly waving the ribbon over her head. Halfway across the meadow, the ground opens up to reveal a silver-red staircase. The stepmother and her daughters hurry down the steps, anticipating a great fortune at the bottom, only to have the ground swallow them up, sealing their fate. Sylva retrieves the silver ribbon lying on the grass and presses it to her bosom. Years later, after she is married and has children of her own, she bequeaths it to her daughter.

Another fairy tale rooted in feminist sensibilities is Jeanne Desy's *The Princess Who Stood on Her Own Two Feet*. In Desy's tale, the villain is not a wicked stepmother but a crass and insensitive prince. Unlike other contemporary fairy tales that draw their inspiration from classical sources, *The Princess Who Stood on Her Own Two Feet* relies on its own story line. Like the princess in its title, the tale stands on its own two feet.

The princess in Desy's story is beautiful, intelligent, and possessed of many talents. Not only can she easily tally the contents of the royal treasury on an abacus, but she is able to master any subject presented to her by the royal tutors. In addition to her intellectual prowess, she is artistically inclined: she plays the zither with ease and also designs exquisite tapestries. She also happens to be very tall. The only thing the princess lacks is love, for there is no man in the kingdom who is a suitable match.

The princess does, however, have an affectionate companion, a golden-haired Afghan hound with thin, aristocratic features who was given to her by a friendly wizard. Faithful and true, the animal keeps the princess company during the day and sleeps at the foot of her bed at night. But the princess is the first to admit, "a dog is a dog and not a prince." And the princess longs to be wed.

One day a prince from a neighboring kingdom is sent by his parents to propose a marriage alliance with the princess that will benefit both kingdoms. A betrothal feast is arranged, and the princess nearly swoons in her chair when she sets eyes on the prince. He is more handsome and dashing than she ever imagined. So delighted is she to have him as her prospective husband that she spends the entire feast holding hands with him under the banquet table.

After the meal is over, it is time for dancing. The royal troubadours take out their instruments and begin to play a waltz. The prince asks the princess to honor him by dancing the first dance, and she rises to accept his invitation. But the moment she stands up, a great shadow passes over his face. The prince stares at the princess in disbelief.

"What is it?" she cried. But the prince would not speak, and dashed from the hall.

For a long time the princess studied her mirror that night, wondering what the prince had seen.

"If you could talk," she said to the dog, "you could tell me, I know it," for the animal's eyes were bright and intelligent. "What did I do wrong?"

The dog, in fact, could talk; it's just that nobody had ever asked him anything before.

"You didn't do anything," he said, "it's your height."

"My height?" the princess cries out in astonishment. "But I am a princess. I'm supposed to be tall." She points out that height is part of her royal heritage, and that everyone in the royal family is tall. But the dog explains to her that while that might be true, men from other kingdoms like to be taller than their wives.

"But why?" the princess asks. The dog fumbles for an answer but cannot come up with one. It makes as little sense to him as it does the princess.

The matter of height, of course, is a metaphor for the power differences between men and women. The prince cannot tolerate a wife who is taller than he, for it suggests that she may eclipse him. He cannot even bear to discuss the matter. Perhaps he doesn't fully understand it himself. All he knows is that her height disturbs him, so much so that he calls off the wedding and returns home.

The princess really doesn't understand the reason for the prince's departure but wants to set things right. She rushes to the wizard and asks whether he can make her shorter. The wizard sadly explains that such a feat is not within his power. He can make the princess fatter or thinner, even change her into a raven, but he cannot do anything about her height. Despondent and depressed, the princess takes to her bed.

Meanwhile, the king and queen have convinced the prince to reconsider his decision and to give the match another chance. He agrees and returns to the castle, where the princess is languishing in her bedroom. Standing by her bedside, he naturally towers over the princess, thereby rekindling his earlier attraction to her.

The prince notices that the princess has become pale from lying indoors so long and offers to take her out for some fresh air. He invites her to go horseback riding, for on a horse, as in a chair, the princess is no taller than he. But during the ride the princess's horse stumbles and throws her to the ground. When the prince assists her to her feet, he once again is reminded of how much taller she is than he.

The princess sees the displeasure in his face and immediately crumples to the ground, crying out, "My legs, I cannot stand." The prince picks her up and carries her back to her room, his chest puffed up with manly pride. Since she cannot stand, he once again looms over her.

The princess spends the next few weeks in bed "recuperating." But she finds herself increasingly bored as the days go by. It's not the most pleasant thing in the world for an energetic and talented young woman to be cooped up in her room all day.

Since she was often idle now, the princess practiced witty and amusing sayings. She meant only to please the prince, but he turned on her after one particularly subtle and clever remark and said sharply, "Haven't you ever heard that women should be seen and not heard?"

The princess sank into thought. She didn't quite understand the saying, but she sensed that it was somehow like her tallness. For just as he preferred her sitting, not standing, he seemed more pleased when she listened, and more remote when she talked.

The princess decides to stop talking, once again sacrificing her pride in order to placate the prince. She communicates her wishes on a slate to him and to her servants, but late at night, when no one is around, she satisfies her need to engage in intelligent conversation by conversing with her faithful dog.

The prince is less than satisfied with this arrangement. He is annoyed by the affection the princess lavishes on the animal. The dog senses his days are numbered and says as much to the princess. When she tells him she doesn't know what she would do without him, he replies, "You'd better get used to the idea. The prince doesn't like me." And so saying, he slumps to the floor and dies, sacrificing himself for the princess's happiness.

The grief-stricken princess is inconsolable. She wraps her faithful companion in the folds of her dress and sets out to bury him. On the way to the grave site, she is intercepted by the prince, who callously remarks, "I thought you got rid of that thing weeks ago."

"What you call 'this thing,'" the princess tells him, "died to spare me pain. And I intend to bury him with honor."

The prince is surprised to hear the princess speak and comments on the fact that she is talking.

"Yes," she smiles, looking down on him. "I'm talking. The better to tell you good-bye. So good-bye." That might have been the end of it, but when her mother, the queen, hears what happened, she becomes agitated.

"Well, my dear," the queen said that night, when the princess appeared in the throne room. "You've made a proper mess of things. We have allegiances to think of. I'm sure you're aware of the very complex negotiations you have quite ruined. Your duty as a princess . . . "

"It is not necessarily my duty to sacrifice everything," the princess interrupted. "And I have other duties: a princess says what she thinks. A princess stands on her own two feet. A princess stands tall. And she does not betray those who love her." Her royal parents did not reply. But they seemed to ponder her words.

That night the princess slips out of the castle to visit the grave of her beloved pet. Standing by the grave site, she considers all she has given up for love.

"How foolish we are," she says aloud. "For a stupid prince, I let my wise companion die." She places a white rose on the grave and waters it with a silver watering can.

On her way back to the castle gate, she hears a noise in the dark and looks up to see a handsome horseman. The rider has long golden hair and aristocratic features, and she senses that he could be a prince. She notices that his banner is a white rose on a black background. The princess asks if he can lower it so that she can examine it more closely. He brings the banner close to her face.

"Death," she breathed.

"No, no," he said smiling. "Rebirth. And for that, a death is sometimes necessary." He dismounted and bent to kiss the princess's hand. She breathed a tiny prayer as he straightened up, but it was not answered. Indeed, he was several inches shorter than she was. The princess straightened her spine.

"It is a pleasure to look up to a proud and beautiful lady," the young prince said, and his large eyes spoke volumes. The princess blushed.

"We're still holding hands," she said foolishly. The elegant prince smiled, and kept hold of her hand, and they went toward the castle.

Stories like *The Moon Ribbon* and *The Princess Who Stood on Her Own Two Feet* use a fairy-tale format to suggest ways in which stereotyped images of women—and men—can be reshaped through fantasy. A fairy tale need not feature a passive heroine, a savior prince, or a malevolent older woman to make sense, although many contemporary tales still include a witch. The heroines in these stories have a sense of humor, actively establish themselves as free-thinking individuals, and, most important, make choices that serve their own interests. In Judith Viorst's abbreviated rendering of the Cinderella story entitled. . . *And Then the Prince Knelt Down and Tried to Put the Glass Slipper on Cinderella's Foot*, the heroine takes a second look at the prince when he arrives at her door with the glass slipper. In the clear light of day, she notices he has a funny nose and is not nearly as dashing as he looked the night of the ball. Quickly deciding he is not for her, she pretends the slipper is too tight and thus cannot get her foot into it. Like the princess who stood on her own two feet, Viorst's Cinderella and other fairy-tale heroines of the future may decide to satisfy their own desires rather than allowing themselves to become the object of someone else's. They may weigh the options available to them, and not be blindly swept away by considerations that in the long run may not be self-fulfilling.

What do reconstituted and revised fairy tales say about the future of fairy tales in general? Is it likely that stories like *Snow White, Sleeping Beauty, Hansel and Gretel,* and *Rumpelstiltskin* will fall by the wayside and be replaced by tales that are more culturally relevant or politically correct? Will the fairy tales of the twenty-first century come to occupy the bedtime hours of children and supplant the tales of the eighteenth and nineteenth centuries?

Probably not. New tales notwithstanding, classic fairy tales penetrate our inner worlds in ways that are difficult to duplicate. Few stories can excite and entertain while touching on personal matters that affect us so profoundly. There is no other story like *Hansel and Gretel* when it comes to gluttony, no adventure like *Jack and the Beanstalk* when it comes to greed. When Walt Disney was pressed to do a sequel to the enormously successful *Snow White and the Seven Dwarfs,* he replied, "Top dwarfs with dwarfs? Why try?"

Though the time-honored tales of our childhood will continue to weave their magic spells, the means by which they are told are likely to change. Fairy tales, it will be recalled, were originally communicated through oral storytelling. Recounted at family gatherings and children's bedsides, they were largely spread by word of mouth and formed a part of everyday social discourse. Over time the stories came to be transmitted through the written word by writers like Basile, Perrault, and the Grimm brothers, who collected and recorded them in books. But even this has changed. In the past half-century, fairy tales have evolved into a visual art form, in large part owing to the pioneering work of Walt Disney and the Disney studio. Nowadays even book versions of the classic tales are accompanied by illustrations based on the work of Disney artists. It is difficult to think of the seven dwarfs today without conjuring up Sneezy, Sleepy, Doc, and the rest. The villain of *The Little Mermaid* is not a generic witch but the dreaded Ursula complete with thickly arched eyebrows and overflowing bosom.

As a result, visual icons and visual representations have increasingly come to dominate fairy tales. Though the stories are still told and read, children are often introduced to the exploits of Snow White, Cinderella, and Dorothy through feature films and videos. Every time the Disney organization puts its stamp on a fairy tale, box office records are broken. Not only have films like *The Little Mermaid* and *Beauty and the Beast* enjoyed great success, but every few years anniversary editions of the Disney classics attract new audiences. The Disney organization has yet to exploit the huge potential of *Hansel and Gretel* or *Jack and the Beanstalk*, but a harp that sings and a hen that lays golden eggs would seem to be an animator's dream.

WHAT THE FUTURE HOLDS

Trends already in the making suggest that fairy tales will become increasingly wedded to information and computer technology as we enter the twenty-first century. One children's computer program, for example, presents *Jack and the Beanstalk* in a decidedly untraditional manner. The program, part of the Learning Company's Reader Rabbit Reading Development Library, uses a computer format to tell the story in one of three ways. An opening screen asks young viewers whether they would like to have Jack's adventure told by an anonymous storyteller (the "classic" version), by Jack himself, or by the giant. All three versions follow the same story line, differing only in the perspective chosen.

When Jack is the narrator, the story reflects his feelings and naturally favors his particular point of view. Sent by his mother to sell Milky-White, Jack announces, "I was sad because I would miss our cow." When he trades Milky-White for the beans, he lets the reader know how resourceful he is: "I had made a clever trade," he declares triumphantly. His mother in the computer version, as in the original, fails to share his enthusiasm.

Jack's version, as might be expected, downplays his avaricious tendencies. It depicts him less as a greedy youth than as a preadolescent Robin Hood, a fearless adventurer who sets out to revenge the ills done by the giant to his fellow villagers. The giant in the computer rendering is portrayed as a thief: "Long ago, the people in Jack's village had three special treasures . . . golden coins, a hen who laid golden eggs, and a harp. Then a giant came and took them all." No mention is made of Jack's greedy inclinations. He merely wants to recoup what rightfully belongs to his neighbors.

When the story is told from the giant's perspective, we get a different picture. He lets the viewer know that Jack is responsible for his difficulties right off the bat: "My trouble started because of a boy named Jack," the giant announces. In the course of presenting himself to the viewer, the giant does not try to deny that he is greedy and has acquisitive tendencies. Indeed, he is quite forthright about who he is: "I am a giant and I love gold," he declares. "When I see golden treasures, I take them."

Once the giant finishes introducing himself, he goes on to describe the events that take place in the story, leading up to the now-familiar chase scene. Roused by the cries of the golden harp, he pursues Jack and follows him down the beanstalk. "I was right behind him," he tells the child watching the drama unfold on the monitor. He sees Jack get the axe from his mother and immediately recognizes the danger facing him. "I knew that if the beanstalk broke, I would fall a long, long way down!" the giant remarks. He then goes on to describe the events that follow:

> *WHACK! WHACK! The beanstalk snapped.*
> *I had already jumped off it.*
> *I was safe but I was not happy!*
> *My treasures were down in the village!*
> *And I could never go there again!*

The giant is spared death, but whatever momentary relief he experiences is tempered by feelings of emotional isolation. He watches the festivities below and laments his situation.

> *The people of the village had a feast.*
> *They danced to the songs of my golden harp.*
> *They gave Jack some of my golden coins.*
> *Did anyone think about ME?*

I wanted to have a feast too, but we only had beans.
I hate beans!

Not only does the ogre manage to escape death, his plaintive remarks enlist the reader's sympathy. On top of everything else, he has to settle for beans while all the others indulge in more delectable fare.

While the computer version of *Jack and the Beanstalk* encourages an empathic response ("Did anyone think about ME?"), it fails to address greed in any meaningful way. There nevertheless is something to be said for promoting compassion and understanding. In taking the role of the giant, young children get to experience what it feels like to be ostracized—not to mention the prospect of having to eat beans.

The opportunity to immerse oneself in multiple role-taking opens up a whole range of possibilities. If *Jack and the Beanstalk*, why not *Snow White*, or even *The Wizard of Oz?* It is entirely possible that an innovative programmer sometime in the not-too-distant future will develop a game that deposits young audiences into the Land of Oz, allowing children to take the parts of Dorothy's three companions. Perhaps becoming the Cowardly Lion could help a child deal more directly with unspoken fears of intimidation, or teach children how to overcome unfounded fears. Perhaps putting oneself in the Tin Woodman's shoes would enable children to deal with feelings of victimization before they too become "heartless." By encouraging identification with helpless victims, new millennium fairy tales may, in the words of the Tin Woodman, help keep children from "ever becoming cruel and unkind."

The ultimate merging of computers and fairy tales eventually leads to the world of virtual reality. Someday not too far in the future a young child may be able to don a computerized headset and "walk" down the yellow brick road. Perhaps a child will become Jack and actually scramble down the beanstalk—or alternately become the giant and chase after Jack. The fairy tales of the future may find a child scaling a castle wall to wake a sleeping princess or experience what it is like to try on a glass slipper. Combining the fantasies of the eighteenth and nineteenth centuries with the technology of the twenty-first offers infinite variations on those age-old excursions into the self we call fairy tales.

WHITHER THE WITCH?

But what about the witch? Will her position in the fairy-tale world of tomorrow be altered as the classic tales of yesteryear become more interactive? Chances are it will. One thing is certain: she will not go away. The witch is an immutable part of the self and will not—cannot—be relegated to a technological trash bin. It will not be possible simply to drag her over to a trash icon on a computer screen and dispose of her with the click of a mouse. The character of the witch, and her place in the human psyche, suggests that she will continue to be a force to contend with.

But she may not always have to die. As fairy tales evolve, it is likely that accommodation with the witch may become more significant than her elimination. As children become older and more mature, they increasingly come to learn—as do Dr. Jekyll and Dorian Gray— that efforts to eradicate the bad side of the self are doomed to fail, and that eliminating the witch can lead to tragic outcomes. A willingness to engage the witch, not merely dispose of her, may turn out to be a positive development when it comes to psychological growth. Perhaps Gretel *can* convince the witch to become a vegetarian. The ability to control and tolerate one's sinful side can be a path not only to self-acceptance but to acceptance of others.

The tales of Grimm and Perrault that feature conventional witches and sequences in which they meet their end will nevertheless continue to prevail for the simple reason that they offer young audiences an important way of dealing with troublesome impulses. The world of three-, four-, and even five-year-olds is a world of absolutes. Black is black and white is white. There are no in-betweens. Fairy tales that include the death of a witch or a comparable witch figure provide children with a powerful tool to deal with tendencies that are not easily dealt with in more conventional ways.

Older children, in contrast, are likely to respond to tales that allow for "conversations" with the evil presence in the story. The very act of engaging the witch, the ability to experience what she thinks and feels, can be growth-enhancing. As children mature, "kill thine enemy" needs to evolve into "know thine enemy." Whether the witch does or does not die may not be as important as the opportunity to interact with her. Children need opportunities to become conversant with parts of themselves they are going to have to deal with for the rest of their lives.

What about adults? What will the fairy tales of the future offer older audiences? Can the tales that over the years have been appropriated by children inject some meaning into a world where tragedy is an everyday occurrence, where sexual scandals fill the nightly news, where children shoot other children, and where ecological disasters loom on the horizon? Is there a "somewhere over the rainbow" where "troubles melt like lemon drops"? Is it even possible to make out the rainbow through all the smog?

The fairy tale historian and social critic Marina Warner believes it is. She maintains that fairy tales fulfill and will continue to fulfill important functions for adults. She argues that fairy tales help us imagine another life. They allow us to tell alternative stories, to conjure up worlds where happy endings are possible. Fairy tales, she believes, strike a chord of optimism that resonates deep in the hearts of all human beings.

Many nevertheless would argue that it is naive to look for answers to life's problems in tales where evil is eliminated by simply waving a wand, where princes always show up on time, and where everyone lives happily ever after. It seems so simple, so utterly removed from reality: the need to make a living, to stay healthy, to make sure our loved ones are safe. All these concerns, however, depend on our ability to form and maintain meaningful relationships. And this means confronting tendencies that can threaten and undermine our dealings with others. Fairy tales serve this function in adulthood as much as they do in childhood. By addressing human frailties, they use fantasy to illuminate problems that adults repeatedly face in their quest to lead more fulfilling lives.

The interplay between fantasy and reality is examined by Robert Coover in *Briar Rose*, a modern retelling of *Sleeping Beauty* that explores the nature of courage, suffering, and unrequited love. Coover does this by alternately telling the story through the eyes of the prince, the princess, and a witch/fairy charged with watching over the sleeping beauty as she waits to be rescued from her hundred-year sleep.

In Coover's rendition, the prince is clearly conflicted about his quest. He questions the ordeal he must undergo to release the princess from the spell. Should he risk his life to rescue her? Is she worth the effort? Will she turn out to be the woman of his dreams? Doubts surface in his mind as he takes in the broken bodies of the countless warriors who have already tried to rescue the sleeping princess. Surveying their lifeless bodies strewn throughout the deadly hedge surrounding the tower, he wonders, like the Cowardly Lion, whether he has the courage to press on, and whether he is caught up in some sort of existential test.

> The bones of his ill-fated predecessors clatter ominously in the assaulted branches, and the thorns, exposed by his cropping of the blossoms, snag in his flesh and shred what remains of his clothing. But he is not frightened, not very anyway, nor has he lost any of his manly resolve to see this enterprise through, for he knows this is a marvelous and emblematic journey beyond the beyond, requiring his unwavering courage and dedication.

The princess, in the meantime, slumbers away, drifting in and out of endless sleep, immersed in fantasies, many of which are erotic in nature. At one point, she is wakened—or so she thinks—by a band of ruffians who have broken into the castle. They take time out of ransacking her room to rape her. Suddenly the drunken intruders are transformed into her father's knights, and she wonders whether all this is really happening, or whether she is only dreaming.

In another sequence, the princess wakens to find not one but three "princes" standing by her bed. One is a wizened old gentleman, another a leprous hunchback, and the third a good-looking young man.

She asks which one kissed her, glancing longingly at the handsome one. "We all did," replies the old man, "and now you must choose between us." The princess is about to select the handsome prince when the leper reminds her that beauty is only skin-deep. Physical beauty, he tells her, lasts but a season, but spiritual beauty lasts an eternity. The princess falls back on her bed, as confused as ever. "You're making my head ache," she tells her visitors.

When the prince of her dreams finally shows up, he wonders whether he has the right castle. The maiden in the bed is less than he expected. He wanders about her bedchamber for a while, casually fingering the furniture and looking at himself in the mirror. He has heard rumors about other sleeping princesses waiting to be rescued. What if this princess isn't the real one? He turns and abruptly leaves the room. The princess is left wondering whether her true prince will ever come.

> She lies alone in her dusky bedchamber atop the morbid bed. Perhaps she has never left it, her body anchored forever here by the pain of the spindle prick, while her disembodied self, from time to time, goes aimlessly astray, drifting through the castle of her childhood, in search of nothing whatsoever, except distraction from her lonely fears (of the dark, of abandonment, of not knowing who she is, of the death of the world), which gnaw at her ceaselessly like the scurrying rodents beneath her silken chemise. If she is asleep, it does not feel like sleep, more like its opposite, an interminable wakefulness from which she cannot ease herself, yet one that leaves no residue save echoes of an old crone's tales, and the feeling that her life is not, has not been a life at all.

During all this time, the witch/fairy bears witness to the events taking place. She regales the comatose princess with stories, interweaving elements of Basile's tale with those of the tales of Perrault and the Grimm brothers. She tells the princess she has mothered twins who were delivered while she was asleep. In retelling the different versions of the story, the fairy muses about all the anguish her magic has caused and reflects on the forces of good and evil swirling within her.

The fairy recognizes that many of her stories, even when by her lights comic, have to do with suffering, often intolerable and unassuaged suffering, probably because she truly is a wicked fairy, but also because she is at heart (or would be if she had one) a practical old thing who wants to prepare her moony charge for more than a quick kiss and a wedding party, which means she is also a good fairy, such distinctions being somewhat blurred in the world she comes from.

Coover's "reinterpretation" of *The Sleeping Beauty* leaves us wondering about the nature of unfulfilled desire. The story forces us to consider the line that separates sex from longing, striving from fulfillment, agelessness from premature death. Clearly these are issues that occupy adults more than children. But the basic idea—fostering identification with various characters—is not that different from what we find in the Rabbit Reader version of *Jack and the Beanstalk*. In Coover's tale, however, the reader is drawn more deeply into the complex interior of the fairy tale so as to illuminate issues that are part and parcel of human existence.

A contemporary perspective on fairy tales is adopted by Geoff Ryman in his novel *Was*. Drawing his inspiration from *The Wizard of Oz*, Ryman describes a Dorothy very different from the Dorothy created by L. Frank Baum. Ryman's story begins with Dorothy arriving in Kansas, having been sent to live with her Aunt Em and Uncle Henry following the death of her mother from diphtheria. Accompanying her is her pet dog, Toto.

Life on the farm turns out to be harsh and unyielding. Not only does Aunt Em humiliate Dorothy by forcing her to perform onerous tasks, but her Uncle Henry molests her, causing her to become withdrawn and embittered. Weaving fragments from Judy Garland's life with sequences from the movie, Ryman describes how Dorothy's attempts to cope with her oppressed existence. After years of emotional torment, she finally escapes to Wichita, where she becomes a prostitute. The ill-fated heroine of *Was* spends the last days of her life in a nursing home, truculent and half-demented, fantasizing about a land called Oz where Munchkins live and salvation lies at the end of a yellow brick road.

Ryman's dark tale plumbs the depths of *The Wizard of Oz* using Dorothy's "previous existence" to draw us into the painful world of childhood. His story is the story of every child who longs for an absent mother, of those children subjected to psychological and physical abuse, of the painful choices people make in order to survive. But most of all, Ryman's sad but uplifting story illustrates the redemptive power of fantasy, demonstrating how the world of the mind can imagine a better life when reality deals us a bad hand.

Tales like *Briar Rose* and *Was* introduce adult readers to a universe of fairy tales that draw their inspiration from familiar stories all of us know and cherish. In addition to these, there are fairy tales from the Perrault-Grimm era that exist in unexpurgated form but are rarely read. Because they contain violent material or were thought to be too suggestive, they simply were relegated to the dustbin of history when fairy tales were making the transition from adult stories to children's tales. Many nevertheless possess an undeniable charm and are refreshingly contemporary in nature.

The Adroit Princess, described earlier, is one. Featuring a heroine who is clever, adventurous, and courageous, the story can easily stand alongside any number of feminist fairy tales in which the heroine takes her destiny into her own hands. The adventure of Finette, with its themes of sexual duplicity, infidelity, and jealousy, is as pertinent today as it was 150 years ago and has much to say about the complex nature of male-female relationships.

Then there is *The Juniper Tree*. Deemed inappropriate for young children in its time because of its violent imagery—and a bit too graphic even today for young children—the story speaks to issues of parental preferences and relationships between siblings, issues with which all parents are familiar. A similar case can be made for the currency of stories like *Donkeyskin*, which raises issues of sexual abuse, and *The Pig Prince*, which contrasts physical and spiritual love.

The wheel comes around. Fairy tales that originally were the exclusive property of adults may once again find an audience among older readers. If they do—and there is evidence this is already taking place—fairy tales are likely to enjoy a renaissance in the new millennium.

Fairy tales are ultimately a celebration of life. Both enchanting and empowering, they are as timely today as they were hundreds of years ago. The underlying dynamic—the age-old struggle between good and evil—resonates between the lines of *Snow White*, *Cinderella*, and *The Wizard of Oz*, as it will in the as yet unwritten stories of the twenty-first century. For this reason, the witch will continue to be a major presence in fairy tales, sensitizing us to forces within ourselves that pose a challenge to our sense of who we are. Her destruction is not an act of vengeance, nor even cruelty. It merely reminds us that sinful tendencies are a part of everyday existence, and that we must do battle with them if we wish our lives to have a fairy-tale ending.

APPENDIX I
Using Fairy Tales

$\mathscr{P}$arents, teachers, and child therapists intuitively recognize that fairy tales offer a unique window into the emotional lives of children. As a psychologist, I am often asked how individual tales can help a child deal with particular issues. Which stories are especially useful for children troubled by their greediness? Can fairy tales help a child who is inclined to tell lies? What might you read to a little girl who is intensely jealous of her younger sister—and feels guilty about it to boot? People also want advice on practical matters. How does one go about engaging a child in the stories? What kinds of questions might you ask to connect the tales to the child's emotional needs?

In the pages that follow, I offer concrete suggestions that address these concerns, with the understanding that one always needs to keep in mind a child's ability—and willingness—to explore personal matters. Since children differ in their readiness to assimilate emotional insights, the suggestions should be seen less as hard and fast prescriptions than as beacons to illuminate themes a child is ready to address. This appendix is organized around these themes and the fairy tales that best bring them to life. It also contains capsule summaries of key tales and can thus stand on its own as a reading guide. The numbers in parentheses refer the reader to chapters in the book that contain fuller discussions of the individual stories.

VANITY

Snow White (3) is the classic story of vanity run amok. Not only is the queen obsessed with being the fairest in the land, but Snow White's desire for a comb and pretty ribbons reveals her own vain tendencies. Encourage children to make this connection by asking them, "Why do you think Snow White invites the disguised queen into the cottage even though the dwarfs repeatedly warn her not to?" You can also alert children to the narcissistic elements in the story by asking them to compare Snow White and her stepmother. How are the two different? How are they alike? Children should be made aware that the two characters share an excessive interest in how they look.

The dwarfs' decision to put the young princess in a glass coffin demonstrates how all-encompassing vanity can be. The transparent enclosure turns Snow White into an object of display and diminishes other aspects of her personality. Asking children, "Why do you think the dwarfs choose a glass coffin rather than the more traditional wooden one?" helps them appreciate the meaning of the dwarfs' decision.

Cupid and Psyche (3), though strictly speaking not a fairy tale, includes many of the elements typically found in fairy tales. Not only does it demonstrate the pitfalls of vanity, but it is ideally suited for introducing children to Greek mythology. The story tells of Venus's effort to destroy Psyche because she is convinced that the girl threatens her position as the most beautiful woman in the world. Children can be asked why they think Venus is so intent on destroying Psyche. How do they feel about Venus's reaction? Engage the child by raising the question of how important physical appearance is, and whether it is healthy to let looks dominate one's life.

A key ingredient in *Cupid and Psyche* is the "jar of beauty" that Venus orders Psyche to retrieve from the underworld. Ask children to speculate about what precisely is in the jar (face lotion? wrinkle cream? blush?) and why Psyche feels compelled to open it even though she is warned not to. Why does Psyche expose herself to danger when she already is so beautiful? The answer, of course, is that Psyche herself is vain. The issue raised by the jar, one that children enjoy debating, has to do with the *source* of beauty. Does it come from without—from the contents of a jar—or from within?

Ricky with the Tuft (11) examines the role that physical appearance plays in relationships. A story by Charles Perrault, whose collection also includes *Cinderella* and *Little Red Riding Hood*, it tells of two princesses, one intelligent yet unattractive, the other beautiful but stupid. By examining the relative importance of physical beauty, the story can help children who worry about their looks. In the story, the sister who is intelligent is valued more than the one who is pretty. Children can be helped to examine their own values by asking them to imagine which princess they would rather be, and why. Teachers especially will find the story useful in their efforts to confront teasing in the classroom since much teasing is based on outward appearance.

Ricky with the Tuft is also valuable for teaching the need to keep one's word. The princess who is stupid promises to marry Ricky, a homely prince, in exchange for the gift of intelligence. But when she is endowed with intelligence, she becomes too clever for her own good and tries to worm her way out of the bargain. Encouraging children to consider how Ricky feels when the princess goes back on her word helps them know how people feel when promises are broken, or when they are deceived.

The Emperor's New Clothes (3) raises issues of public presentation of self and the deceptiveness of looks. Children delight in the tale of the vain, self-deceiving ruler who winds up as a subject of ridicule when a mere child sees through his charade. The tale empowers children by conveying that adults aren't always right. And children, when asked, are usually happy to tell of times they felt they were right and their elders were wrong.

Andersen's story also says something about blindly following others. Ask young listeners about times they went along with playmates in order to be part of the crowd: "How did you feel about your decision afterward? Were you sorry? Did you get into trouble?" *The Emperor's New Clothes* does double duty by opening children's eyes to the corrupting nature of peer pressure.

GLUTTONY

Hansel and Gretel (4), the quintessential tale of gustatory self-indul-
gence, demonstrates what can happen when one's appetite gets out of
hand. While Hansel and his sister have good reason to be hungry,
they continue to devour the witch's cottage after eating their fill, thus
subjecting themselves to peril. In reading the story to a child, ask for
examples of real-life "perils" associated with overeating, such as
tummy aches or losing a taste for a particular food. One can also raise
the complex question of obesity. Is it always the result of overeating?
Is the fat person to blame? What is the ideal body image? Since even
elementary school children diet, and eating disorders begin at
younger and younger ages, *Hansel and Gretel* can be a powerful vehi-
cle for stimulating talks about healthy approaches to food.

The tale can also initiate discussions of resourcefulness. Draw attention to Hansel's ingenuity—bread crumbs to mark the path—as
well as Gretel's cleverness in luring the witch into the oven. Also
point out that it is Gretel who figures out how to cross a lake so she
and Hansel can get home. Invite children to contribute examples of
times when they too have drawn on inner resources to solve a difficult problem.

Little Red Riding Hood (4) describes the consequences of wolfing
down one's food. Playful prodding can induce young listeners to consider the connection between the wolf's ravenous appetite and their
own tendencies to overeat. The same kinds of questions raised by
Hansel and Gretel in regard to gluttony can be raised about *Little Red
Riding Hood*.

The Grimm version of the story, *Little Red Cap* (4), is especially useful in this regard. Here the heroine and the grandmother join forces
to outwit the wolf by drowning him in a trough of water. Children
should be helped to understand that the wolf perishes because he cannot control his ravenous appetite—the trough contains water that has
been used to boil sausages. The Grimm version also lends itself to a
consideration of female resourcefulness, for it is the heroine and her
grandmother rather than a woodsman who devise a way of outwitting
the wolf.

Where the Wild Things Are (4) is a contemporary tale of conflicts in which food figures prominently. The child protagonist, Max, is sent to his room without dinner after he becomes unruly and threatens to eat his mother up. Alone in his room, he embarks on a fantastic adventure in which he encounters the "wild things," a ferocious bunch of creatures that he ultimately tames.

The story can help a child to talk about unmanageable impulses, especially anger. A question like, "Can you tell me about your wild side?" prompts children to talk about worrisome parts of themselves. In the same vein, one can relate Max's attempt to control the wild things to efforts on the child's part to control unruly tendencies. This can lead to a consideration of ways in which anger is expressed at the dinner table, since children often refuse to eat as a means of expressing discontent. "Can you think of other ways that Max might indicate he's unhappy?" is a way of stimulating interchanges between parent and child regarding food and eating.

ENVY

Cinderella (5) and other related stories are essentially about jealousy, particularly among siblings. As children listen to these stories, they often connect the jealousy of the protagonists with their own jealous feelings. A good way to get children to talk about these feelings is to ask, "Is anyone in the family treated better than the rest?" This is a guaranteed springboard for lively discussions of envy when children are reluctant to bring up such matters on their own. *Cinderella* also relates to persecution and victimization, so that teachers can use it to initiate discussion about children picking on other children in school. Use the story to get the child to imagine Cinderella's feeling when she is tormented by her sisters: "Can you describe how you might feel if you were in Cinderella's place?"

Children tend to be most familiar with the Perrault rendition of *Cinderella* since Disney used it as the basis for his film. But the Grimm version, *Aschenputtel* (5), dramatizes the envy of the sisters and the persecution by the stepmother more effectively. Though it contains scenes of mutilation, it features a poignant scene in which the dead mother symbolically returns in the form of a tree to care for her daughter. Parents should take time to explore this part of the story with children, for it touches on issues surrounding abandonment and addresses children's deepest fears: "Will my parents leave me if I am bad?" or, "How will I survive if I am left all alone?"

One can substitute *The Moon Ribbon* (12), a contemporary Cinderella tale, for the Grimm version if the mutilation in the latter story seems too disturbing. The tale approaches jealousy in a relatively nonviolent manner while retaining its thematic core: the rivalry between the sisters and the heroine. Like *Aschenputtel*, the story includes a meeting with the spirit of the deceased mother, providing another opportunity to talk about abandonment and spiritual continuity. The same issue is raised in *Rashin Coatie* (5), a Scottish Cinderella tale, *and Yeh-hsien* (5), a Chinese tale.

The ribbon in *The Moon Ribbon*, a memento left to the heroine by her mother before she died, can inspire discussion of favorite dolls, teddy bears, and other playthings that fill an important niche in children's lives. Termed "transitional objects" by psychologists, these special objects have emotional significance beyond their value as playthings: they provide young children with comfort and solace by symbolizing parental love.

Younger children usually have no problem recognizing this on a gut level, but older children are sometimes ashamed of clinging to these objects. Knowing that others have similar attachments can help dispel embarrassment and allay fears that their ardor for these playthings is infantile or even abnormal. One can kindle interchanges about transitional objects by simply asking a child to talk about his or her favorite toy, following this up with, "How does it help you when you feel sad (lonely, picked on, etc.)?"

The Frog Princess (5), a Russian fairy tale, features a competition among three sisters-in-law who vie for the favor of their father-in-law, the king. One of the princesses is a frog, a fact that leads to hilarious sequences involving bread-baking and frenzied dancing. Like *The Moon Ribbon*, *The Frog Princess* allows children to consider ways of dealing with jealousy in relatively nonviolent ways—in this instance, through competition. Ask children about times when they had to compete with others. How did they feel when they won? When they lost?

The Frog Princess is highly engaging in that it is one of the few fairy tales that conveys its message through humor. Another attraction is that the story shows a strong heroine taking control of the situation (the competition) instead of a heroine who relies on the prince to help her out of her predicament. The story thus is useful in presenting to young girls an alternative vision of fairy-tale heroines. You can draw attention to this by asking young listeners, "How is the princess in the story different from princesses in other fairy tales?"

Deceit

The Goose Girl (7) depicts the price one pays for taking "let's pretend" too seriously. A story in the Grimm brothers' collection, it tells of a servant woman who usurps her mistress's identity in order to marry a prince in a distant land. Upon her arrival, she tricks the court into believing she is the true princess.

To the extent that the story is about unhappiness with one's identity, children can be asked to comment on dissatisfaction or satisfaction with who *they* are. "Who would you like to be if you could take another person's place? Why would that be better than who you are now? What would you gain? What would you lose?" Questions like these help children appreciate that getting one's wish fulfilled often comes at a price.

The Goose Girl also gives children a chance to explore feelings about leaving home. Children who have to move to new surroundings because of parental separation or divorce often have little opportunity to talk about the trauma of separation or about what it feels like to be thrust into a new environment. Tap into these feelings by asking children to put themselves into the shoes of the princess, who also has to leave home. "Can you tell me how you think the princess feels?" usually is enough to get the ball rolling.

The Frog Prince (7) tells of a princess who reneges on her promise to let a frog sleep in her bed for fetching her ball from a well. Early versions of the story describe the erotic implications of the princess's promise, but the children's version focuses more on the princess's attempt to get out of her promise. Ask children to reflect on instances when they too lied to get something they wanted very badly. "Can you remember a time when you told a fib to get something you wanted very much?" often suffices. Encourage the child to speculate on how the frog feels when the princess goes back on her word. By having children experience what it feels like to be the victim of a broken promise, the story can be used to nurture empathic skills.

Rumpelstiltskin (7) explores the consequences of telling lies by recounting the story of a miller who lies to the king about his daughter's alleged ability to weave gold from straw. In reading the story to children, ask them to come up with a reason for the miller's preposterous claim: "Why do you think the father comes up with such a silly story?" Help them to understand that he lies in order to puff himself up in the king's eyes. Young listeners should be encouraged to describe instances in which they themselves have told fibs to exaggerate their accomplishments. They also should be made aware that the miller's lie has dire consequences in that it places his daughter's life in jeopardy, and that their own efforts at self-aggrandizement may also produce unpleasant results.

Rumpelstiltskin also considers the circumstances under which it may be permissible to lie. The miller's daughter lies to the king—and to Rumpelstiltskin—in order to save her life. Children sometimes lie to spare the feelings of others—telling Grandma they love her birthday gift, for example, when they really don't. They also may lie to avoid undeserved punishment, as may happen in homes where children are severely punished for committing minor infractions. The story thus can be used to help children sort out some of the moral dilemmas involved in telling lies.

LUST

Fairy tales that have sexual overtones typically do not deal with sex per se, but with precocious sexuality—"sex before its time." Sexual messages in fairy tales are usually conveyed indirectly so that the child does not have to deal with subject matter he or she is unable to handle. *The Little Mermaid* (8), for example, never makes explicit the connection between the heroine's lack of legs and the absence of a vagina, even though this constitutes an underlying dynamic in the story. Rapunzel's illicit pregnancy (8) is never spelled out, even though it is the reason she is banished by the witch; the story mentions only that her apron no longer fits about her waist. And the nature of the princesses' nocturnal escapades in *The Twelve Dancing Princesses* is only hinted at by the fact that they leave their bedroom in the dead of night to rendezvous with twelve handsome princes and do not return until the following morning.

The stories nevertheless can be helpful in exploring the physical and psychological aspects of sexual attraction with older children (between the ages of nine and eleven, for example) since many children in this age range are subjected to a great deal of information and misinformation about sex. Children can be asked at what age it is appropriate to start dating or attending mixed parties. With younger children, it is best to accent the tender and sentimental nature of the feelings between the characters, allowing the sensual elements in the story to rise naturally to the surface when the child is more mature and better prepared to deal with them. At a time when children are increasingly exposed to the more tawdry aspects of sex on television and in magazines— when five-year-olds ask their parents what oral sex means after hearing about it on the nightly news—it can help to read stories in which attraction between a man and a woman is presented in the more general context of commitment and caring.

GREED

Jack and the Beanstalk (9) ranks high among fairy tales that have greed as their focus. Children who listen to the story often are impressed by Jack's cleverness and daring, ignoring the fact that Jack is as greedy as the giant. Call the child's attention to this by pointing out that Jack steals the golden harp after he already has a source of endless wealth. A good question to pose is, "Why does Jack climb the beanstalk a third time when he already possesses a hen that lays golden eggs?" To get children to explore their own greedy inclinations, ask them to compare Jack's behavior with instances in which they too hungered for more than they really needed. A good starting point is to have young listeners describe their reactions the last time they visited a toy store.

The Fisherman and His Wife (9) is uniquely suited for very young children because of its straightforward plot. In the story, a magic fish awards a fisherman and his wife all their wishes after the fisherman spares his life. The fish grants them a castle and endless riches, but the fisherman's wife is never satisfied. As with *Jack and the Beanstalk*, youngsters can be asked to consider times when they behaved like the fisherman's wife.

The story also gives children a chance to experience what it feels like to be on the other end of the giving-getting continuum. How do they feel when they give something to someone compared to how they feel when they are given something? The story helps young listeners explore the joys of generosity—the beneficence of the fish—as well as the consequences of selfishness.

The Juniper Tree (9) raises issues about favoritism in families and the lengths to which some people will go to satisfy greed. The story tells of a stepmother who plots to dispose of her stepson so that the family fortune will go to her and her daughter. It is probably best to avoid reading this story to very young children since it contains a scene in which the stepson meets a gruesome death. Older children, however, may benefit from what the fairy tale has to say about greed as well as about loss. Children often feel responsible for misfortunes that befall a family, such as divorce or death. The daughter's conclusion that she is to blame for her brother's death can open up discussions about misplaced responsibility and unwarranted guilt. The scene in which the sister gathers up her brother's bones and lovingly plants them under a tree is a poignant reminder of the caring bond that exists between siblings.

SLOTH

Pinocchio (10), the tale of a puppet who must overcome his lazy ways in order to become "a real boy," is a classic depiction of sloth and its consequences. The original story by Carlos Collodi is book-length, but specific sequences—described in Chapter 10—can be culled out since young children have a limited attention span. Critical incidents in the story are the cricket's warnings to Pinocchio about the consequences of not going to school, and the Blue Fairy's admonitions about avoiding work. Ask children to speculate on why the cricket and the Blue Fairy feel so strongly about this subject. What are the long-term implications of laziness, of failing to do schoolwork? Children can be invited to recount times in their own lives when they were too lazy to do what was asked of them.

Most children have seen the Disney version of *Pinocchio*, so that the differences between the film and the original story can be compared while reading the story. This teaches young audiences that there can be different versions of a story—different truths—and that each can emphasize different things. Lying, for example—portrayed in the film by the growth of Pinocchio's nose—is but a minor part of the Collodi original, occupying only a page and a half in a book of over two hundred pages. But since most children are familiar with the film, the nose episode can be used to explore the social aspects of lying. Some questions you can ask in the course of reading the story are, "Can other people tell when you are lying—and how do you know?" and, "Can you tell when someone is lying to you?"

The Three Spinsters (10) depicts how maternal influences contribute to industriousness. The story of a lazy girl who is promised in marriage to a prince because the prince's mother, the queen, believes the girl is industrious and loves to spin, illustrates the potential rewards of hard work. But the girl has never bothered to learn how to spin. She is saved by the magical appearance of three women—maternal icons who symbolize the innate potential for hard work—who spin the flax for her and prove to be her salvation.

The story can be combined with historical facts about spinning (provided in Chapter 10) to help children, especially young girls, appreciate the role that spinning played in women's lives in years gone by. Ask listeners to consider the kinds of work opportunities available to women then and now: "How is working with your hands different from working with your head? What rewards derive from each?" This line of questioning can be supplemented with questions like, "What do you want to be when you grow up?" so as to explore the more general topic of work and self-esteem.

Mother Hulda (10), another story in the Grimm brothers' collection, raises issues of laziness, diligence, and responsibility. The story describes two sisters who are direct opposites of one another when it comes to work. The industrious sister falls into a well and there encounters a powerful witch who shelters her in exchange for performing household tasks; when it is time to leave, the witch—Mother Hulda—showers the girl with gold. Her sister travels to the bottom of the well expecting similar good fortune, but she is a laggard and refuses to perform the chores assigned by Mother Hulda; when it is time for her to leave, she is showered with pitch as her "reward."

Mother Hulda is particularly appropriate for very young children because of its absorbing imagery: the magic land at the bottom of the well features apples that cry out and loaves of bread that speak. It also is one of a number of stories that lends itself to play reenactments. Using a circle drawn on the floor to represent the well, yellow confetti for gold, and black confetti for pitch, teachers can use the story to make the message of industriousness versus sloth more palpable.

BEYOND SIN:
LONELINESS, LEAVING HOME, AND ILLNESS

Vasilisa the Beautiful (6), yet another Russian fairy tale, recounts the story of an orphaned child forced to live with Baba Yaga, a ferocious witch, and the doll that figures in the heroine's survival. The scene at the beginning of the story in which the dying mother bequeaths the doll to her daughter can help children confront hidden fears about the loss of a parent. As with the ribbon in *The Moon Ribbon* (12), the doll opens a window for children to talk about favorite objects—dolls, stuffed animals, and "security blankets"—and how these objects help deal with loneliness.

Toy Story (6), a cinematic fairy tale, is a particularly valuable story for dealing with children's apprehensions about moving. The toys in the story—Woody (the protagonist's old standby) and Buzz Lightyear (a new arrival)—come into conflict at a time when the protagonist is preparing to move to a new neighborhood. The struggle between Woody and Buzz reflects the inner struggle between the security of the familiar and the desire for change.

The story's meaning can be enhanced by pointing out how each of the toys in the story reflects tensions in the child. Children can be asked to talk about "Woody feelings" and "Buzz feelings" as a way of getting them to reconcile conflicts surrounding a move—or any other significant change in their lives. Specific responses to questions a child may raise come easily if one bears in mind that Woody and Buzz are transitional objects and symbolically represent a child's need for love and support.

The Velveteen Rabbit (6) is an excellent story for exploring feelings of loneliness that result from extended illness and enforced isolation. The central character in Margery Williams's story is a young boy who is confined to his room while recuperating from a bout of scarlet fever. The story includes a conversation between the boy's favorite playthings—the Velveteen Rabbit and the Skin Horse—about what it means "to be Real."

Make sure young listeners know what is meant by "Real" in the context of the story, since children often assume that it has something to do with turning into a live animal. The true meaning has less to do with returning to the wild than with being loved and cherished. Parents reading the story to their children should take time to dwell on the part of the tale in which the Skin Horse explains this to the Rabbit, making sure the child understands the message. Even though the Velveteen Rabbit is destroyed toward the end of the story—the boy's doctor worries that it harbors scarlet fever germs—it continues to live, so to be speak, because it is loved.

❧❧   ❧❧   ❧❧

The suggestions in this appendix present just a few ways of making fairy tales more growth-enhancing for children. Adults who love the stories will discover other creative interventions, and children themselves, ever imaginative and ever inventive, will surprise us with observations uniquely their own.

APPENDIX 2
Finding Fairy Tales

𝕿he number of books on fairy tales is vast. In addition to the standard collections and scholarly treatises, there are tales from almost every imaginable part of the world. To avoid making the bibliography bloated and unwieldy, I have included only those books I personally have found useful and fun to read. The entries include brief annotations to help readers decide which books might of particular interest.

FAIRY-TALE COLLECTIONS

Beauties, Beasts, and Enchantment: Classic French Fairy Tales, translated by Jack Zipes (New York: NAL Books, 1989), features a highly stylized version of "The Adroit Princess" and a number of other "salon" fairy tales.

The Blue Fairy Book, collected by Andrew Lang (London: Longmans, Green Co., 1889; reprint, New York: Dover, 1965) is the volume in the Lang "color" fairy-tale series that contains the stories with which most people are familiar. Less familiar tales can be found in the Yellow, Red, and Gray volumes.

The Complete Grimm's Fairy Tales, translated by Margaret Hunt (New York: Pantheon Books, 1944), contains all 220 of the Grimm tales, including "The Juniper Tree."

Don't Bet on the Prince: Contemporary Feminist Fairy Tales in North America and England, edited by Jack Zipes (New York: Methuen,

1986), is a collection of contemporary tales by noted feminist writers and includes "The Moon Ribbon" and "The Princess Who Stood on Her Own Two Feet."

English Fairy Tales, compiled and edited by Joseph Jacobs (London: The Bodley Head, 1968), was first published in 1890 and includes classic tales from the British Isles, such as "Jack and the Beanstalk" and "Rashin Coatie."

Hans Christian Andersen: His Classic Fairy Tales, translated by Erik Haugaard (New York: Doubleday & Co., 1978), includes eighteen of Andersen's most acclaimed tales, including "The Little Mermaid," and "The Emperor's New Clothes.

Household Stories by the Brothers Grimm, translated by Lucy Crane (London: Macmillan & Co., 1886; reprint, New York: Dover, 1963), contains fifty of the most popular tales by the Grimms, accompanied by handsome illustrations by Walter Crane.

Il Pentamerone (The Tale of Tales) by Giambattista Basile, translated by Sir Richard Burton (New York: Liveright, 1927), is full of rich language and bawdy sequences. It features "The Princess Who Couldn't Laugh," "Talia, Sun, and Moon," "Cat Cinderella," and forty-seven other tales.

Perrault's Fairy Tales (New York: Dodd, Mead, & Co., 1921; reprint, New York: Dover, 1969), contains eight of the original tales included in Perrault's *Contes de ma mère l'oye* (Tales of Mother Goose). This collection features "Little Red Riding Hood," "The Sleeping Beauty in the Woods," and the version of "Cinderella" adapted by Disney.

Russian Fairy Tales, translated by Norbert Guterman from the collections of Aleksandr Afanas'ev (New York: Pantheon Books, 1945), is a rich collection of Russian tales that includes "The Frog Princess," "Vasilisa the Beautiful," and other stories featuring characters like Korchoi the Deathless and the ubiquitous Baba Yaga.

INDIVIDUAL STORIES

Briar Rose by Robert Coover (New York: Grove Press, 1996), a Sleeping Beauty story for adults, is told from the perspective of the prince, the princess, and a delightfully wicked fairy.

The Moon Ribbon and Other Stories by Jane Yolen (London: J.M. Dent and Sons, 1976) includes a refreshingly different take on the classic Cinderella tale.

Pinocchio by Carlo Collodi (New York: McGraw-Hill, 1982) is the complete story and it contains all the sequences left out of the Disney film.

The Princess Who Stood on Her Own Two Feet in *Stories for Free Children*, edited by Letty Pogrebin (New York: McGraw-Hill, 1982), is a modern-day fairy tale featuring a resourceful princess and a less-than-gallant suitor.

Was by Geoff Ryman (New York: Knopf, 1992), chronicles Dorothy's life before Oz and is meant for adult audiences. This account of her life in Kansas presents a very different view of Aunt Em and Uncle Henry.

Where the Wild Things Are by Maurice Sendak (New York: Harper & Row, 1963) is a twentieth-century fairy tale of food, rebelliousness, and letting your wild side take over.

The Wizard of Oz by L. Frank Baum (Chicago: George M. Hill, 1900) contains no Hunk, no Zeke, and no Miss Gulch. Found here instead are Kalidahs, Quadlings, and a land populated by fragile people made of china.

ANALYSES AND COMMENTARIES

Kate Bernheimer, ed., *Mirror, Mirror, on the Wall* (New York: Anchor Books, 1998). Women writers—including Margaret Atwood, Fay Weldon, and Linda Grey Sexton—talk about the impact of fairy tales on their lives.

Bruno Bettelheim, *The Uses of Enchantment* (New York: Knopf, 1976). Analyzing how fairy tales help resolve oedipal conflicts through fantasy and wish fulfillment, this is the classic psychoanalytic work on fairy tales by a noted child psychiatrist.

Ruth Bottigheimer, ed., *Fairy Tales and Society* (Philadelphia: University of Pennsylvania Press, 1986). Includes articles on topics ranging from the way women are depicted in fairy tales to the use of fairy tales in psychotherapy.

Clarissa Pinkola Estés, *Women Who Run with the Wolves* (New York: Ballantine, 1992). Explores the impact of folklore and fairy tales on women's psyches from a Jungian perspective.

Steven Swann Jones, *The Fairy Tale* (New York: Twayne, 1995). A slim volume packed with insightful essays, including one on the influence of classic fairy tales on *Where the Wild Things Are* and *The Cat in the Hat*.

Maria Tatar, *The Hard Facts of the Grimms' Fairy Tales* (Princeton, N.J.: Princeton University Press, 1987). Discusses sex and violence in fairy tales, children as victims, and the stepmother-witch connection.

Marina Warner, *From the Beast to the Blonde* (New York: Farrar, Straus & Giroux, 1995). A scholarly analysis of the place of fairy tales in history, religion, and culture. Beautifully illustrated.

Jack Zipes, *Happily Ever After* (New York: Routledge, 1997), is a socioeconomic analysis of the place of fairy tales in the culture industry, including their depiction in film. Includes chapters on *Pinocchio* and *The Lion King*.

✤ INDEX ✤